Who Killed
John Maynard Keynes?
Conflicts in the Evolution
of Economic Policy

Who Killed
John Maynard Keynes?
Conflicts in the Evolution
of Economic Policy

W. Carl Biven

DOW JONES-IRWIN
Homewood, Illinois 60430

© RICHARD D. IRWIN, INC., 1989

Dow Jones-Irwin is a trademark of Dow Jones & Company, Inc.

Project editor: Jane Lightell
Production manager: Ann Cassady
Designer: Mike Finkelman
Compositor: Publication Services, Inc.
Typeface: 11/13 Times Roman
Printer: R.R. Donnelly & Sons Company

LIBRARY OF CONGRESS
Library of Congress Cataloging-in-Publication Data

Biven, W. Carl.
    Who killed John Maynard Keynes?
    Includes index.
    1. Keynesian economics.   2. Keynes, John Maynard,
1883-1946.   3. Chicago school of economics.   4. United
States—Economic policy—1945- . I. Title.
HB99.7.B54 1989   338.973   88–33526
ISBN 1-55623-149-0

Printed in the United States of America

1 2 3 4 5 6 7 8 9 0 DO 6 5 4 3 2 1 0 9

This book is dedicated to my son, Russell.

ACKNOWLEDGMENTS

It is not possible to list all of the individuals to whom I am indebted, one way or the other, for their help in the writing of this book. But there are those that I must thank by name..

The advice of Donald Hardy and Arthur Rittenberg in the early stages of the project was invaluable. Robert Carney, Kong Chu, John Hooper, and Henry Thomassen gave generously of their time to read drafts of the manuscript. Their comments have been most helpful. I alone, of course, am responsible for what is in this book. My brother, Tony Biven, read each chapter as it came out of the word processor. Writing is a lonely business, and his warm encouragement made it easier. Last, but not least, my wife and children gave me the gift of patience when I was absent from family events while working on this book. To all of these, I am deeply grateful.

To keep from distracting the reader with footnotes, the sources for quotations and other appropriate acknowledgments are listed in a set of notes at the end of the book.

TABLE OF CONTENTS

Who Killed
John Maynard Keynes?
Conflicts in the Evolution
of Economic Policy

CHAPTER 1

THE DEATH OF KEYNES

Robert Lucas, professor of economics at the University of Chicago, is a major contributor to modern developments in economics. If one can imagine economists being described in the same terms as hotshot jet pilots such as Chuck Yeager, who flew the experimental planes at Edwards Air Force Base in the 1950s, Lucas has "the right stuff."

A scholar of Lucas's ability merits attention; when he speaks, people listen. His comments at a conference held in the latter part of the 1970s were published under the title "The Death of Keynes." Lucas was not speaking of physical death, of course. For John Maynard Keynes, the man, died and was buried at Westminster Abbey in 1946. Lucas was declaring the end of Keynesian economics.

This book is about Keynes but, even more, it is about a larger story in which his ideas happened to play an important part; it is about the debate of the last five decades over economic issues and about the controversies in the evolution of modern economic policy. After World War II the United States abandoned, as did the other leading industrialized countries, a *laissez faire*, or "hands off," approach to economic problems. The story of the decades since the war is about the struggle to put something in its place; the struggle to come to an agreement, as a matter of political judgment, on how. much government ought to be involved in the economy and to define, on a purely technical level, the limits of our ability to influence economic events.

For the first three decades after the war, something of a consensus developed that can be described by the label "Keynesian economics." Sometime in the 1970s, this agreement broke down. What was left, at least in academic circles, is described by Lucas as "total chaos . . . the end of consensus economics." Some economists would think Lucas's description a little strong, but there is no question that there are sharp differences among professionals on key issues of theory and policy.

Economics is a soft science, meaning that it is not as successful in predicting events as the physical sciences. The success of scientists and engineers in landing a spacecraft on the moon within a thousand yards of the designated landing target is something social scientists can only view with envy. In economics, competing theories can exist side-by-side for decades. Economists cannot perform the controlled laboratory experiments to eliminate decisively one of the contenders. They must wait for time to provide the data for testing propositions and, even then, the historical signals are not unambiguous.

Because economics is not an exact discipline, the human factor assumes importance. There is more room for the individual scholar's own subjective judgment, preconceptions, and biases. Analytic effort is preceded, as one of the important economists of this century, Joseph Schumpeter, once said, "by a preanalytic cognitive act that supplies the raw material for the analytic effort." Since empirical results often fail to prove conclusively the truth or falsity of a theory, the development of economic analysis becomes more personalized. As Arjo Klamer, whose interviews with a dozen economists are published in his fascinating book, *Conversations with Economists,* has written, economists "not only construct models . . . they philosophize, appeal to common sense, and talk about other economists and their work. Economics involves the art of persuasion. . . . This process leaves room for nonrational elements, such as personal commitment and style."

It is possible for two Nobel Prize winners in economics to give a President diametrically opposed advice on a specific problem. In fact, they have done so. One could not blame the layman for wondering who these people are and where they are coming from. That is why I have chosen to tell the story of the controversies in the evolution of economic policy in the last half-century in terms of the human beings who were involved in the debate about theory and the design of policy strategies. In one of his most frequently quoted statements, Keynes wrote that "the ideas of economists and political philosophers, both when they are right and when they are wrong, are more powerful than is commonly understood. Indeed the world is ruled by little else. Practical men, who believe themselves to be quite exempt from any intellectual influences, are usually the slaves of some defunct economist. Madmen in authority, who hear voices in the air, are distilling their frenzy from some academic scribbler of a few years back."

By far the most important economist participating in the debate was Keynes himself. He was not the only one; other scholars who have had an impact appear in these pages. But his work, *The General Theory of Employment, Interest and Money*, is the most influential book in economics written in this century, the book that started the "Keynesian Revolution." It is surprising the degree to which this treatise, written in 1936, is still the focus of much of the controversy among scholars about how the economy works. There is hardly a meeting of the American Economic Association, the annual assembly of the best and the brightest, at which a session on some aspect of Keynes's ideas does not find its way into the program. For those who are sympathetic to the main thrust of his ideas, he is obviously important. For those who reject all or part of his theory, Keynes still provides, in some measure, a point of reference for explorations in other directions. His ghost, even after half a century, presides at the debate about economic issues. For this reason I have used Keynes and his work as a point-counterpoint motif for this book, which sketches the postwar development of economic policy.

The next chapter provides a brief profile of Keynes, the man. The two chapters that follow explain the key points of his theory and how it affected policy at the zenith of its influence in the 1960s, in what came to be called the "Age of Keynes." By the 1970s, a sharp reaction to Keynes, particularly from a school of thought that came to be known as "monetarism," had come to have a major impact on the policy debate. Chapters 5 and 6 explain the main points of monetarism and describe its influence on the Federal Reserve. Keynes's vision was basically short-run; he said little about the long-run expansion of the economy. His followers, particularly in the 1960s, adapted his model for practical application to the problem of long-run growth. Economic growth is one of the main problems of our time, and we will explore it in Chapter 7. In Chapter 8, we move to the 1980s. One of Keynes's more practical policy contributions was the use of the government's budget as a tool to stabilize the economy. He would have been fascinated by the experiment of the Reagan years known as "supply-side economics," the topic of Chapter

8. Keynes participated in the international conference that designed the international financial system put in place after World War II, described in Chapter 9. We shall see how this system collapsed in the early 1970s and was replaced by still another arrangement. Some of our key economic problems today arise from the international connection. Finally, the quality of economic life in the United States, as we enter the decade of the 1990s, is the subject of Chapter 10. The details are different from the England of the 1930s that Keynes knew, but the basic problem of human welfare in the unfolding of economic events is the same, a concern he inherited from the rich tradition of the Cambridge school in which he was trained.

Are Keynes's ideas no longer relevant? Is Keynes "dead" in the sense that Lucas meant and, if so, who or what brought about the demise of Keynesian economics? Or is it a classic case of mistaken identity and Keynes still lives with his theories still germane to the problems of our day? We will sift the evidence on these questions later, but before that we have a lot of ground to cover. Besides, it would ruin the story to reveal the solution to the mystery at the very start of the tale.

CHAPTER 2

KEYNES

John Maynard Keynes was born in the same year in which Karl Marx died, 1883. The contrast between these two towering figures of modern social science could hardly be more striking.

Marx was the German-born radical who forecast the doom of capitalism. Surviving pictures show his piercing eyes staring from his bearded countenance like an avenging Jehovah. The ironic twist in his story is that he found political asylum in England, the leading capitalist nation of his day. When Marx left the quiet of the British Museum, where he spent much of his life in research for his voluminous writings, it was to meet in the underworld of revolutionaries who plotted the overthrow of the existing social order. Marx's death went unnoticed by English society, oblivious to the enormous impact he would one day have on the lives of billions of human beings. Only a handful of people were present when his friend and colleague, Friedrich Engels, delivered his graveside remarks in a cemetery in a suburb of London.

In sharp contrast to Marx, Keynes was part of the English Establishment. There is a gentry element in his family connection, as Joseph Schumpeter said in a memorial essay. Keynes's parents were part of the intellectual community. His father, John Neville Keynes, was himself an economist and logician who taught at Cambridge and served for many years as Registrar for the university. In the best tradition of the English upper class, young Keynes was educated at Eton and King's College. His loyalty to these institutions was deep, and he lectured at King's College, with some interruptions, throughout his life and served for years as Bursar, administering the college's finances with great skill. To a degree uncommon for scholars he intermingled his academic career with a life of action. He held influential posts in government and served as adviser to various London bankers.

This is the bare outline of Keynes's life. It is worth our time, here at the beginning before we get too engrossed in his economics, to dwell at some length on Keynes, the man, if only to satisfy the curiosity of those with only a vague idea of who Keynes was. For this deeper insight into his personality we must go to Bloomsbury.

Bloomsbury is a neighborhood in west central London, but this geographic detail is incidental. The important part is what the label *Bloomsbury* stood for—a group of gifted people and the culture they created.

Those who belonged to the Bloomsbury group were drawn together from two different directions. One was Cambridge; the majority of Bloomsbury had studied there. They were bonded together in close intellectual and emotional ties as undergraduates through a student society known as the *Apostles* to which most of the members of Bloomsbury had belonged.

THE APOSTLES

The Apostles is an old Cambridge society, founded in 1820. Tennyson, the poet, was an Apostle while a student. The members viewed their relationship with a seriousness that has an antique quality today, and they selected initiates carefully.

Keynes was elected an Apostle during his first year at Cambridge in 1903. Perhaps closest to Keynes among the members was Lytton Strachey, who later set a new style in the art of biography in his *Eminent Victorians*. Also a member of the Society was E.M. Forster, author of such novels as *A Passage to India* and *A Room with a View*. One can sketch a mental image of the dress and surroundings of the Apostles and the later gatherings of Bloomsbury—the high-set collars for the men, the long dresses for the women, the Edwardian drawing rooms—from the costumes and sets in recent movie adaptations of Forster's novels. Other contemporaries and members included Desmond MacCarthy, later editor of *The New Statesman* and literary critic for the *Sunday Times*, and Leonard Woolf, author and publisher and husband of the brilliant, but tragic, novelist Virginia Woolf. Membership in the Apostles continued after undergraduate days and some remained active. It was not unusual for Keynes, as a young man of 20, to sit in small, intimate discussion groups that included not only his contemporaries but distinguished Apostles some years his senior, like Bertrand Russell and Alfred North Whitehead, both established mathematicians and philosophers.

The interests of the members and the flavor of their discussions differed with each new generation. During Keynes's student days they were absorbed in the philosophy of G.E. Moore, 10 years senior to Keynes but also an active Apostle. His *Principia Ethica* was published shortly after Keynes was elected to the Society. This treatise dominated the Apostles' debates and provided a frame of reference for most of them for the rest of their lives.

To understand Moore's attraction, a little background is useful. To begin with, these students were part of an elite group. In the early 20th century, the English educated only a small part of the population at the university level. The curriculum was designed to produce a specific result. For the most part students "read" in mathematics, the classical languages, or philosophy. The training was deliberately nonvocational and graduates went into the learned professions, education, or public service; they were not expected to go into business. As one of Keynes's biographers has said, "they were a product of a very English reaction to industrial life, based on the cult of dead languages, chivalry, moral utopias, and the rejection of commercial careers." Whatever positive impact this educational philosophy had for the individual, the effect on British commercial and industrial leadership has been an interesting subject of debate. In any event, it was as natural for its products to engage in intense metaphysical discussions about fundamental questions of life as it is for American college students to discuss the relative merits of Pac-10 football versus the Big Ten.

Philosophical debate at Cambridge in Keynes's day was set in the background of a revolt against the Victorian Age. Queen Victoria died in 1901. By the time of her death, the basic value system of the period that bears her name was already under challenge. From society's point of view, the Victorian code of conduct resulted in a stable social structure. The twin obligations of frugal living and hard work produced a type of behavior to enhance the rise of capitalism. On the other hand, the demands that the Puritan ethic placed on the individual in the name of a higher and social good were suffocating.

The tension caused by this conflict between the demands of social duty and the individual's need for the simple joy of living finally brought to a head the philosophical debate to which Moore's *Principia* was a major contribution. The decay of religious beliefs reinforced this reevaluation and search for an alternative ethical system.

What did Moore say? Instead of emphasizing the requirements of conscience, as did the Puritan ethic, Moore gave priority to states of consciousness. Of highest value in human behavior were personal relationships and the enjoyment of beautiful objects. Right living was to be found in total commitment to friendships and aesthetic experience. "The appropriate subjects of passionate contemplation and communion," Keynes later wrote in describing the impact of Moore's ethics on himself and his contemporaries, "were a beloved person, beauty and truth, and one's prime objects in life were love, the creation and enjoyment of aesthetic experience and the pursuit of knowledge." The followers of Moore specifically repudiated a life of action, such as politics or the pursuit of wealth. "Salvation" was a totally individual experience. In terms of personal conduct, they rejected social conventions and mores. The demands of proper behavior were to be determined in each case by the intuition and judgment of the individual.

BLOOMSBURY

Members of this Cambridge set, imbued with the philosophy of G.E. Moore, were major contributors to the cultural milieu that was Bloomsbury. Another influence came from the Stephen sisters.

Vanessa and Virginia, along with their two brothers, Thoby and Adrian, were the children of Sir Leslie Stephens, a philosopher, once a Fellow and tutor at Trinity College, Cambridge. Later involved in a literary career, he was the editor of 26 volumes of the *Dictionary of National Biography*. From one of the leading Evangelical families of Victorian England, Stephen became an agnostic in his early life, though he continued to take seriously Victorian conventions. Vanessa and Virginia cared for him in his old age with filial devotion. Subject to melancholy, he made unreasonable demands on those around him, particularly in his later life. After his death at the age of 72, the children left the family home in South Kensington and took up residence in the less fashionable Bloomsbury. The four children were still relatively young; Sir Leslie had had his children in later life. Vanessa, the oldest, was only 25 when her father died. Their move to Bloomsbury was an act of liberation from a depressing Victorian home.

The Gordon Square residence of the Stephen children, presided over by two beautiful and independent young women, became a center for gatherings of bright, creative people. The Cambridge connection was established through the older son, Thoby, who had studied at the university. Friends like Lytton Strachey, who had finished his studies at Cambridge and moved to London, found the Thursday evening "at home" gatherings at the Stephen's a welcome opportunity to replace in Bloomsbury the intellectual and social environment they had known in Cambridge. Before long a basic group was established and carried on in the tradition of an informal salon. Its members had either been Apostles or had some connection with the Stephen family. Included in early Bloomsbury, in addition to Lytton Strachey, was his brother James Strachey, translator of Freud. E.M. Forster and Desmond MacCarthy were members along with Duncan Grant, an artist and a cousin of the Stracheys. So, also, Roger Fry. Fry was older than the other members, 17 years older than Keynes, and was already well established in the art world, both as an artist and administrator. He served for a time as director of New York's Metropolitan Museum. He had been a member of the Apostles while a student. Clive Bell, who also knew the others at Cambridge, was an art critic who later married Vanessa. Keynes was one of the later members to become attached to the group.

As the bond among the members increased, they took up residence in Bloomsbury. The somewhat imprecise boundary of Bloomsbury contains a number of squares—Gordon Square, Fitzroy, Tavistock, Bedford, and Brunswick Squares. "They are still very pleasant places in which to wander," we are told in a recent article in the travel section of *The New York Times* by Vanessa's son, Quentin. "The houses have a certain tall Victorian grace about them." Vanessa and Clive Bell took over the Stephen house at 46 Gordon Square following their marriage. Virginia and Adrian moved to Fitzroy Square, providing a second base for the Bloomsbury group, and others moved close by. Over time there was much shuffling around and exchange of residences—Keynes eventually took over 46 Gordon Square—but the members remained within easy walking distance of each other, a colony of intellectuals and artists. Nothing remains in these houses today to remind us of the fascinating individuals who lived in them. The residence at 46 Gordon Square is owned by the University of London, as are most of the old houses in the area, and is used for classrooms and a student snack bar.

To find evidence of the presence of Bloomsbury one must go 50 miles south of London to Sussex where several of the members acquired country homes. Virginia and Leonard Woolf had a place; Keynes bought an estate named Tilton. But the focal point of Bloomsbury South was Charleston Farm which belonged to Vanessa and Clive Bell. There was always much coming and going, and some members of the group lived at Charleston for long periods of time. It is an unusual place. Over the course of half a century, Vanessa, Duncan Grant, and other artists painted the walls and ceilings, decorated the furniture, and designed the carpets and fabrics. Quentin Bell, Vanessa's son who made pottery as a child, remembers the house as filled with artists. "And they were monsters," he is quoted as saying. "They'd take the pots right out of my hands and start painting them." In the end they created their own personal art gallery and left a unique legacy from an age long past. Duncan Grant, the last of the original *Bloomsberries*, died there in 1978 at the age of 93. Charleston, handed over to a trust, has been restored under the careful eye of Quentin Bell and is now open to the public. In an improbable turn of events, part of the funds to finance the restoration came from fund-raising expeditions to Dallas by Quentin Bell and his sister, Angelica Garnett, with assistance from others including the actress Lynn Redgrave. A new type of soap, wrote one reporter, "Bloomsbury Comes to Dallas."

The influence of Bloomsbury, its ideas of art and literature, gradually spread beyond the boundaries of its close-knit circle as its members began to publish their books and exhibit their paintings. One of the more visible exposures of the general public to Bloomsbury was the post-impressionist exhibit brought to London by Roger Fry in 1910. Fry had assembled a large collection of the works of Cezanne, Gauguin, and Van Gogh. The paintings had been done several decades before the exhibit but shocked the rather staid English public which greeted them with laughter and derision. Bloomsbury took up the cause of post-impressionism. A second exhibit in 1912 was dominated by such modern artists as Picasso and Matisse, but nine English painters were also represented, three of them members of Bloomsbury—Vanessa Bell, Duncan Grant, and Fry. Over the course of his career, Roger Fry had a strong influence on English taste.

Bloomsbury also became supporters of the Russian Ballet of Diaghileff, who introduced to London audiences the brilliant performances of Nijinsky. A prima ballerina in the group, Lydia Lopokova, later became Keynes's wife.

It has been said that the members of Bloomsbury were better publicists than creators. Their painters would not be ranked at the highest level of English artists. Perhaps only Virginia Woolf would be placed in the top class in literature. But their influence, for their short time on stage, was impressive. Reaction to the Bloomsbury cult by those outside the inner circle was mixed. They were admired, they were hated; but they were not ignored. Nor will they soon be forgotten. They left a massive record of their personal lives and activites. The published diaries of Virginia Woolf make up five volumes; her letters, six volumes. Her husband, Leonard Woolf, wrote a five-volume autobiography. In the 1930s Bloomsbury survived as a memoir club in which the members shared recollections of their lives and activities in papers read to each other at meetings. It is a record that is a scholar's delight; the work on Bloomsbury by historians and sociologists is approaching the status of a cottage industry.

We come now to the titillating part of Bloomsbury behavior. The Cambridge Apostles brought with them into the group their commitment to Moore's *Principia Ethica*. It was passed on to those in Bloomsbury who were not members of the Society. They easily embraced Moore's emphasis on aesthetic enjoyment as a part of the good life. They also readily accepted the priority given to human friendships, but with a twist that Moore had not intended. Roy Harrod, student and colleague of Keynes, discreetly omitted from his authoritative biography published in 1951 any mention of Keynes's sexual preferences. The reason for this omission is clear enough. He did not want to create blocks to an objective examination of Keynes's economics which was still novel and controversial. By the latter part of the 1960s biographical research had established that Keynes, along with other members of Bloomsbury, was homosexual.

It is more correct to say that Keynes was bisexual. He quite clearly was homosexual for 20 years prior to his marriage, at the age of 42, but apparently was happily adjusted after his marriage to Lydia

Lopokova. There was in Bloomsbury an almost endless combination of affairs with members of the same and opposite sex. Bloomsbury was described by one wit as a place "where all the couples were triangles and lived in squares." Critics might see the moral code of Bloomsbury as a reaction to Victorian hypocrisy at best and, at worst, an attempt to justify, in terms of Moore's philosophical system, any behavior in which they wished to indulge. In his memoir on his early beliefs written three decades after his student days at Cambridge, Keynes expressed reservations about rejecting social conventions and substituting personal judgment. Chastened by the savage bloodletting of World War I and the collapse of the world's economies during the Great Depression, he reflects that he and his friends were not aware "that civilization was a thin and precarious crust erected by the personality and the will of a very few, and only maintained by rules and conventions skillfully put across and guilefully preserved. . . . It did not occur to us to respect the extraordinary accomplishment of our predecessors in the ordering of life (as it now seems to me to have been) or the elaborate framework which they had devised to protect this order."

What all of this has to do with Keynes's economics, if anything, is not clear. The uninitiated might think it farfetched to link Keynes's sexual behavior to his theories, but some biographers and sociologists have had a field day in an attempt to make the connection. A 1984 biography, for example, says in the preface that "in composing this volume, a close textual analysis of Keynes's various writings has been undertaken in order to determine and to demonstrate what neuroscientists would describe as his 'cognitive style'. . . . The time has come," it continues, "to penetrate the mask of myth and legend that surrounds the life of Maynard Keynes and to rediscover the whole, authentic man." Some may find a psychological profile less useful for interpreting Keynes's economics than would others.

KEYNES AS ECONOMIST AND STATESMAN

In a certain sense Keynes was not of the innermost circle of Bloomsbury. Its main focus was art and literature, and Keynes's main interests were not in these fields. Not without literary talent, his memoir recounting negotiations with a German diplomat, Dr. Melchior, following the armistice of World War I is a distinguished example of the genre. Throughout his life, Keynes maintained a sharp interest in the visual arts, ballet, and theater and gave generously of his own funds and administrative talents to assist a number of art projects. In an interesting escapade during World War I, he went to Paris for an art auction while the city was under bombardment from "Big Bertha," the legendary cannon designed by the Germans for shelling at long distances. He had learned of the auction of major works of French artists and talked the Treasury into appropriating the necessary funds to acquire these treasures for England. A practical side benefit, he argued, would be help for the French balance of payments. Keynes began his own rather extensive art collection with purchases at this auction of some works by Cezanne, Ingres, and Delacroix. The driving force behind the establishment of an arts theater at Cambridge, he was personally involved at times in its management. Also a leading contributor to the establishment of the Arts Council through which government funds were channeled for the support of the arts, he played an important role in the rebuilding of Covent Garden and other art facilities damaged in the bombing of London during World War II. He was an avid book collector including original editions of the works of Isaac Newton. But despite his lifelong attachment to art, he could not match the aesthetic level of the inner core of Bloomsbury.

A difference in orientation also caused tension with Bloomsbury. Keynes was, by his very nature, an activist. His distinguished career in government was in conflict with the central tenets of Moore's philosophy, which gave the highest priority to friendships and contemplation of the beautiful and frowned on the world of action. In a sense Keynes lived, throughout his life, in two worlds, the contemplative world of Bloomsbury and the world of affairs.

Keynes's involvement in a life of action was partly due to his own temperament. Practical problems presented an interesting challenge. Despite a talent for theoretical work (Bertrand Russell once described Keyne's intellect "as the sharpest and clearest I have ever known"), his interest in economics leaned heavily to the applied. Keynes did not care for theory for its own sake and quickly lost interest in the abstract unless he saw a practical application. Another asset, particularly useful in a soft science like economics — was his sharp sense of intuition. Keynes's natural inclinations were reeinforced by his Cambridge training in economics. The dominant force at Cambridge during Keynes's studies was Alfred Marshall, who was responsible for establishing economics there as a separate discipline. Marshall thought of economics as a branch of applied ethics and lent his prestige to the Cambridge tradition that the final purpose of economics was to improve the human condition. The self-centered orientation of Bloomsbury was counteracted, in Keynes, by this Cambridge influence.

While he was capable of egalitarian sentiment, his public concern was heavily conditioned by class consciousness. Keynes and his friends had no doubt that they were part of an elite class. Bloomsbury was not interested in reaching the masses. They were quite explicit. Civilization depended on a lower class to perform the menial tasks to satisfy human wants; the creative force was represented in an endowed aristocracy free to maintain and advance the boundaries of civilization. With the exception of Keynes, the members of Bloomsbury were not wealthy people. But they had just enough inherited wealth to live the good life and devote their considerable talents to the higher purposes of artistic creation.

Keynes reflected this sense of superiority in a number of interesting ways. He could be brutal in his appraisal of others who did not quite fit his standard. He had an odd preoccupation with peoples' hands. In his evaluation of Woodrow Wilson, whom he observed at the Paris Peace Conference after World War I, Keynes noted, among other things, that "his hands, though capable and fairly strong, were wanting in sensitiveness and finesse" and went on to add that "the first glance at the President suggested not only that, whatever else he might be, his temperament was not primarily that of the student or the scholar, but that he had not much even of that culture of the world which makes M. Clemenceau and Mr. Balfour as exquisitely cultivated gentlemen of their class and generation."

Keynes's emphasis on the importance of an upper class in social arrangements had two effects that are related to his later work in economics. For one thing, he was never tempted by the doctrines of communism. After a visit to Russia with Lydia Lopokova, he wrote in 1925:

> I sympathize with those who seek for something good in Soviet Russia. But when we come to the actual thing what is one to say? For me. . . Red Russia holds too much which is detestable. Comfort and habits

let us be ready to forgo, but I am not ready for a creed which does not care how much it destroys the liberty and security of daily life, which uses deliberately the weapons of persecutions, destruction, and international strife. . . . How can I adopt a creed which, preferring the mud to the fish, exalts the boorish proletariat above the bourgeois and the intelligentsia who, with whatever faults, are the quality in life and surely carry the seeds of all human advancement.

He also found unappealing the socialist position of the British Labor Party, an attitude shared by the other members of Bloomsbury with the exception of Leonard Woolf, who was active in Labor Party politics.

At the same time that he opposed government ownership of the means of production, Keynes saw a role for government to act as a counterweight to the private sector. It was not an inherent desire for strong government. His feelings in this matter were an extension of class consciousness. The "managing" of the national currency in foreign exchange markets or compensatory fiscal action to stabilize the economy could be safely entrusted to an intellectual elite that could be counted on to manage things properly and to guide the general public in the right direction. He had tremendous confidence in the power of reason to control human affairs.

Involvement in public service was a gradual process. Keynes took the civil service examination after finishing his undergraduate studies at Cambridge. The subject in which he scored the lowest was economics. "Evidently I knew more about economics than my examiners," he commented. He chose to work in the India Office. During his stay there he became an expert on the Indian monetary system. As a result of this experience Keynes produced his first book, *Indian Currency and Finance,* considered to be one of the better statements of the gold exchange standard. Some of the ideas that he was later to propose in his recommendations for an international monetary system to be put in place after World War II were presented in embryonic form in this work.

After two years of service in the India Office he returned to Cambridge where he made his commitment to a career in economics and settled into academic life. He received a fellowship at King's College, lectured, wrote, and became editor of the *Economic Journal,* the journal of the Royal Economic Society, while still in his 20s. Keynes maintained his London contacts with the Bloomsbury group and with his business interests. Successful speculation in the foreign exchange market and the stock and commodity markets made him a man of modest wealth. He had a fascination with risk, a feeling for the big plunge. This is not a common trait of economists.

The tranquility of Cambridge life was disturbed by the coming of World War I. Keynes went back into public service at the Treasury where he worked throughout the war. Throughout his life he had a capacity for hard work. Good at cutting through the heart of a problem and preparing recommendations in position papers, he rose in the councils of government as his talent became more recognized and contributed at the highest decision making levels. Following the Armistice he went to Paris for the Peace Conference as senior representative of the Treasury empowered to speak for the Chancellor of the Exchequer. He also served as deputy for the Chancellor on the Supreme Economic Council.

Keynes had a ring-side seat at the Peace Conference with a chance to observe directly the world leaders in action—Wilson of the United States, Clemenceau of France, Orlando of Italy, and Lloyd George of Great Britain. There were great hopes that the negotiations would open the possibilities for a new era of peace and prosperity. Like any person of sensitivity, Keynes was sickened by the bloodletting of the static trench warfare that cut down the youth of Europe, including many of his Cambridge friends and acquaintances. Even as the conference proceeded he had firsthand information, through official reports, on hunger in Europe among the civilian population. Keynes became distressed by the terms of the treaty as they began to develop. The reparations imposed on Germany he thought too punitive, a Carthaginian peace that would make for an unstable political balance in Europe. For his own part he submitted a plan for the rebuilding of Europe that foreshadowed in some ways the Marshall Plan introduced for reconstruction of the war-torn economies after World War II. Shortly before the signing of the Treaty in June 1919, he resigned his Treasury position in protest of the terms of the Treaty and returned to England. Going to Charleston, he worked at white heat on a book attacking the terms of the treaty, *The Economic Consequences of the Peace*. It was published in December 1919. One of the more famous personal declarations in political literature, it almost immediately made him internationally known.

The book is a biting criticism of the terms of the Treaty. In some ways a polemic, it is probably unfair in some of its judgments.

Keynes later felt himself that he had been too harsh in his comments on President Wilson who was given heavy-handed treatment. But in its central thrust, the broad assessment of the defects of the Treaty, the book has survived the judgment of time rather well. The strident tone of the tract is probably explained, in part, by his feeling of a need to atone to his Bloomsbury friends for his part in the war. A number of the Bloomsbury group were pacifists and some of the men conscientious objectors. His relations with Bloomsbury were chilled by the silent—and sometimes not so silent—disapproval of Keynes for his part in the war effort. The sharpness of the attack in *The Economic Consequences of the Peace* was probably accentuated by his need to reestablish his Bloomsbury credentials.

It was in the years following his return to Cambridge after the war that his major contributions to economics were made. His *Treatise on Money*, published in two volumes in 1930, would have, he thought, a major impact on the field. It was not, as it turned out, well received. A rethinking of the main themes of the *Treatise*, along with a preoccupation with the causes of the Great Depression, led him to the insights of *The General Theory*, which was published in 1936. Only a handful of substantive contributions were done after the completion of this major work, for he went back into the Treasury with the coming of World War II.

It is probably true, as it has often been said, that Keynes worked himself to death during the war. His contributions to the financing of the war, to negotiations for a postwar loan from the United States, to the debate over the establishment of the International Monetary Fund—the proposal offered by the British and rejected in favor of the American draft is known as the Keynes Plan—were unremitting. He suffered a heart attack in 1937; his work in behalf of the war effort probably contributed to the final attack that took his life at Tilton in 1946.

Much honored for scientific contributions and his service to government, he became Lord Keynes, Baron of Tilton, in 1942. He seems to have been one of those fortunate people who are reasonably content with how the important things in their lives turned out. Asked toward the end of his life what he would have done differently, Keynes answered, "I would have drunk more champagne."

What are we to make of this man in a word of brief summary? There is no question that he was brilliantly creative and strongly committed to what he saw as the public good. Fiercely patriotic in his own way; he was tenacious in negotiation when British interests were involved. Those who knew him have conflicting opinions of his personality. He was arrogant and overbearing, he was considerate and generous, depending on who is speaking.

Sometimes the shrewdest observers are children. Quentin Bell remembers as a child crossing Chichester Harbour on a ferry in the company of Keynes and other adults. It was a warm day and Keynes had taken off his hat and laid it upside down within easy reach. Its shape reminded the child of a boat. Bell threw it into the water and remembers it "gently, rather jauntily, riding up and down upon the little waves." The hat was duly retrieved by boatmen and Bell remembers being "a little surprised that the grownups did not share my ecstatic delight. Neither then nor later," he reports, "did I see Maynard lose his temper." Patience with a little boy who has just thrown his hat in the water can make up for a lot of arrogance.

CHAPTER 3

KEYNES AND THE CLASSICS

Every great truth begins as a heresy. History does not build monuments to scientists who only repeat what is common knowledge; great minds are great because they confront a ruling orthodoxy. To understand those who make important contributions to human thought, you must begin with the state of the science at the moment of discovery.

The body of doctrine that dominated economic theory at the time Keynes was writing is usually called *classical economics* and to understand Keynes we must have some notion of what it was all about. There is a further payoff to a short trip through this historic teaching. In recent developments in economic theory and in practical policy debate, there has been a return to the economics of the pre-Keynesian period. In some ways we have come full circle. We need to know something about the classical school of thought not only to understand Keynes but also to follow current controversy.

THE CLASSICAL ECONOMICS

Keynes's most important objection to classical economics is related to one question: is a capitalistic system self-regulating in the sense that it automatically tends toward full employment? Is such a system capable of recovering from the periodic slumps to which it is subject without government intervention? Up until the Great Depression economists generally held that capitalistic systems have built within them a mechanism for automatic self-correction. Should such an economy slide into a depression—with all the damaging effects on human lives and social organization—forces automatically go into effect to check the contraction and restore the economy to a level of full operation. The system was held to be, in a sense, an automated system with its own circuit of feedback and capacity for self correction.

The basic stabilizing mechanism in this model is the pricing system. If a product is not moving as well as a manufacturer expects, it may be that it is poorly designed and low in quality. In that case, it's back to the drawing board. Suppose though that the product is competitive in design and quality but still there are unsold inventories. Then we come to the issue that is central for economic analysis; the price is too high to clear the market. Demand is not great enough at the quoted price to move the amount supplied. If the price were lowered consumers would buy what is being produced.

It is important in this theory that not only must prices for output change when necessary but also the prices of inputs used in the production process. If the wage rate, the price of labor, is too high in terms of what employers can pay, for example, some people who want to work are not able to find a job and unemployment appears. The price of funds needed for purchase of plant and equipment is the interest rate. When consumers cut back on consumption spending, funds saved are channeled into the hands of investors through financial markets for purchase of capital goods. If the interest rate is too high, demand is not sufficient to absorb the supply of funds and consumer saving is not returned to the spending stream in the form of investment. The way to eliminate both the surplus of labor and capital funds is for the prices of these two inputs, the wage and the interest rate, to drop. If these two prices are lowered, there is some price level at which markets clear. Workers who are willing to work at a lower wage are employed and the amount that consumers wish to save at a lower interest rate is absorbed into investment.

The idea of a self-regulating market is due to the genius of Adam Smith who published his book, *The Wealth of Nations*, in the same year Thomas Jefferson drafted the Declaration of Independence. We take for granted the free market system as part of our familiar environment. But in historical terms it is a relatively recent invention. Economies in ancient and medieval times were basically command economies where price and other details of trade were determined by the governing authority. A large number of the world's economies today, starting with the Soviet Union, are, of course, still command economies.

The power of the market system to bring into agreement intentions of buyers and sellers, and thus effect an "efficient" allocation of resources, is only one of its advantages. Another is its power to motivate through the promise of reward for economic contribution. Adam Smith's great insight is the possibility of reconciling individual self-interest and the public good through a free market system. In Smith's vision human energy is mobilized as individuals compete with one another, each seeking their own reward. While sellers are free to make their own market decisions motivated by self-interest, they are, at the same time, prevented from exploiting consumers in price and product quality because of competition from other sellers also seeking their own reward and rivals for share of the market. Through competition individual self-seeking is converted into what Smith called an *invisible hand* of control. Greed is turned to public purpose. "Harnessing the 'base' motive of material self-interest to promote the common good is perhaps *the* most important social invention mankind has yet achieved," writes Charles Schultze, chief economic adviser to President Carter. "Turning silk into a silk purse is no great trick, but turning a sow's ear into a silk purse does indeed partake of the miraculous."

The most sophisticated version of the pricing system in a free market was developed by the French economist, Leon Walras, whose book, *Elements of Pure Economics*, was published about a decade before Keynes was born. In order to understand Walras's contribution we need to take a brief side trip.

Economic decisions usually involve things that are measurable, like amounts sold, price, and income. It is possible in economics — more so than in the other social sciences — to reduce a problem to numbers. Economists think in mathematical terms; an economic relationship comes up on their mental screens as an algebraic equation. The amount of a product (x) that consumers demand depends, among other things, on the product's price (y). The lower the price the more the public buys. Carrying the analysis of the pricing system further, economists observe that the sales of a product also depend on the prices of other products with which it competes for the public's dollar. If the price of steel falls, sales of aluminum are adversely affected. We could think of the economic system as described by a large set of equations with an equation for each product showing the relationship between the sales of that product and its own price and the prices of competing goods. The market sales and price can then be found for each item by solving for all the x's and y's in the set of equations. A model of this kind, described here in skeleton form, is called a *general equilibrium model* and is Walras's contribution to economics. It is not something one would bring up for discussion during halftime at a game between the Bears and the Raiders, but it is a tool of major importance in modern economic analysis.

In the real world of McDonald's hamburgers, VCRs, and Startrek movies, buyers and sellers find the values for the x's and y's —sales quantities and prices—that clear all markets through a process of trial and error. If there are surpluses or shortages of goods, prices adjust until the amounts demanded and supplied are equal. Equations describing the demand and supply for inputs are also included in the system. If there is an excess supply of labor on the market, wage rates adjust until unemployment is eliminated. The general equilibrium model is a representation of the classical self-adjusting mechanism in its most elegant form. If prices and wages do not correctly reflect underlying conditions of supply and demand, buyers and sellers interacting in markets force the necessary price changes. The free market works like a giant computer finding the values of all of the x's and y's that bring supply and demand into line through a process of adjustment.

The tilt of history at this moment is in the direction of free market control as a form of economic organization. The record of socialist experimentation in this century has been disappointing in terms of the standard of economic efficiency. Critics of capitalism claim, of course, that a free market system produces undesirable social effects and that such a system must be modified to be acceptable. Precisely how and to what extent it ought to be supplemented by government action provides the subject matter for continuing debate. But there is evidence that the ability of the free market to allocate resources efficiently, for all of its faults, is robust. The historical shift in choice of social forms is illustrated by the introduction of free market features in some of the socialist nations of Eastern Europe, in China and, most recently, in the Soviet Union.

To appreciate the power of a decentralized market to bring order to the operation of an economy one must observe a country where a free market does not exist. For example, one could observe Russia. Since the days of Stalin, production, marketing, and price decisions have been made in the Soviet Union by a government planning agency. Resources are first taken off the top for defense purposes. Since Soviet output is only a little over half of U.S. production, matching gun for gun and rocket for rocket preempts a larger proportion of available output than it does for the United States. The sacrifice required to maintain a competitive military posture is greater. After defense has been provided for, another share of resources goes to expand the industrial base. What is left over in production capacity goes to consumers.

The planning commission has determined the amount of the various types of consumer goods to be produced. For goods to be absorbed in an orderly way in any economy, consumer standards for quality and product design must be satisfied and price levels must be set so that planned production—that amount and no more—is sought for purchase by the public. In the decentralized economies of western nations, a failure to maintain quality and product appeal is signaled by a loss of market share. The ultimate penalty for not reacting is bankruptcy. Once quality is assured in a free market system, price must be adjusted in response to market reaction to a level that consumers are willing to pay and that covers the cost of production. In the Soviet Union where market feedback is sluggish and often ignored, it has not been uncommon for unsold goods to accumulate in huge inventories. Subsidies for enterprises have compensated for inefficiencies. Planning authorities have also frequently missed setting the price at a level that balances output with demand. They have often priced it too low, in which case there are shortages and people want to buy more at the low price than the production plan allows. Queues or waiting lines in front of stores, a common sight in the Soviet Union, are a sure sign that the price that clears the market has not been chosen. The typical housewife spends an inordinate amount of time shopping as she goes from store to store to find one that has not run out of stock.

When prices and profits do not operate as a signaling system, planners must resort to other signals. In the Soviet Union one target commonly used in the past is the output quota. A firm's success or failure has been determined by whether or not the firm has produced its assigned output. A number of interesting puzzles arise in administration of such a system. Something as simple as defining the unit for measuring output can involve a problem. If glass output, for example, is measured in terms of square yards, the glass produced is made so thin in an effort to spread raw materials, frequently in short supply, that it is too brittle to be usable. When output is measured in terms of pounds or tons, products are too weighty. Khrushchev is said to have once complained that the comrades were producing chandeliers so heavy the ceilings would not support them.

Another fascinating problem has arisen when socialist countries within the Soviet orbit trade with one another. Since they have each determined prices in an arbitrary way, it is impossible to decide on the terms of trade in exchanges among themselves on a rational basis. To solve the problem, prices for equivalent products set in capitalistic markets have been used as a benchmark. Marshall Goldman, a U.S. expert on the Soviet economy, reports that when a Soviet economist was asked how these trading partners would decide on prices when the revolution is complete and all capitalistic systems have disappeared, "he answered with a knowing wink, 'We will keep one country capitalist just for this purpose.'"

In the early Stalin years when the Soviet Union was in short supply of most goods it was possible to organize the economy along paramilitary lines for production decisions without doing a large amount of damage. In the more advanced stage of industrialization at which the economy has now arrived, inefficiencies created by rigid, bureaucratic direction seriously retard growth momentum and weaken the industrial base on which political power depends. Gorbachev, representing a younger generation of leadership, is attempting to decentralize the decision-making process as a part of *perestroika*. Substantial reforms, if achieved, will have a traumatic effect on a society that has lived with a command system for well over a half-century. Even those who welcome the changes must learn to adapt to a new way of thinking. A nation of people lacks the pricing expertise that is second nature to sellers in a market economy. Whether they can overcome the resistance of a vast bureaucracy that has a stake in the planning apparatus is yet to be determined.

THE CLASSICAL THEORY OF MONEY

Returning to our main theme, the classical economists assigned to price the crucial role of resource allocation and maintaining the stability of the economy. There is a further, important point in classical theory to be noted.

When we use the world *price* in this discussion we mean *relative price*. Suppose that given demand and supply conditions, oranges are twice as valuable as apples. If the correct relative value holds in a primitve barter system it would take two apples to get one orange. In a more advanced economy where everything is measured in terms of money, the appropriate relative value would be reached if oranges were priced, say, at $10 and apples at $5. The correct relative value would also hold if oranges were priced at $20 and apples at $10. The *relative price*, the two–for–one relationship, is the same in the two cases, but the *general price level* or the *average price* is not. The price level in the second case is double that of the first.

We can speak of a general level of prices, and changes in that level, only when money is a part of market transactions. In a barter economy only relative prices exist, the ratio at which goods exchange for one another. Fluctuation in the general price level, an inflationary or deflationary pattern, is a disease peculiar to economies advanced enough to have a money system.

The second major problem with which classical economists wrestled is what determines the general level of prices and this question led them to the *quantity theory of money*. The quantity theory is one of the oldest theories in economics. A sophisticated version can be found in tracts over two centuries old. Because of its importance the theory deserves a somewhat formal discussion.

The quantity theory can best be explained in terms of a relatively simple relationship which is stated as follows:

$$MV = PQ$$

The *M* on the left-hand side of the equation stands for the amount of money in circulation. The symbol *V* stands for the *velocity* of money or its turnover rate. D.H. Robertson, a student and colleague of Keynes, tells a story to illustrate the idea of velocity in a book entitled *Money*, first published in the 1920s. It is one of the few books on economics that could be described as charming and it has been kept in print. It is best known for the whimsically appropriate quotations from *Alice in Wonderland* with which Robertson starts each chapter. In the story which Robertson tells to illustrate the idea of velocity, two Englishmen, Bob and Joe, decide to become enterprising businessmen, pool their money, and buy a barrel of beer to take to Epsom Downs to sell on Derby Day for sixpence a pint.

After buying the beer Bob had threepence left and Joe had nothing. It was a hot day and as they carried the beer along the road they became thirsty. Bob decided to stop for a rest and have a pint of beer, giving Joe his threepence as half of the purchase price. Joe decided to join Bob for a glass and gave him the threepence back. By now the end of the story is predictable. The threepence kept exchanging hands until the beer was gone. Turning over rapidly, the threepence bought the entire supply.

On the right side of the equation, P stands for the general price level or the average level of prices and Q stands for the units of output exchanged. Looking at the equation as a whole, the left side, MV, the amount of money in circulation times the number of times each dollar is used on the average, is a measure of total spending. The right side, PQ, the average price times the number of units sold, is a measure of income received by sellers. The equation really says that total spending equals total income, an obvious statement but, nevertheless, a useful way to think of activity in an economy.

The classical economists went beyond the obvious. The Q in the equation they thought of as unchanging because they believed that the economy tends toward full employment. In relatively short periods of time in which the population is fixed, only one level of output is produced if we assume that everyone that wishes to work is working. The velocity they thought of as depending on customs such as how often people are paid and how often they pay their bills. It also depends on the simple technology of money movement, whether money is circulated by riders on horseback or by electronic networks. Payment customs and technology do not change frequently so that velocity was assumed to remain unchanged for long periods of time. The V and the Q, then, are thought of as constant in classical reasoning. If the V and the Q are constant, then it must be true that if you change the money supply on the left side of the equation, the price level on the right side of the equation changes also. More precisely, the price level changes in proportion to the change in the money supply. Double the money supply and the price level doubles. We have arrived at the punch line of this dialogue, the *quantity theory of money*.

Two key points make up, in summary, the substance of classical economic theory which Keynes took as his starting point. Full employment is reached automatically through relative price adjustments. The general price level is determined by the amount of money in circulation and does not affect relative prices.

There is a schizophrenic quality to classical logic. Economic events are split into two separate types of behavior. The first involves real goods and services, the guts of what economic activity is all about. The second involves money. The two dimensions have little to do with each other. Relative price and output levels can be precisely determined in a barter economy, a world without money. Money makes the exchange of goods more efficient but is neutral as far as the level of output is concerned. This assertion, the *neutrality of money*, is a central doctrine of classical economics and has been reincarnated in recent theories. Does an increase in the money supply stimulate production and employment? Some influential economists would answer this question today by saying no, except as a purely transitory effect. We will return to this issue later.

KEYNES AND THE CLASSICAL ECONOMICS

Classical economics dominated English thought for a century and a half before *The General Theory*. It is difficult to exaggerate the powerful grip it had on conventional thought at the time Keynes was writing. In order to get a hearing for his novel proposals, he first had to challenge its basic premise. "If heretics on the other side of the gulf are to demolish the forces of nineteenth-century orthodoxy," Keynes wrote in *The New Republic* about a year before publication of *The General Theory*, "they must attack them in their citadel. . . . I was brought up in the citadel and I recognize its power and might."

The central thrust of Keynes's *General Theory* is an attack on the classical doctrine that the economy has the capacity for self-correction. It is not surprising that someone in the 1930s would challenge the thesis that the system reacts efficiently to eliminate unemployment. In 1933, the worst year of the Great Depression in the United States, unemployment reached 25 percent of the labor force. One out of every four workers could not find a job. This can be compared to the highest annual employment rate recorded after World War II, just under 10 percent in 1982. The other major industrialized nations shared in this trauma. Britain had severe unemployment not only in the 1930s but also in the 1920s; for most of the interwar period the British economy did not perform at an acceptable level. Social unrest was widespread.

The power of *The General Theory* to persuade was not simply that it pointed to the impotency of classical theory in explaining the economic catastrophe of the 1930s. The gap between theory and reality was a fact known to everyone and it is a truism, often repeated by economists, that you can't beat a theory with a fact alone. An historical happening like the Great Depression could represent only a temporary departure from normal and be unconvincing as a rebuttal to traditional thinking. You can only beat a theory with a theory. Keynes's claim to serious consideration was based on his analysis of why the traditional doctrine failed and his new and apparently more realistic theoretical framework for studying the fluctuations of a capitalistic economy. He offered a different vision, a novel interpretation of the world economic catastrophe of the 1930s, which came not from some crank with a naive solution for bettering mankind, but from someone accepted as a legitimate member of the professional establishment. In Keynes the man and the moment met.

As we have seen, the basic mechanism for self-correction in the classical theory is the pricing system. The first question to which Keynes addressed himself in his famous book was why the pricing mechanism didn't work as planned.

One answer to the question involves an appeal to the simple fact that prices are "sticky." In order for the classical system to work, prices must be flexible. They rise and fall as the condition of the economy requires. The fact is that some prices change infrequently. Agreements between buyers and sellers, between employers and workers often involve long-term commitments, either formal or informal. Prices in some cases may not change for extended periods of time. If prices are not flexible, then the basic adjustment mechanism cannot operate and serious departures from full employment can occur.

While Keynes recognized the problem of price stickiness, he went beyond this to argue that even if prices are flexible, adjustments may not restore an economy to full employment. He was highly sensitive to the role of expectations, partly because of his own speculative adventures in commodity and foreign exchange markets. In a depression, a sharp fall in prices and wages might stimulate demand by presenting consumers with tempting bargains and employers with low wage opportunities, but it might also set off a wave of pessimistic expectations that cause consumers and investors to revise spending plans downward despite the inducement of lower prices. The efficiency of the market in stabilizing the economy is still, after 50 years, one of the key controversial issues among economists. There is even debate as to precisely what Keynes said on the matter. But it is clear that he thought that the market is not powerful enough to prevent serious departures from full employment. To the argument of classical economists that the pricing mechanism would restore a condition of full employment in the long run if given the chance, Keynes made his famous reply, "in the long-run we are all dead."

If the system is not automatically self-stabilizing, then some form of government action to compensate for a failure of private spending may be appropriate. One approach would be monetary policy, variation in the money supply by central bank authorities. In terms of the equation, $MV = PQ$, a recession is a fall in output (Q) below the level that would be produced at full employment. This could only happen in the classical model as a temporary occurrence. In the Keynesian world, it could be a persistent problem. If output fell below the full employment level, why not increase the money supply (M) on the left-hand side of the equation? Employers reacting to an increase in sales stimulated by an increase in the money supply would sell off excess inventories and hire workers to increase output.

Interestingly enough, Keynes was not enthusiastic about this approach. His doubts and the doubts of the Keynesian economists who followed him opened the way for one of the major economic controversies of the postwar period. We will return to this debate later.

Rejecting monetary policy as a viable option for counteracting recessions, Keynes turned to another tool, fiscal policy. Fiscal policy is probably his most original contribution in terms of public policy recommendations. It involves the use of the government budget to compensate for private spending. If private spending is insufficient to bring the economy to a level of full employment, government should increase its spending to add to private outlays. An alternative to an increase in government spending would be a decrease in taxes to stimulate private expenditures. In either case the budget moves in the direction of deficit.

This recommendation may not sound unusual in an age in which

we have come to accept massive Federal deficits with a certain amount
of equanimity, but in the 1930s, when the principle of the balanced
budget dominated thinking in public finance, the idea seemed terribly
radical.

Keynes was suggesting in his fiscal policy recommendations a
new way of looking at the budget. Instead of the standard public
accounting rule of matching receipts and expenditures, he suggested
a different budget principle. The budget should be thought of as a
counterweight to the private sector. Whether the budget is balanced
or a deficit or surplus incurred should depend on the state of the
economy; a deficit in recessions to increase total spending, a surplus
in periods of high prosperity to reduce total outlays when there is
danger of inflationary pressure. This new tool, fiscal policy, absorbed
a lot of attention from researchers who followed Keynes.

These two points, 1) that the economy does not necessarily
tend toward full employment and 2) that the government should
compensate for the failure of the market to maintain full employment,
are what, in practical terms, the *General Theory* was all about.
Keynes made his argument with an elaborate theory which provided
a base for developments in economic analysis for the next several
decades. The whole field of macroeconomics, which deals with the
behavior of the national economic environment, started with Keynes.
But the practical implications of his work do not seem, looking back
50 years, to be all that revolutionary. The most controversial point
then, and probably now, is the assertion that the capitalistic system is
not self-stabilizing because it opens the door for government action.

In many ways Keynes was conservative. He was looking for
a way to conserve the existing capitalistic structure which he felt
could not survive repetitions of a social calamity like the Great
Depression. The conservative aspect of Keynes's work is emphasized
by the negative Marxist reaction to the theme of *The General Theory*.
Marxists assert that capitalistic systems are eventually torn apart by
internal stresses due to such things as recurring depressions. Once
they collapse, they are replaced by socialist systems. Marxists look
upon Keynesian economics as an attempt to shore up an inherently
faulty system and delay the historic arrival of socialism. They save
their choicest invective for those who attempt to thwart the will of
history.

One of the problems of assessing the impact of Keynes's work is that the term *Keynesian* has been made to carry a lot of freight; it has been used to describe experiments in public policy that have little relationship to what Keynes wrote. One observer has commented that "it is probable that the Athenians did not execute Socrates so much for the things he had said as for the things they thought he had said." A paraphrase of this statement would also be true of Keynes. He is sometimes blamed for things he never said. There is no question but that he opened the door for acceptance of government involvement in the macroeconomy, a development of major historical importance. It is not accurate to attribute to him, as some of his critics are inclined to do, prime responsiblity for the development of the welfare state. The welfare state, in some form, would have come about if Keynes had never lived.

CHAPTER 4

THE AGE OF KEYNES

With the start of World War II, shortly after publication of *The General Theory*, the problem facing industrialized nations was suddenly no longer the unemployment of the depression years but the marshalling of resources for prosecution of the war. When economists and statesmen turned their attention again to the problems of a peacetime economy, Keynes was dead. He had attended a meeting on international financial arrangements in Savannah in early 1946, became ill there, returned to England, and died a few months later. The debate about postwar economic issues went on without him.

While the impact of Keynes's economic ideas on economists and policymakers has been significant, it is not easy to trace the precise path of this influence.

EARLY RECEPTION

First reaction to *The General Theory* by economists was mixed. Confronted with a novel doctrine, many of the older generation tended to be skeptical. The more flexible, younger economists, frustrated by the contradiction between the classical theory of the self-stabilizing economy which they had been taught and the widespread unemployment of the Great Depression, quickly became caught up in discussion of the new ideas. Paul Samuelson, a 20 year old graduate student at Harvard at the time of the publication of Keynes's book (later to be the first American to win the Nobel Prize in economics) has described the excitement of the moment as he experienced it. "*The General Theory* caught most economists under the age of thirty-five with the unexpected virulence of a disease first attacking and decimating an isolated tribe of south sea islanders."

In economics seminars around the country *The General Theory* became the topic of discussion. Kenneth Galbraith has told the story of "how Keynes came to America." Most would probably agree that "Harvard was the principal avenue by which Keynes's ideas passed to the United States." Alvin Hansen became one of the best known Keynesians. Keynes provided little detail on the implementation of fiscal policy. Economists such as Hansen worked at providing the specifics. Policymakers from Washington who were struggling with the real world problems came to Boston for his weekly seminars. There was a two-way street. Graduates of Harvard and other leading universities, trained in Keynesian thinking, took jobs in Washington and brought the new ideas to New Deal agencies.

Keynes's work on *The General Theory* happened to coincide with work on the development of the now familiar accounting system designed to measure the performance of the economy. This effort by a number of people—including as a major contributor Simon Kuznets—resulted in procedures for estimating the Gross National Product, a measure of national production activity now published quarterly by the Department of Commerce and followed closely by those monitoring the economy for government and private corporations. The Gross National Product and its components, such as spending on consumption by the general public and on plant and equipment by business, are the key magnitudes whose behavior Keynes's theory was designed to explain. The newly available information raised the level of consciousness of the informed public about matters of Keynesian concern. It also provided the basic data that economists needed to test empirically the economic relationships which he emphasized. And test they did.

The discipline of econometrics, which uses real world data to determine the precise way in which economic events are actually related, was still in its infancy. Early American econometricians worked with agricultural prices and quantities attempting to specify such things as the demand for wheat. These data, long collected by the U.S. Department of Agriculture and readily available as public information, provided the observations needed for the statistical analysis that is the heart of econometrics. Keynesian theory and the new Gross National Product accounts opened up the possibility of a broader focus to econometric research, the behavior of the national economy. Lawrence Klein of the University of Pennsylvania was one of the pioneers, with a first crude attempt in the 1940s to describe the U.S. economy with a small set of equations. From such beginnings came an industry. Today econometric models designed for forecasting the Gross National Product, too large to solve were it not for high speed computers, are routinely sold to industry and government.

The most influential instrument for spreading Keynesian ideas to the masses of undergraduates was the text written by Paul Samuelson, published in 1948. Samuelson's *Economics* was the first introductory text to incorporate the Keynesian model.

KEYNES AND PUBLIC POLICY

New ideas are seldom implemented by governments so as to satisfy the standards of intellectual purists. Keynes, with his long experience in public service, would not have been surprised that acceptance of Keynesian thinking by policymakers was uneven and incomplete, quite removed from the neat textbook presentation. Some of Keynes's ideas had influence, others did not. Some Keynesian policies were implemented but the stimulus came from a non-Keynesian source.

Keynes's most practical policy recommendation, for example, use of the government budget as a counterbalance to the private sector to prevent short-run oscillations in the economy, was not entirely original. Experiments in compensatory spending had been tried on a number of occasions before publication of *The General Theory*. Public works programs were initiated by some states before World War I. Herbert Hoover proposed bunching needed public works projects in periods of economic slowdown. Sweden experimented in the early 1930s with the idea of balancing the budget over the business cycle, with deficits in time of depression and compensating surpluses in times of prosperity.

The public works programs of Roosevelt's New Deal preceded *The General Theory* by several years. Keynes addressed an open letter to the President in late 1933 in the *New York Times* urging Roosevelt to use government expenditure to stimulate the economy. The President and Keynes met later in 1934. The meeting was not a particular success. Roosevelt is quoted as complaining to a cabinet member, "He left a whole rigamarole of figures. He must be a mathematician rather than a political economist." The President was probably never comfortable with the new theory of finance. He had run against Hoover in the 1932 campaign charging his opponent with fiscal irresponsibility for running budget deficits and pledging to stop "this dangerous kind of financing." His initiation of public works projects, followed by budget deficits, was based on simple pragmatism. You could not let people starve. But eventually, after some order is restored, one should move back to the old time religion of balancing the budget. Roosevelt was never really comfortable with his departure from financial orthodoxy.

The most convincing evidence that a stimulative budget policy could move the economy in the direction of full employment came from the massive defense spending of World War II. Once rearmament started, unemployment quickly evaporated. This laboratory demonstration of the effectiveness of fiscal policy, along with the unwillingness of millions of discharged service men and women to accept a return to the massive unemployment of the 1930s, probably had more to do with national acceptance of more active government after the war than the musings of economists. The stage was set for the Employment Act of 1946.

The first version of this act was introduced by Senator James E. Murray of Montana, an unusual combination of wealth and liberal political philosophy. One of the wealthiest members of the Senate, he sponsored over his career a number of bills related to social issues, health, education, labor, and social security. Senator Murray's bill had a strong Keynesian tone. The President was required to submit to Congress annually a "national production and employment budget." This budget should provide a forecast of the amount of private and governmental spending likely to take place in the coming year. It should also present an estimate of the amount of total expenditures necessary to bring the economy to a full employment level. Should the projected spending fall short of what was needed for full employment, the President should submit to Congress a plan for federal outlays sufficient to supplement private spending by the necessary amount.

The compromise bill that finally passed was much more general in theme, a broad commitment to a prosperous economy. "It is the continuing policy and responsibility of the Federal Government to use all practical means consistent with its needs and obligations and other essential considerations of national policy. . . to promote maximum employment, production and purchasing power." Part of the reason the bill passed with almost unanimous consent is its vague language. The act does not say precisely, for example, what the "maximum employment" target is. "All practical means" is not spelled out. Some members of Congress interpreted the phrase to imply forceful fiscal action along the lines of the Murray bill; others interpreted it to mean something less interventionist, a report, say, by a committee assigned to investigate the problem. Instead of requiring the President to submit to Congress a "national production and employment budget," the act simply requires the President to submit a general report on the condition of the economy "together with such recommendations for legislation as he may deem necessary or desirable."

History sometimes smiles on political affairs. It is lucky that the final version of the act is rather general. In 1946 we did not know enough about national economic management to implement the type of program that Murray had in mind. Nor do we know enough today. The vagueness of the Employment Act's commitment, however, has long bothered those of more activist inclination. There was an attempt in the Humphrey-Hawkins Act of 1978 to give more precise content to the original bill, for example, by defining in specific numerical terms what is meant by full employment. This bill has failed in practice to bind Presidents in a more precise way. The requirements of the act remain vague.

Despite its generality, the act still represents a landmark; a formal statement of a rejection of the principle of government neutrality in the face of serious unemployment (the *laissez-faire* policy that guided most of our history) and an acceptance of the propriety of some type of government concern for economic prosperity. A change in national attitude would have occurred if Keynes had never written his famous book. The time for some form of government commitment had arrived. But the act is consistent with Keynes's rejection of the classical doctrine that the economy tends automatically to full employment and requires no human intervention. Perhaps both the Employment Act and *The General Theory* were part of a larger phenomenon, a growing consciousness that government failure to act in the face of serious unemployment was no longer acceptable. What Keynes did was to provide the theoretical framework that made this changing public attitude intellectually respectable.

FISCAL POLICY AFTER THE EMPLOYMENT ACT

There were four recessions during the terms of Presidents Truman and Eisenhower, — 1948, 1953, 1957, and 1960. All were relatively mild compared to the depression of the 1930s. In these recessions fiscal action was limited to the stimulation of the automatic stabilizers, a budget impact that requires a word of explanation.

There is a certain amount of stabilizing capability built into our fiscal system that requires no discretionary decision by Congress. If the economy moves into a recession, government receipts from income taxes fall since the income on which these taxes are based has also fallen. On the other side of the budget, some outlays, such as unemployment insurance, are automatically increased when the economy moves into a recession. In an economic expansion taxes and outlays behave in the opposite way, tax receipts rise and expenditures fall, and have a restraining effect that moderates inflationary tendencies. In summary, the budget has an anticyclical property. It moves in the direction of deficit at the low point of the business cycle and toward surplus in the expansion phase; passive deficits and surpluses, if you will, that are caused not by conscious changes in budget provisions by legislators but simply in response to movements in the economy.

If there is any improvement in our understanding of the effect of the budget on the behavior of the economy as a result of the Keynesian debate, it is with regard to this automatic feature. Politicians before Keynes would have instinctively reacted to a budget deficit, even one arising from depressed business conditions, by feeling some obligation to urge a decrease in government outlays or an increase in taxes. Policymakers today would recognize such action as not only inappropriate but probably counterproductive. An increase in taxes during a recession would aggravate economic conditions by reducing private spending power.

The Committee for Economic Development (CED), formed in 1942 by a group of business executives who leaned toward the progressive end of a conservative political persuasion, accepted the idea that a public finance rule that calls for an annually balanced budget is inappropriate. They argued that deficits are sometimes helpful. The policy target, they argued, should be a balanced budget at full employment. The rhetoric of fiscal policy discussions today, couched in terms of a full employment or high employment budget, can be traced in part to this early contribution of the CED.

Fiscal actions during the Truman and Eisenhower administrations were primarily of this passive, automatic stabilizing variety. Tax reductions were implemented by a Republican controlled Congress in two of the four recessions that occurred during the Truman and Eisenhower years but probably not for compensatory reasons. Congress lowered rates and increased exemptions just before the recession that began in late 1948. The revenue act was passed over the President's veto. Truman and his advisers were still preoccupied with inflation, the problem of the postwar transition period. Scheduled tax decreases were also allowed to take place in 1954 under Eisenhower, an appropriate action given the recession of 1953–1954. Neither of these cuts were made to compensate for a short-term economic slowdown although the timing was fortunate. Equity considerations and the encouragement of private initiative provided the underlying motivation. The first explicit commitment to Keynesian fiscal policy as a stabilizing tool came with the Kennedy administration.

CAMELOT

John Kennedy ran his presidential campaign of 1960 on the general theme of "getting the country moving again." For his chief adviser on economic strategy, he chose Walter Heller of the University of Minnesota. Heller was 20 years old at the time. *The General Theory* was published, one of the younger generation influenced by Keynesian economics in the 1930s and 1940s. When he joined Kennedy a little over two decades later he was a leading Keynesian economist and remained throughout his life one of the more visible representatives of this school of thought. He served in an official capacity in two administrations, Kennedy's and Johnson's, and was a consultant to a number of Democrats during presidential campaigns, Stevenson, Humphrey, Carter, and Mondale.

The position to which Kennedy appointed Heller was Chairman of the Council of Economic Advisers, a committee of three economists provided for by the Employment Act of 1946. Their role was to assist in the preparation of the annual economic report and to advise the President generally on matters of economic policy.

The economic report is one of the more important statements of an Administration's economic game plan. It actually consists of two parts. The first, a presentation of general themes and about a dozen pages in length, is the official report of the President. This is followed by 200 pages of detailed analysis by the Council. When reference is made to the economic report of the President, it frequently means the report of the Council. The difference between the two parts of the report became important in a curious episode involving Donald Regan, who was serving at the time as President Reagan's Secretary of the Treasury. Unhappy with policy positions of the Council, particularly that of Chairman Martin Feldstein with whom he disagreed on key issues, Regan advised the public to read the first part, the President's report, and tear up the remaining part, the report of the Council. For dramatic effect at a nationally televised session he preceded to do just that, to rip apart a copy of the report. The formation of economic policy is not always a harmonious process.

In any event it was to the position of Chairman of the Council that Kennedy appointed Walter Heller. The other two positions on the Council and the staff recruited to support it were filled by an unusually able group of economists. James Tobin of Yale, Kenneth Arrow of Stanford, and Robert Solow of MIT were later to win the Nobel prize. Heller, Tobin, Solow, and Gardner Ackley of Michigan were to serve as presidents of the American Economic Association. Though not an official member of the Council, Paul Samuelson was available as an informal consultant.

Part of their function, as the Council members saw it, was education; to educate not only the President but also Congress and the general public in a new way of thinking about economic matters. James Tobin observed that Kennedy "came into office without any firm understanding or conviction in macro-economic matters. . . . Innocent of economics on inauguration day, he was an interested and an apt pupil of the professors in the Executive Office Building."

There was at the time a wide variety of Keynesian economists, as there still is today. Heller and his group represented a type of thinking that called for only modest changes in the government role in capitalistic systems. They recognized the power of the free market in the allocation of resources and the determination of production decisions. The central problem of a capitalistic system, they argued, lies in its instability, a tendency to lapse into periods of depression and unemployment. This instability can be dampened by judicious use of fiscal policy. Once full employment is assured, the old classical model, in which there is interplay of private interests in a market of freely determined prices and production quantities, can be counted on to allocate efficiently the use of the nation's economic resources. The only new wrinkle is the use of government spending and taxes to reinforce the spending of the private sector to insure full employment. This line of thinking represented the mainstream economics accepted by a majority of Keynesian economists of the day, as well as by Keynes himself in *The General Theory*. Because of its melding of the traditional economics with Keynesian theory, it came to be called the *neoclassical synthesis*. This version of Keynes was the one presented to a more general public in successive editions of Samuelson's *Economics*.

Shortly after the inauguration Heller began working on the idea of a tax cut to stimulate the economy, a proposal formally made by Kennedy in 1963. The plan was to be sold explicitly and in a straightforward way as the modern approach to budget policy.

In a widely referred to commencement speech that Kennedy delivered at Yale University in 1962, he called for a rethinking of the national approach to economic problems. "The great enemy of the truth is very often not the lie—deliberate, contrived, and dishonest— but the myth—persistent, pervasive, and unrealistic. . . . Today I want to particularly consider the myth and reality in our national economy." Myth or not, the idea of a balanced budget remained for the most part the conventional truth in the early 1960s and selling the idea of deliberately running a deficit was a bold move. In an interview with *The New York Times* shortly before his death, Heller tells of taking to the White House a draft of another Presidential speech for Kennedy to review. Kennedy who was a speed reader covered it rapidly and indicated his approval. The brevity of the deliberation bothered Heller. "My God, Mr. President," he reported himself as commenting, "don't you know I have you saying something in there that no other President has ever said—that a deficit under certain circumstances can be a good thing; that there are constructive deficits and destructive deficits and it depends on the circumstances? He said 'well, all right, let me take another look at that.' And so he went back and he looked at that part," Heller further reported "and he changed one sentence, just very moderately, and then he tossed it back to me and said 'let's go.'"

The tax cut plan presented to Congress in 1963 and formally passed under President Johnson in 1964 was more innovative and ambitious in intent than the simple rescue of an economy caught in a deep recession. The economy was not in a recession at the time; it was simply growing at a sluggish rate. What the Council had in mind was somewhat sophisticated.

The Council used the expression *potential GNP* to describe the output the economy could produce if we were at full employment. If the economy were at less than full employment then actual production would be less than potential and there would be a *GNP gap*. Estimates of this gap measured in billions of dollars were reported in the President's *Economic Report*. The gap was presented as the cost of unemployment, the output we could have had but did not due to an excessive jobless rate. A GNP gap can exist even if the economy is in an expansion phase of the cycle. If business is growing, but at a sluggish pace, unemployment appears. The unemployment rate when the Administration took office was a little under 7 percent. A tax cut would cause the economy to expand more rapidly, according to the plan, and draw more workers into jobs.

In addition to this problem of failure to reach the potential level of output, there was still another matter to be considered, the long-term growth of the potential GNP. As the nation's population grows over time the number of people looking for jobs each year gets larger. New job openings must be created. If the ability of the economy to produce, as measured by the potential GNP, does not grow then workers will be unemployed. The Council then had two goals in mind as a result of fiscal action: 1) to stimulate the economy so that existing capacity would be fully utilized and 2) to cause this capacity to grow over the long run at a rate sufficient to absorb workers coming into the labor force.

To achieve these two goals, the tax proposal had both short-run and long-run features. There was a tax cut for consumers to stimulate spending by the general public and cause production to expand in response to increased sales. Other tax changes incorporated in the proposal included direct advantages to business to encourage investment in capital equipment. Such investment both stimulates the economy now and also increases capacity to produce over the long run. The tax cut for consumers reinforces the direct investment incentives in the tax changes since additions to plant and equipment are more likely to take place when consumption levels are high.

In presenting its argument for the tax cuts, the Council cited particularly the high rates that people paid on the final increments of income. The top marginal rate at the time was 91 percent. These high rates were hurting incentive to invest, it was argued, imposing a *fiscal drag* on the economy, preventing it from increasing long-run capacity, and locking the nation into an unacceptably high unemployment rate. The supply-siders of the Reagan Administration cited the long-run feature of the tax cut of 1964 and its positive effect on the economy as precedent for the tax bill of 1981.

THE PHILLIPS CURVE

There is another part to the thinking of the Kennedy advisers that is important to understand not only for tracking this particular episode but also for following the debate between the Keynesians and their critics that emerged later in the 1960s and 1970s. This part of the policy strategy is explained in terms of what came to be called the *Phillips curve*.

A.W. Phillips, after whom the curve is named, came from an interesting background of experiences. His education was as fragmented and casual as Keynes's was traditional and elitist. Born in New Zealand he dropped out of high school at the age of 15 to become an apprentice in an electric utility plant. Completing his apprenticeship at 20, he rousted about for a year seeing the country, working at times as an electrician and at others pursuing adventure as the mood caught him. At one point he joined up with a buffalo and crocodile hunter, a Crocodile Dundee type, whom he met in the Northern Territory. In his own words, they "shot a few crocs but not enough to make big money." In 1937 he decided to see the world, an urge not uncommon for the youth of the isolated lands of New Zealand and Australia. He headed for Britain by way of China and Russia. When he was only one day at sea on a Japanese ship on which he had booked passage, Japan declared war on China. A detour to Japan was followed by an adventurous trip through Mongolia, to Siberia, and on to Moscow on the Trans-Siberian Railway. From there he traveled to London where he found work with an electric utility. Joining the service when the war started, he was sent to the Pacific, taken prisoner in 1942, and spent three years in Japanese prisoner of war camps

Given a choice of being demobilized in New Zealand or the location where he joined the service, Phillips chose the latter and was returned to London. Taking advantage of an educational grant for veterans he enrolled at the London School of Economics and was 35 when he finished his undergraduate work. His academic career may have ended there had he not caught the attention of some members of the faculty with a machine that he built in the garage of a friend. The gadget was based on a mathematical model that he had developed describing the economy as a series of flows representing variables such as spending and income receipts. The demonstration machine consisted of transparent, plastic pipes filled with colored water simulating action in the economy. One could turn a valve labeled "interest rate," for example, and a flow representing investment spending would increase. The new investment, in turn, would enlarge the flow of national income. The invention, a hydraulic version of a computer game, was later produced by a plastics company and a number were sold to some major universities. It provided an interesting distraction at a national meeting of the American Economic Association in the 1950s as otherwise staid economists crowded around the Moniac on exhibit, twisting the knobs to change the flows in plastic pipes. The design was an impressive achievement for someone with only a smattering of undergraduate economics courses and Phillips was encouraged to stay on for further study.

Phillips's professional career lasted about two decades from the time he was appointed an assistant lecturer at the London School of Economics until he had an incapacitating stroke at a relatively early age in Australia where he had gone to accept a professorship at the National University. Forced to end his professional life early, he produced a modest amount of research in economics compared to other well-known economists. But among his scientific papers is one that hit the jackpot, one of the most frequently cited articles written since World War II.

Phillips's research was based on wage and unemployment data going back into the 1800s that had been collected by several economists at the London School. One of them suggested that Phillips might want to work with some of these numbers. The result of his efforts appeared in a British economic journal in 1958. Subjecting the data to statistical analysis, Phillips concluded that over the period 1861 to 1957 money wages rose as the unemployment rate fell. When this simple relationship is plotted on a graph, the result is what came to be known as the Phillips curve. Money wages are related to the prices of the goods that workers produce, of course, and the Phillips relation was later transposed by other economists to a form relating the price level and the unemployment rate. In this version, the Phillips curve suggests that when the unemployment rate falls there is a tendency for the economy to experience inflationary pressure. This result had been anticipated by earlier studies, including work done three decades before by Irving Fisher of Yale, one of the first American economists to gain recognition outside the United States. This earlier research failed to get much attention. Phillips's article happened to come at the right time. There are not many examples of economic research with such immediate impact. Samuelson included the Phillips curve in the fifth edition of his famous textbook, published in 1961. Within three years of the publication of Phillips's original paper, his curve became part of the standard economic model.

The uninitiated might wonder why this finding would cause any excitement in the first place. Phillips himself thought it a matter of common observation that when the economy expands there is a dual effect. The unemployment rate falls and there is some upward pressure on prices. In his mind the formal statistical analysis simply confirmed the expected and provided a quantitative estimate of the distribution of the effect in the two directions. The reason for the unexpected interest in Phillips's article must be explained in terms of the developments that preceded his work.

Keynes was primarily concerned with unemployment, as were most economists during the 1930s. While his theory could also be applied to the other major social problem, inflation, his main preoccupation while writing *The General Theory* was with the issue of the day. Keynes took it for granted that in a severely depressed economy government fiscal policy designed to stimulate business would reduce unemployment without causing inflationary pressure. As long as there are unemployed workers anxious to take jobs, employers need not pay higher wages to attract labor. More workers can be hired at the same wage the work force is already receiving. Expansion does not exert upper pressure on prices. Only when the economy reaches full employment and employers have to compete for more workers is there an upper pressure on wages and eventually on prices. This line of reasoning suggests an *either-or* situation. Up to the point of full employment there is no inflationary pressure; inflation sets in only if the economy attempts to expand beyond the labor resources available for work. To put the matter another way, there is no conflict between the goal of full employment and the goal of price stability. Keynes had the subtlety of mind to know that this statement of the matter is an oversimplification; price pressure can develop at less than full utilization of resources. But the commonplace view developed that as long as government ends the fiscal stimulus when full employment is reached, the economy arrives at the blissful state of full prosperity without inflation.

There was some concern during the 1950s that this expected outcome did not match the actual performance of the economy. Even though there was excessive unemployment in that decade, there was still upper pressure on prices. Phillips's analysis was consistent with this real world behavior. According to the Phillips curve, even before the economy reaches full employment prices start to rise. It might not be possible, in a word, to have both full employment and price stability.

Fortunately, this bad news had a good news counterpart. In Phillips's results the amount of inflation incurred, if full employment were the national objective, would be small enough to fall within reasonable bounds. This finding was confirmed for the United States by research done by Paul Samuelson and Robert Solow. A year after the appearance of Phillips's article they presented to a meeting of the American Economic Association the results of a Phillips curve fitted to American data. Their research showed that in the United States the unemployment rate could fall as low as 4 percent without raising the inflation rate above 3 percent.

To fully appreciate what these numbers mean in practical policy terms requires further comment. The measurement of unemployment is centered around the concept *labor force*, which can be defined as including all those people who are in the job market. There are a number of niceties that statisticians include to make the term operational, but basically the labor force is made up of those who have a job or are looking for work. The unemployment rate is the number unemployed, those looking for work, taken as a percentage of the labor force. It is reported monthly in newspapers and also on national television, if 15 seconds of time are available on the day the number is released by the Bureau of Labor Statistics.

In order to have full employment, as most observers understand the term, the unemployment rate does not have to fall to zero. In a large labor market such as the United States there are always people who are in transition between jobs. Workers who are displaced by the bankruptcy of a company, decide to change jobs, or are simply coming into the labor force for the first time enter a search path looking for employment. There are in the labor market *frictions* that slow job movement, frictions that include such things as imperfect information about where a suitable job can be found or a lack of fit in terms of the worker's skills and the requirements of the job opening. Because of these frictions, finding a job requires time and there are always some people in the search process. This frictional unemployment is not a social problem provided that the search is not unduly prolonged. The definition of full employment, then, allows for some unemployment. Once it's known how much frictional unemployment is normal for an adaptable labor force, it can be determined how much unemployment would constitute the *full employment unemployment rate*. If a society is committed to full employment, this contradictory and awkward sounding measure provides the target of public policy.

In the early 1960s the consensus of economists would probably have placed the amount of frictional unemployment at about 3 percent. This would define the full employment unemployment target. The Kennedy Administration announced in the 1962 economic report an interim target of 4 percent. The selection was based on the Phillips curve results obtained by Samuelson and Solow. The unemployment rate could not be pushed below 4 percent because a 3 percent rate of inflation was as much as the country could bear. The dollar was at the time in the early stages of its problems with other currencies (a matter requiring the bold action of devaluation by Richard Nixon a decade later), and it was thought that an inflation rate above 3 percent would trip an undesirable reaction in foreign markets. The administration realized that the unemployment target was on the high side and introduced programs for retraining unskilled workers to make the labor force more flexible and able to move more rapidly through the job search.

The 4 percent target became, through constant repetition in the news media, a number cut in stone. It remained for a decade the unofficial national employment target. During the 1970s it was recognized that the rate that reflected the amount of labor market tightness implied by the 4 percent figure in the early 1960s had drifted upward due to such things as changes in the makeup of the labor force. Specifically the labor force now had a larger proportion of women and teenagers, both of whom tend to enter and exit the labor force more frequently than middle-aged males. The proportion of inexperienced teenagers has declined in the 1980s, a change that has moved the full employment rate back down by some unknown amount. The equivalent full employment target of unemployment today would probably fall somewhere between 5 and 6 percent. In 1987 and 1988 the rate fell to a little above 5 percent without setting off strong inflationary pressure.

What the Phillips curve did was to justify a statement of national policy goals in terms of a tradeoff. Policymakers are presented, according to the Phillips relation, with a menu of choices. They can have lower unemployment, but at the cost of higher inflation; they can have less inflation but at the cost of higher unemployment. As political choices reflecting the preferences of their constituents, Democrats would presumably opt for lower unemployment and Republicans for price stability.

TROUBLE IN CAMELOT

The heart of the Kennedy package can be summarized in a few basic postulates. Federal compensatory action to enhance the performance of the economy is appropriate. Tax cuts for consumers and business can be used to stimulate the economy to operate at its full potential and to insure a more robust growth rate. The policy outcome is not perfect but it is possible to achieve a low level of unemployment with a modest amount of inflation.

The experiment was widely acknowledged to be a success. The unemployment target set by the Administration was reached in the mid-1960s and inflation was even more modest than the Phillips curve data predicted. Similar experiments were tried elsewhere. Most of the democratic countries undertook some form of demand management after World War II. It is not clear who first used the expression but observers began to speak of *fine tuning* the economy through government action.

Those who had suffered through Economics 101 as undergraduates may have taken some quiet satisfaction in late 1965 from recognizing the face staring at them from their newstands on the cover of *Time* magazine. One of the symbols of the success of the new economics was that the subject for *Time*'s cover story for the year's final issue was none other than John Maynard Keynes. *Time* was almost euphoric in its description of Keynesian economics.

> Today, some 20 years after his death, his theories are a prime influence on the world's free economies, especially on America's, the richest and most expansionist. In Washington the men who formulate the nation's economic policies have used Keynesian principles not only to avoid the violent cycles of prewar days but to produce a phenomenal economic growth and to achieve remarkably stable prices. . . . Now Keynes and his ideas, though they still make some people nervous, have been so widely accepted that they constitute both the new orthodoxy in the universities and the touchstone of economic management in Washington. . . . Those ideas are so original and persuasive that Keynes now ranks with Adam Smith and Karl Marx as one of history's most significant economists.

The euphoria was not to last long. The irony of the Keynesian episode is the brevity of its dominance as a theory of public policy and the speed with which events conspired to weaken confidence in its central claims. The news item immediately preceding the Keynes cover story in the December 31, 1965 issue of *Time* was about medical treatment for the wounded in Vietnam. The Keynes story and the Vietnam story are not unrelated. The imbalances caused by the war broke the rhythm of the Keynesian experiment. More was demanded than the economy could deliver when a major military initiative was added by President Johnson to an already robust economic expansion and the ambitious programs of the Great Society. The result was the inflation that bedeviled the economy for over a decade.

There were in fact Keynesian solutions available for the strains caused by the Johnson foreign policy initiative; a cutback in government programs to compensate for increased military spending or a tax increase to cover the additional government outlays and to withdraw spending power from the private sector. These unpopular options pressed upon Johnson by his economic advisers were rejected by a President under intense political challenge over the war in Vietnam. Dislocations in the economy were allowed to develop and the reputation of Keynesian economics, by association, was damaged in the process. At the very peak of success the Age of Keynes became a part of history. Those who observe today belligerent disagreement among economists about the basic model of how the economy works may now look back in nostalgia at the consensus and heady confidence that prevailed in the first part of the 1960s, in the place that "for one brief shining moment was known as Camelot."

CHAPTER 5

MONETARISM

Keynesian economics, born in the Great Depression, was preoccupied with the problem of unemployment. It has been described, and not without reason, as depression economics. When the key social problem shifted to inflation with the start of World War II, Keynes changed the focus of his analysis. In *How To Pay For the War*, a pamphlet he wrote in 1939, he addressed the inflationary problem that the war created.

Keynes has often been depicted as a crude inflationist. He was not and could be eloquent in deploring a fall in the currency's purchasing power, a fall that is the mirror image of a rise in prices. "Lenin was certainly right," he said in an often quoted passage. "There is no subtler, no surer means of overturning the existing basis of society than to debauch the currency."

Keynesian economics can be applied to the problem of a general price increase as well as unemployment; but it should also be said that it is less potent in its explanatory power when used to analyze inflation. The rise in prices that started with President Johnson set the stage for a counterrevolution to exploit the limitations of the Keynesian paradigm. This counterrevolution is described under the label *monetarism*.

INFLATION AS A SOCIAL PROBLEM

Of the two great pathologies of a free market system, unemployment and inflation, inflation is the more subtle in its impact and more pervasive in number of people affected.

The heart of the inflation problem is that it redistributes income.

If all wages and prices rose in the same proportion during inflation, family economic positions would be unchanged. Price tags in stores would be higher, but the number of dollars in wallets would also be larger. The amount of goods and services people could buy, the standard of living, would be unaffected. In an inflation, though, all wages and prices do not rise in the same proportion; some salaries and wages do not adjust for price increases as well as others. Some families end up with less real purchasing power than they would have had there been no inflation; others end up with more.

In itself there is nothing unusual about a redistribution of income and wealth. Governments routinely make distributive decisions in the process of raising public revenue. It is almost impossible to design a tax that is neutral in its effect on incomes. But there is a big difference in redistribution by government and the redistribution that occurs with inflation. Citizens participate in tax decisions and, in the political interaction, complaints are registered and concessions negotiated. From inflation there is no appeal. It strikes like the hand of fate; it takes income or wealth from some and gives to others without due process of law or basic concerns of equity.

The negative effects of inflation are most dramatic in the case of a hyperinflation. In the famous German inflation of 1923 prices rose on an hourly basis. Workers and employers negotiated wages each morning to correct for inflation of the previous day. Employees were paid twice daily. One of the children in the family waited by the factory gate at noon for the working parent who brought the paycheck to the child; the child, in turn, ran to a store where the other parent waited to convert the currency into goods before price increases made earnings worthless. In every inflation there is a general flight from money. In the German hyperinflation creditors hid from debtors to avoid payment in worthless paper. As the domestic value of the currency collapsed, its value relative to other currencies dropped also. At the height of the inflation the entire mortgage debt of Germany, fixed in terms of marks, could be purchased for a handful of American currency.

The hyperinflation of 1923 left such a deep wound in the collective psyche of the German people that they still have intense feelings about the priority of price stability. In the 1980s the Reagan administration made repeated efforts to persuade German officials to adopt stimulative economic policies in the hope that rising German income would lead to increased purchase of American goods and relief in the U.S. balance of trade deficit. American pressure consistently met with stubborn resistance. Even with the historically high German unemployment rates of the 1980s, policymakers were unwilling to risk inflationary pressure.

In periods of milder inflation steps can be taken to avoid the adverse effects of a general price increase. Lenders, for example, build into interest rates a premium to allow for inflation. If prices are expected to rise 10 percent, 10 percentage points will be added to interest rates and market rates rise by that amount. Some wages and other income payments are tied to a cost-of-living index and are automatically corrected for inflation. Wealthholders shift their holdings out of money or assets fixed in terms of money. The public adapts to inflation, but the usual adjustments do not solve the problem completely. Some have more know-how and assets to hedge against inflation than others or benefit by the way in which government transfers are indexed.

Beyond the actual harm done by inflation there is the psychological damage. Surveys have shown that even those who gain from inflation feel aggrieved by a rise in prices. Few people have a good sense of their overall balance sheets. Shoppers are acutely aware of an increase in the cost of groceries but forget that the loss is counterbalanced by capital gains in the value of homes, which rose more rapidly in price during the inflation of the 1970s than the cost-of-living index. Even comparatively mild inflations leave a residue of social frustration.

Over the last 50 years the inflation record in the United States has been mixed as one would expect. The price level actually dropped during the Great Depression. Consumer prices were 20 percent lower in 1939 than they were in 1929. World War II and its aftermath brought inflation as wars always do. Modern wars are costly to fight and taxpayers resist the increase in taxes necessary to pay for the war as it is waged. Governments raise taxes to the level citizens tolerate and pay for at least part of the rest by printing new money. The excessive creation of new spending power causes inflation and inflation is another form of taxation. People keep more dollars as taxes are kept below what is necessary to cover the cost of the conflict, but the dollars buy less. In wars purchasing power is extracted from the public either through normal types of taxation or through inflation.

The postwar period can be conveniently divided into two parts. Over the entire 15 years that include the 1950s and the first half of the 1960s, consumer prices rose about 20 percent; a modest amount on an annual basis by today's standards. For the 15-year period including the last half of the 1960s and the 1970s, prices rose about 175 percent or almost nine times as fast. Even this inflation rate is far short of the classic hyperinflation. But it is large enough to have aroused public indignation and shift the policy debate from unemployment to price stability.

MONETARISM

Inflation is one of the primary economic problems to which the classical economists addressed themselves. Their explanation of inflationary pressure is embodied in the famous quantity theory of money that was examined in an earlier chapter. The price increases of the 1960s, 1970s, and 1980s prompted a return to the quantity theory of classical economics restated in modern terms. For a look at this revival of classical doctrine, we must go to the Midwest.

The city of Chicago is still Carl Sandburg's grain stacker of the world, but it is also many other things. Among them, it is the home of the University of Chicago. The university's economics department has long had its own carefully differentiated personality. Its traditions have been formed by a long line of distinguished economists, from Frank Knight, who did pioneering work in the theory of risk and uncertainty, through more recent scholars such as Milton Friedman, about whom we will have much to say, to a younger generation including Robert Lucas.

The tradition at the University of Chicago has several dimensions. One of them is a fierce belief in the organizing power and efficiency of a free market economy and the mischief of government interference with market decisions. In this tradition all types of price interference are an anathema and government regulation should be kept to the absolute minimum. It is, basically, *laissez-faire* economics, singular not only in the intensity of its commitment to the efficiency of market interaction but also in the breadth of problems to which market solutions are thought to apply. At Chicago free market principles have been extended beyond purely economic matters and used to analyze broader social phenomena traditionally the province of sociology, including such topics as marriage and the family. One expanded area of application is described under the phrase *law and economics,* an approach in which legal decisions are deeply embedded in economic criteria. The law and economics group has been a major influence at the university's law school. Among former students whose views were shaped by this school of thought are Robert Bork and Douglas Ginsburg, both later nominated by President Reagan for a position as justice on the Supreme Court. Bork was particularly influenced by Aaron Director, a leader in the law and economics group.

A second tradition at Chicago is an emphasis on monetary theory and this leads us to Aaron Director's brother-in-law, Milton Friedman. Millions of Americans have read Friedman's column in *Newsweek*, where for years he shared space on alternate weeks with Samuelson, or have seen him on television, particularly in his series on economics, from which came *Free to Choose*, a best selling book coauthored with his wife, also an economist. The force of his personality has dominated the movement known as *monetarism*.

Keynes was already 30 years of age when Friedman was born in Brooklyn in 1912. His parents' story is the story of most immigrants of the period, the struggle to make ends meet. Friedman recalls that his mother worked as a seamstress in a clothing factory to supplement the family income. His father died when he was 15 years old. Without financial support from his family, he went through college and later graduate studies, on sheer brainpower, supported by a series of scholarships at successive levels of his education.

Friedman's undergraduate training was at Rutgers where he was influenced by two young members of the faculty, Arthur Burns and Homer Jones. Burns was later to become Chairman of the Council of Economic Advisers under Dwight Eisenhower. Though Eisenhower liked Burns personally, he was not, apparently, greatly interested in economics. The young Vice President, Richard Nixon, was and listened with care to Arthur Burns. When Nixon became President, he appointed Burns Chairman of the Federal Reserve Board. Homer Jones served for years as director of research at the St. Louis Federal Reserve Bank, the one bank of the twelve Federal Reserve banks with a research staff of strong monetarist persuasion. It was through Jones's influence that Friedman went to Chicago for graduate study in economics. He eventually received his doctorate from Columbia University to which he had transferred when offered more adequate financial support. After a brief stay in government and at several other universities, he came back to Chicago where he did his major work.

Friedman strongly embraces the free market ideology of the Chicago school. Among his many contributions to application of the free market to social policy is his proposal for an all volunteer army, an idea that has been implemented. He has also argued for, and created interest in, an educational voucher system that would provide government funds but permit students to pick their own school, an arrangement that would expose educators to the pressure of market competition. The main contribution of Friedman, however, has been in the area of monetary studies.

In his early career Friedman, like most young economists of the time, worked within the Keynesian analytical framework. Research done in 1941 on the war-induced problem of inflation, for example, is couched in Keynesian rhetoric. At Chicago he gradually moved away from mainline Keynesian economics to a return to classical thinking. In a famous essay, "The Quantity Theory of Money—A Restatement," published in 1956, he presented in modern form the classical monetary theory.

In the analysis of the early Keynesians, control of the money supply is quite secondary to management of the government budget in its effect on the economy. To put the matter in other terms, monetary policy executed by the Federal Reserve is subservient in importance to fiscal policy as a stabilization tool. Friedman's major contribution has been to reestablish the importance of money in economics. His first impact was on economists as he began to persuade members of the profession of the importance of his views through a series of books and articles. Had public events not intervened, the discussion might have remained an esoteric subject of controversy in abstract economic journals. As inflation became a national problem in the late 1960s and 1970s, however, Friedman's ideas entered the public forum, debated in a variety of general publications and, eventually, in committees of Congress. For Friedman in the 1970s, as for Keynes in the 1930s, the man and the moment met.

DOCTRINE OF MONETARISM

It is not easy to summarize in a few words the essential ideas of monetarism. There are, nevertheless, some key beliefs that generally define the boundaries of monetarist doctrine.

First and foremost is the reaffirmation of the classical quantity theory of money that says that inflation is primarily related to the behavior of the money supply. Inflation, in Friedman's oft-quoted statement is "everywhere and always a monetary phenomenon." Inflation follows from excessive creation of money and if money creation is not excessive, inflation cannot occur.

This central theme can be best understood by returning to the equation of exchange discussed in an earlier chapter, $MV = PQ$. The MV on the left side of the equation, by way of reminder, represents the total spending of a given time period, the amount of money multiplied by the turnover rate of money, the velocity. The PQ on the right-hand side represents total income, the quantity of goods sold times the average price received. It can also be thought of as the Gross National Product, the dollar value of the output of the economy.

A regular increase in the money supply, M in the equation of exchange, is necessary to accommodate the long-term growth in output, Q, that takes place as the economy expands through time. Given the historic economic growth record, about 3 or 4 percent is the appropriate annual money growth target. Money can increase by this rate without exerting upward pressure on P. If, however, M is increased at a rate faster than the growth in Q, an increase in P, that is, inflation, occurs.

The central theme emphasized in monetarist doctrine is that inflation in the postwar period, as in every other historic occurrence, has been due to an excessive creation of money. Monetarists argue that Keynesians, in their preoccupation with fiscal policy, diverted attention from, and misunderstood, the role of money in the economy. This is the heart of the Keynesian-monetarist debate. There is a lot of detail, not easy to follow. Developed here is a brief summary of the key issues, a summary necessary to understand the major policy debates of the last quarter century.

As a return to classical economics, monetarism reaffirms the key classical proposition that the economy is inherently stable. Like classical economists, monetarists argue that the economy has a capacity for self-correction. When lapses from full employment occur, automatic adjustments take place to restore the system to full operation. In terms of the equation of exchange, Q, total ouput, tends to the full employment level.

Monetarists argue that the historic record supports this belief. For example, they point out that the economy has been reasonably stable since World War II. There have been eight recessions in the postwar period, relatively short in duration and mild by prewar standards. Monetarists look on the Great Depression as a historical aberration and criticize Keynes for generalizing from the depression of the 1930s as though it were the standard case and for presenting a picture of the capitalistic system as inherently unstable. Friedman not only argues that the system has its own capacity for self-correction without need for government intervention, but that one of the main reasons for the disappointing performances that do occur is the bumbling attempts of public officials to manage the economy. The most dramatic case of policy mismanagement that he cites is the Great Depression itself.

There have been many attempts to explain what caused the collapse of the economy in the 1930s. One of the more famous is Friedman's interpretation presented in what has by now become a classic, his monetary history of the United States produced in collaboration with Anna Schwartz. The Depression began in mid-1929 with a decline in production and prices. This downward movement was aggravated by the crash in the stock market in October of that year. Friedman and Schwartz argue that this cyclical contraction turned into a major collapse because of the failure of the Federal Reserve to carry out its responsibility of providing the banking system with the liquidity needed in a time of crisis. From the start of the economic decline in August 1929, to the bottoming out in March 1933, the Federal Reserve allowed the money stock to decline by about one third, a drop over three times as large as previous declines in the U.S. experience. This decrease was accompanied by a banking panic that reduced the number of commercial banks by about one third due to bankruptcies and consolidations. Friedman and Schwartz argue that the duration of the economic decline would have been shorter and the drop less severe had the Federal Reserve supplied the bank reserves needed to cushion the fall. Had it not been for the ineptness of the

Federal Reserve, they conclude, the Great Depression, as we know it, would never have happened.

It is fascinating to read, for its human interest content, the Friedman-Schwartz survey of events inside the Federal Reserve at the time the crucial decisions were made. One of the more colorful characters in U.S. central banking history is Benjamin Strong who served as president of the New York Federal Reserve Bank. Although he was not a member of the Board of Governors that controls the system, Strong nevertheless dominated the early days of the Federal Reserve through sheer brilliance and force of personality. Strong died in 1928 and the locus of power inside the Federal Reserve shifted from the New York Bank and was diffused across the entire system. The Federal Reserve lost its leadership just before facing the greatest challenge of its short history, the collapse of Wall Street in 1929. Friedman and Schwartz cite a statement by Irving Fisher that if Benjamin Strong had not died the Great Depression would not have occurred. To attribute the cause of a major cataclysm like the Great Depression to the mistakes of a small group of decisionmakers, even more to the death of one man, is a surprisingly bold assertion as they recognize. "It is a sound general principle," they concede, "that great events have great origins. . . . Yet it is also true," they add, "that small events at times have large consequences."

There has been considerable debate about the Friedman-Schwartz argument that a sharp drop in the money supply was the cause of the Depression. A large number of economists find it convincing. In any event, the fact that academics and financial analysts have become sensitized to the need for the Federal Reserve to act firmly in a period of financial crisis is at least partly due to Friedman. Memories of the debacle of the 1930s, kept vivid by the Friedman-Schwartz analysis, explain the dispatch with which the Federal Reserve acted in providing liquidity to the financial system in the aftermath of the stock market crash of October 1987.

Friedman's interpretation of the cause of the Great Depression is part of a broader conviction that the instability observed in capitalistic systems is at least partly traceable to government action. In opposition to the Keynesian view that government ought to provide a counterweight to instability in the private sector, Friedman argues that government action itself destabilizes and that the self-corrective process of the free market ought to be allowed to operate with a minimum of government involvement. We should pause for a moment to emphasize the importance of this assertion. His belief represents a return to a view that dominated thinking about economic policy before publication of *The General Theory* 50 years ago.

MONETARY VERSUS FISCAL POLICY

One of the issues involved in the Keynesian-monetarist controversy with important practical implications for policy management is the relative importance of monetary and fiscal policy. The key issue can be understood in an intuitive way by returning to the equation of exchange.

The control of M in the equation of exchange by the Federal Reserve, an institution whose operations will be looked at in detail in the next chapter, is what is meant by monetary policy. If the money supply is changed, what happens to GNP, PQ in the equation, depends on the behavior of the velocity, which Arthur Burns once called money's second dimension. The behavior of velocity is a key theoretical and practical issue in the debate between monetarists and Keynesians.

Keynesians came to the conclusion that monetary policy is relatively ineffective because they thought the velocity of money unstable. With an unstable velocity the effect of a change in M on the GNP cannot be predicted. In a recession, for example, if the Federal Reserve increases the money supply in order to stimulate total spending in the economy, the policy move may be offset by a decline in the turnover rate of money. There is more money but it is being used less. Under these circumstances the ability of the central bank to influence the behavior of the economy is frustrated. To be sure that the economy is stimulated the government should resort to fiscal action, Keynesians argued, an injection of government spending directly into the system or a decrease in taxes that would lead to an increase in private spending.

Classical economists recognized that velocity changes over longer periods of time due to such things as improvements in communications but thought it tends to be rather stable over shorter periods. In this matter also monetarism represents a return to classical thinking with modern revisions. For monetarists V is either constant or behaves in such a way that its behavior can be explained in terms of a small number of variables. If the Federal Reserve changes the money supply, the effect on GNP, the PQ in the equation, can be predicted.

The same line of reasoning led monetarists to believe that fiscal policy has a small effect, at best, on the performance of the economy, for the effectiveness of fiscal policy also depends on the behavior of velocity. If the velocity is constant, then total spending, MV, cannot change as a result of a fiscal action unless the money supply is changed to accommodate the change in government spending or taxes. If the money supply is held fixed, an increase in government outlays would have to be offset by a decrease in private spending leaving total spending unaffected. Fiscal policy works, monetarists say, only when accommodated by monetary action.

A large volume of empirical work has been done to determine how velocity actually has performed in the real world economy and to test the relative effectiveness of monetary and fiscal policy. In an early statistical test done by Friedman and an associate, David Meiselman, monetary policy won hands down. Fiscal policy was shown to be relatively unimportant in its effect on the Gross National Product while monetary policy is a dominant influence. But other researchers made conflicting claims.

After 25 years of empirical research, a general consensus has been reached on some key issues. The views of the early Keynesians that monetary policy is ineffective is no longer accepted. This is probably one of the more dramatic turnarounds in professional opinion in the last 30 years. It is generally agreed that changes in the money supply have a strong effect on the behavior of the GNP and that the Federal Reserve has a key role to play in the behavior of the economy. Keynesians have conceded more in this debate than have monetarists. Keynesians now recognize monetary policy as a major influence on the behavior of the GNP though they still insist that fiscal actions can exert an influence independent of monetary policy. Even if the Federal Reserve holds the money supply constant, they argue, an expansionary fiscal action induces enough of a change in the velocity through indirect effects to permit total spending to increase. While monetarists grant that fiscal actions have an effect, the effect, in their view, is quite secondary to monetary action.

MONETARISTS AND THE PHILLIPS CURVE

A final point of difference, to complete the story of the Keynesians and monetarists, involves the Phillips curve. The monetarist belief that the economy is self-correcting and tends to full employment means that the main effect of a change in the money supply is not on output, except, perhaps, for transition periods, but rather on the price level. Monetarists reassert the *neutrality of money* postulate advanced by the classical economists. In this view the main task of monetary authorities is to see that increases in the money supply, beyond the amount necessary to accommodate ordinary economy growth, do not cause inflationary pressure. Phillips curve studies, however, suggested a tradeoff between price stability and full employment. An increase in money, according to Phillips, affects not only P in the equation of exchange but also Q. The Phillips relationship leaves room for activist monetary policy to stimulate output and employment. It represents one of the final parts of the Keynesian logic requiring a monetarist response.

Friedman challenged Phillips's conclusion—as Edmund Phelps of Columbia University also did independently—in his presidential address to the American Economic Association in 1967 and again in his Nobel prize lecture in 1976 arguing that the Phillips curve tradeoff is spurious. His line of reasoning leads us to one of the most recent episodes in the story.

While the initial article by Phillips presented historical data to show that there is a tradeoff between inflation and unemployment, it did little in the way of explaining why the data behaved as they did. As James Tobin was to say later, the Phillips curve was an empirical fact looking for a theory. Early attempts to explain the relationship concentrated on the mechanics of the labor market. If full employment is to be reached, enough fiscal and monetary pressure has to be exerted to draw even lower skilled workers into employment. Since marginal workers are less productive, their employment causes an increase in cost and an upward pressure on prices. A reduction in the unemployment rate tends to be associated with an increase in the price level.

Friedman offered a different approach to explaining the Phillips curve. There is at any time a number of workers who are unemployed and in a search path looking for a job. If inflationary pressure is exerted by monetary authorities, the money wage rises. A higher money wage might well induce unemployed workers to abandon the search path, accept employment and reduce the unemployment rate as the Phillips curve suggests. This increase in wages is passed on, in the form of price increases, however, to customers who buy the product that labor is producing. This inflation, in turn, eliminates the gain to workers from the increase in money wages, reducing real purchasing power to the level prior to the wage increase. The number of workers willing to accept employment, therefore, goes back to its previous level. While a higher money wage temporarily reduces unemployment, eventually the employment gain is nullified.

In brief, Friedman argues that workers bargain for *real* not *money* wages; that is, not just for dollars but for what the dollars buy. Once they learn to expect inflation, unemployment does not respond to increases in the general price level. When the expected rate of inflation is added to the Phillips equation, the tradeoff between inflation and unemployment disappears.

Initially Friedman's argument had only a modest impact on Phillips curve orthodoxy because it did not fit well the U.S. experience. Workers' price expectations did not, in practice, seem to invalidate a short-term tradeoff between inflation and unemployment. But with the increase in the inflation rate in the latter part of the 1960s and continuing into the next decade, econometric research began to show a weakening of the inflation-unemployment option. The inflationary era of the 1960s and 1970s required a new look at the inflation-unemployment relationship.

The first explanation for the worsening of the tradeoff by mainline Keynesians was in terms of a series of shocks that put intense pressure on the economic system. Among the more dramatic of these events was the increase of petroleum prices by the Organization of Petroleum Exporting Countries in 1974. The increased cost of petroleum imposed by an international cartel was passed on through the marketing system for all products that depend on oil either directly or indirectly. In 1972 and 1973 poor harvests in major growing areas of the world resulted in a short-fall of agricultural production and rapid increases in the price of food and basic commodities which added to overall inflationary pressure. There were other events in an unusual bunching, including a somewhat exotic incident, the disappearance of the anchovy catch (an important source of protein for animal feed) off the coast of Peru.

Monetarists reject, as a fundamental cause of inflation, pressures exerted on cost from whatever source, arguing that such pressures cannot cause prices to rise, except, perhaps, as a temporary event unless the Federal Reserve supplies the new money needed to accommodate transactions at the higher price level. If the Federal Reserve refuses, temporary strains appear but the system is flexible enough to absorb the shock through a downward adjustment of other prices to accommodate the rise in the relative price of a product like oil. Inflation is everywhere and always due to the excessive creation of money.

Even though Keynesians emphasized external shocks as a major cause of the weakening of the unemployment-inflation tradeoff, they gradually began to recognize, over the course of the 1970s, that inflationary expectations were becoming part of the inflation pattern.

RATIONAL EXPECTATIONS

There is an interesting problem connected with Friedman's analysis of expectations. Among the more difficult economic phenomena to analyze is the one in which today's decision depends on some event in the future. As an example, business decisions to spend on capital equipment depend on the forecast of the market for the products that the equipment makes; or, again, people's willingness to buy stocks on the stock exchange depends on what they think stock prices are likely to do in coming quarters. In the Phillips curve case, workers' decisions to accept employment at a given wage today depend on how they think the price level will behave in the future. If you wish to model decisions that link together the present and future, you must decide on a procedure that imitates the way people form expectations about future events.

The mathematical technique that Friedman used has an importance beyond that of the specialist because of the developments that it stimulated. The technique is an error-learning process. If people find that prices rise more in a period than expected, they correct for the error on the basis of this experience. But the correction process, and this is a key point, is sluggish; it is stretched out as data from a number of previous quarters are used in a series of adjustments to form new expectations.

The practical result of Friedman's approach is that workers revise their forecast of price changes gradually. In the meantime they are likely to be mistaken about what is happening to real wages. An increase in the money wage is interpreted by workers (for a time period necessary for the error-learning process to work) as a genuine increase in real wages. Until the correction is complete, inflation leads to lower unemployment. There is a short-term Phillips trade-off even though, eventually, it ceases to exist. In the short period government can affect the level of unemployment.

The question that arises is why people would let themselves be fooled for even a short period of time? The economists who asked this question make up what is known as the *school of rational expectations*.

Much of the work on rational expectations draws from an article written by John Muth in the early 1960s. Muth argued that it is logical for people to utilize all information, current as well as past, in forming expectations about the future.

One application of this idea is to the stock market in what is known as *efficient market theory*. The simplest way to describe it is to say that "you can't beat the market." Unless one has insider information, an advantage that is, by recent experience, not without its perils, each trader in the stock market has the same information available for forming an opinion about the behavior of the price of a given stock. If there is something about a certain stock that makes it look particularly attractive, these facts are common knowledge and are immediately built into the stock's price. It is impossible for one trader to perform better than another except for the advantage gained from the luck of some random event.

Efficient market theory has not escaped the attention of analysts who make a living advising clients on stock purchases. For one of the more practical implications of the theory is that buying and holding a widely diversified group of stocks is likely to have a higher return than active management of a portfolio. Efficient market theory is generally accepted as valid by professors of finance in business schools, and not without reason, for the performance record of diversified, unmanaged portfolios over a long period is better than those professionally managed. On the other hand believers in efficient market theory have some explaining to do since the October 1987 stock market crash. For the theory is based on the assumption of rational behavior and doesn't allow for the mass-psychology exhibited in the one-day, 500-point drop in the Dow Jones average.

Applied to the inflation-unemployment problem, rational expectations holds that not only are past inflation rates considered in estimating future rates, but current developments and information on future events are also incorporated into the forecast. Rational people learn to use all available information about the inflation mechanism in forming expectations. The expectations forming process is forward looking as well as dependent on past information. People don't just react to past experience, they anticipate.

The policy implications of the rational expectations insight are enormous. The main point of Keynes's work is that government has a role to play in preventing unemployment. Friedman and other monetarists represent a return to the pre-Keynesian classical position. They argue that government cannot affect the unemployment picture, except for a short-term interval when it is possible to trade off some inflation for lower unemployment because of the time lag in workers' reaction to a rise in price. The rational expectations school is a return to the classical position with a vengeance. Not even in the short-run is there a role for government involvement. It is not surprising that this school of thought has come to be called the *New Classical Economics*.

The rational expectations movement, while critical of certain aspects of Friedman's methodology, generally reenforces monetarist conclusions. But its influence is broader than this, affecting the design of economic theory for a wide range of problems. Led by scholars such as Robert Lucas and Thomas Sargent, it is one of the more important developments in economics since World War II. The excitement of the rational expectations adventure, particularly for the set of younger economists, is captured in Arjo Klamer's *Conversations with Economists*, which we have referred to before; an unusual book providing, through a series of interviews, a rare, insider's look at the thought world of economists at their most creative. For all the excitement among the initiated, the denouement of this story is not yet revealed by whoever writes the scripts for the story of the dismal science. The conquest of rational expectations has been primarily at the theoretical level. It has had a minimum effect, up to this point, on practical policymakers and still lacks convincing empirical support. Critics state that it implies a degree of price and wage flexibility that doesn't exist in our economy. The hypothesis requires prices and wages to adjust rapidly to expected events; decisionmakers correctly anticipate inflationary pressures and adapt their own wage and price decisions accordingly. In practice, wages and prices appear to adjust slowly and with prolonged lags. Legal and less formal institutional arrangements prevent rapid reaction to inflation even if correctly anticipated. There is an inertia in the wage-price setting process that produces the same result as if workers and price setters formed expectations through a slower, error-learning method. In the transition period following the initiation of an anti-inflationary monetary policy, for example, a large part of the adjustment is in terms of output and employment rather than wage and price restraint.

MONETARISM TODAY

We come now to the point of looking at the current state of the controversy that we have been examining in this chapter. Where do we stand? The answer is that monetarism is itself in trouble.

It is unwise to make excessive claims for any school of economic thought. Economics is a soft science. Theories are hard to verify and changes in underlying conditions can make them less useful. They have their moment in the spotlight and then recede into the background.

Keynesian economics was sorely tested by the inflation of the 1960s and 1970s. How monetarism ran into trouble in the 1980s leads us to examine the Federal Reserve.

CHAPTER 6

MONETARY POLICY

When Americans think of the Federal Reserve they probably think of the tall, imposing, cigar-chomping figure of Paul Volcker who was chairman of the Board of Governors of the Federal Reserve System from 1979 to 1987 and who has become a legend in his own time. When asked in surveys in the 1980s to name the most influential Americans, the man-on-the-street most commonly selected, after Ronald Reagan, Paul Volcker.

This second most influential American headed up, until replaced by Alan Greenspan, one of the more interesting of our government entities. The Federal Reserve is a central bank, a bank that regulates other banks. Its counterpart in England is the Bank of England, in Japan, the Bank of Japan, and in West Germany, the Bundesbank.

The 12 district Federal Reserve Banks which make up the Federal Reserve System operate under the direction of a seven member Board of Governors in Washington. The System is an organizational arrangement with a dual personality; it has both private and public features. The 12 banks are privately owned by the commercial banks in the district that belong to the System; but the members of the Board of Governors and its chairman are appointed by the President of the United States with the advice and consent of the Senate. A creature of Congress, and ultimately answerable to that body, it nevertheless has been given broad powers to act with more independence than the central banks of our major trading partners and is more insulated from political pressure.

The private commercial banks whose actions the Federal Reserve is designed to control are the largest of our financial institutions in size of assets and the most diversified in activities. In one activity, in particular, they are unique. When Willie "the Actor" Sutton, a legendary bank robber of earlier decades, was asked by a prison psychologist why he robbed banks, Willie, somewhat incredulous at the naïveté of the question, answered "because that's where the money is." Willie got it half right. That's not only where the money is; that's where it is created. Most of the money supply consists of checking accounts and to understand the process of money creation you have to look at the operation of banks.

Tradition has it that the fractional reserve system, which is at the heart of modern banking, began with the goldsmith in early modern times. The goldsmith happened to deal in a raw material that was also used as the community's money. A man of some material substance, he was a source of loans and took on the function of a banker. Since he had the most secure facilities in town, people brought him their gold for safekeeping. Eventually they got into the habit, when they wanted to make a purchase, of writing a note to the goldsmith to transfer credit for a portion of their gold to someone else in the community. A crude form of check writing developed and claims against the goldsmith circulated, in the place of gold, in settlement of bills when due.

The use of checks, as an option to carrying gold, was an improvement in the efficiency of money transactions. But something else happened that was more dramatic. The goldsmith realized that most of the community's money never left his vault and he started lending it out. Typically, the borrower would not withdraw the gold but leave it in the goldsmith's possession, retaining the privilege of writing checks against the deposit. When borrowers' claims were added to those of original depositors, total deposits exceeded the gold holdings. The goldsmith had created money.

The reason the system worked, of course, is that depositors seldom removed their gold so that a gold reserve was always available to meet the occasional withdrawal. If all depositors claimed their gold at the same time, the goldsmith could not deliver.

The goldsmith introduced the system of fractional reserves on which modern banking is based. Since banks are required to hold only a fraction in reserve against their deposits, they are able to make loans larger than their cash holdings and, in the process, create new checking accounts. Our money supply is, basically, the monetized debt of commercial banks. The Federal Reserve controls the money supply by limiting or expanding the ability of the banks to create new deposits.

THE TOOLS OF THE FEDERAL RESERVE

The first way in which the Fed controls the banks is through its power to change the reserve requirement ratio, the fraction of deposits that banks must hold in the form of cash. If it is raised, the ability of the banks to lend is reduced. The Fed is also authorized to supply reserves to banks by extending loans for which banks pay the *discount rate*. The Fed encourages or discourages bank borrowing by lowering or raising this charge.

Both of these tools are of limited use. The power to change reserve requirements is a somewhat clumsy tool that doesn't permit delicate adjustment of reserve positions and is used infrequently. There is a long-standing tradition in the Fed that borrowing is a privilege and not a right. The Fed prefers that banks limit their borrowing at the discount window to periods when they are subjected to an unexpected demand for cash. It does not wish banks to finance growth through borrowing from the Fed. Banks tend, therefore, to use the discount window sparingly; if pressed for cash, they are more likely to turn to other alternatives. They may, for example, borrow from banks with excess reserves in the overnight federal funds market, paying the *federal funds rate*. Since lending by the Federal Reserve is constrained by Fed operating policy, changes in the discount rate have, in themselves, a limited effect on bank behavior. The importance of a variation in the discount rate lies more in its information content or what is called *the announcement effect*. When the Fed lowers or raises the discount rate, it sends out a clear message that it is loosening or tightening credit conditions. To be more precise, the Fed is usually confirming a change already underway, a change initiated by using its most sophisticated tool, the open-market operations.

Open-market operations simply involve the purchase or sale of government securities by the Federal Reserve, transactions that cause a change in the reserve position of the banks. If the Fed buys securities, for example, it gives up cash to some seller in the private sector—banks, other financial institutions or simply the general public—and the cash ends up in new deposits in the banks. These cash deposits represent high-powered reserve dollars that can be used for the multiple expansion of credit. If the Fed sells in the open market, reserves of the banks are reduced as private buyers write checks against banks to transfer funds to the Federal Reserve. This is a delicate tool in which the reserves of the banks can be adjusted by small amounts.

There is a second impact of open-market operations. When the Fed buys or sells securities, it affects their price; it causes the price to rise when it adds to market demand with a purchase, or to fall, when it adds to the market supply with a sale. One of the most fundamental relationships in finance is that the price of a security and its yield are inversely related. If one goes up, the other goes down. If the Fed sells a security, the price falls and the yield on the security rises. If the Fed buys, the price goes up and the yield down.

Private securities must compete with government offerings; commercial paper competes with Treasury bills and, at the long end of the market, corporate bonds with long-term government issues. If the Federal Reserve forces rates on government securities up in a credit tightening move by selling government securities, the yield on private debt instruments rises also. The government debt serves as a medium through which the effect of Federal Reserve actions is transmitted across credit markets. Since common stocks compete with bonds, the stock market is also affected by Federal Reserve open-market operations. If the Fed exerts upward pressure on interest rates and bond prices fall, stock prices also move downward. It is very difficult for a bull market to develop in stocks when the Fed has adopted a tight money policy.

Open-market decisions are made by the Federal Open Market Committee which consists of the seven members of the Board of Governors and five presidents of the district Federal Reserve banks. Since the decisions are executed at the open market desk located at the New York Federal Reserve Bank, the president of that bank is an *ex officio* member. The remaining eleven presidents take turns in filling the other four spots on the committee. While all twelve presidents attend the monthly meetings and participate in the discussion, only five of them vote.

Discussions at the meetings are a matter of secrecy; partly, of course, to prevent some market participants, ingenious enough to get prior information about Federal Reserve intentions, from gaining an unfair advantage. But more than that, the minutes are published for general use with a month's delay. There is an air of mystery, to some degree deliberately cultivated, about the actions of the Federal

Reserve. The unknown tends to keep financial markets off balance and, as the Fed sees it, enhances control. James Tobin has been quoted as saying that "Burns smoked a pipe and Volcker smoked a cigar. Both produced smokescreens."

There is a dedicated body of specialists known as *Fed watchers* who make a career trying to pierce through the smoke. The open-market operations are the key to anticipating the credit posture that the Fed plans to adopt. The Fed does not participate in auctions conducted by the Treasury in the initial offering of government securities. It restricts its activities to the secondary market where old issues are traded. This is a telephone market with about three dozen government security dealers participating. In addition to the transactions in securities by phone, the Open Market Desk at the New York Fed interacts with dealers in daily conference meetings that provide the Fed with a source of feedback on the degree of tightness in credit markets, the general state of liquidity, and attitudes and perceptions of participants in financial markets.

Information circulates in the financial community on when the Fed is in the market and when it is not. The problem for observers, though, is that they are not always sure why the Fed is acting. The Fed must react frequently to events outside its control that cause changes in the reserve positions of the banks. These events include such things as variations in the float that arise from the check clearing operations provided by the Federal Reserve and the spending by the Treasury which writes its checks on the Federal Reserve and, in the process, adds to or contracts the reserves held by banks. It is not always easy to separate purchases or sales meant as "defensive" actions to prevent the reserves from deviating from Fed targets and other market actions designed to change the basic credit posture of the central bank. Part of the Fed watcher's expertise is in filtering out the static and identifying Fed activity that conveys information about Federal Reserve intentions.

FEDERAL RESERVE STRATEGY

This brief survey of the mechanics of Federal Reserve control leads to a more important issue, the target strategy used to implement monetary policy. The Fed has as its ultimate target a healthy economy, by which we mean, presumably, an economy that has, under ideal conditions, full employment without inflation. But in its day-to-day operations it must have a more immediate target to govern the use of its basic tools.

The Fed long preferred interest rates as an indicator of the looseness or tightness of monetary policy. Another available target is the quantity of money, a magnitude closely related to the behavior of the Gross National Product. The two targets are not unrelated. They are mutually determined, and this is a subtle point, by the interaction of supply and demand. Money is supplied to the general public by commercial banks whose ability to provide funds depends, in turn, on the reserves that the Fed makes available. If more money is demanded than is supplied—the Fed is limiting reserves—interest rates are forced up. There is some interest rate that should clear the market; that is, there is some rate that brings the quantity of money demanded and supplied into equality where both sides of the market are satisfied. If the Fed feels that a certain quantity of money is appropriate, given current economic conditions, it could aim at that amount of money or, on the other hand, target the interest rate that is consistent with that quantity. The Federal Reserve traditionally operated with the interest rate target.

Without going into detail about some of the more difficult theoretical differences between monetarists and Keynesians, it can be said that the interest rate is given an importance and visibility in Keynesian models that it does not have in monetarist analysis. Keynesians think that the interest rate is the key mechanism that transmits the effect of a change in the money supply to the economy. They have not been uncomfortable, therefore, with the priority that the Fed has traditionally given interest rates in its targeting strategy.

Monetarists sharply disagree. While interest rates have a role in transmitting the effect of Federal Reserve actions in their models, they also feel that the relation between changes in rates and economic behavior is so complex that it is impossible to model precisely. The Fed should forget interest rates and target directly the quantity of money whose relationship to the economy has been found, through empirical research, they say, to be both consistent and predictable. Monetarists also argue that market rates can be deceptive as indicators of the degree of monetary looseness or tightness. If participants in the markets interpret an increase in reserves and the money supply as inflationary, for example, market rates go up instead of down as the Fed intended because of the inflationary premium added by lenders. Low rates may not be an indicator of loose money and high rates may not be an indicator of tight money. Interest rates, according to monetarists, can be deceptive as a guide to Federal Reserve policy.

There is a singularity of theme that runs through monetarist thinking. Monetary policy is the dominant tool for use by government. The ultimate goal is stable prices. The way to maintain the monetary discipline necessary to achieve this goal is through tight control of the money supply. One should not be distracted by misleading targets like interest rates. The money supply is the priority variable.

There is one modification that should be added to this prescription. Friedman claims from his empirical research that while the money supply is dominant in its influence on the economy, it makes its effect felt with a time lag that is both long and variable. If the money supply is changed, the effect on nominal Gross National Product may not take place for 12 months, 18 months, or longer. Further, the precise length of the lag can vary in different time periods. Since you do not know precisely when a change in money will have its effect, the Federal Reserve should avoid attempts to adjust money to counteract movements in the economy. If the Fed, for example, increases the money supply at a faster rate to stimulate the economy in a period of recession, the effect may not be felt until the recession is over and inflationary pressure has set in. In this case the action would have a destabilizing effect rather than the one intended.

Belief in a time lag has led Friedman to argue for a simple rule for the conduct of monetary policy. Friedman argues that the Fed should avoid attempts to fine tune the economy and simply increase the money supply at a constant rate each year to accommodate normal growth, say 3 or 4 percent. The Fed should avoid discretionary action; it should be put, if you will, on automatic pilot. The economy will never be perfectly stable, but economic performance will come closer to the ideal with a constant money increase than it will if the Federal Reserve is allowed the discretion of varying the money supply according to its own inner lights.

Friedman's asceticism in the conduct of monetary policy attracted a number of disciples in the 1970s. Monetarist views were implemented, for example, in some countries in Latin America by former students of Friedman who had arrived at positions of influence in policy circles and were known as *the Chicago boys.* Margaret Thatcher introduced a monetarist policy in Britain. Monetarism here at home first took the form of Congressional resolutions. The Fed's record in avoiding erratic variations of the money supply was less than perfect in the postwar period. Friedman's emphasis on the importance of changes of money and on a steady increase in the money supply had sufficient influence to lead eventually to a Congressional resolution requiring the Federal Reserve to adopt as a target a money supply increase confined to a narrow percentage range and requiring the Chairman of the Board of Governors to announce the range selected in annual appearances before the membership of the banking committees of Congress.

While the resolution nudged the Fed in the direction of a monetarist type of money rule, the constraint imposed on Fed behavior was moderate in practice. While the Fed duly announced monetary target ranges, there was no penalty for missing them, even by rather large margins; it also remained free to change the target range between reporting periods whenever it thought appropriate.

For a genuine movement in the direction of monetarist policy, one had to wait for the arrival of Paul Volcker in 1979.

THE MONETARIST EXPERIMENT

Few, if any, of the people appointed to head up the Federal Reserve were as prepared to assume the responsibilities of the job as Volcker. Princeton trained, with graduate studies in economics at Harvard and the London School of Economics, he has spent most of his professional life in public service. Appointed Under Secretary of the Treasury for Monetary Affairs by Richard Nixon in 1969, he played a key role in the events surrounding the devaluation of the dollar in 1971 and 1973 and gained extensive experience interacting with foreign finance ministers and central bankers during this crucial period. From the Treasury Volcker went to the Presidency of the Federal Reserve Bank of New York, a position that made him an *ex officio* voting member of the Federal Open Market Committee and with responsiblity for supervision of the open market desk.

In October 1979 only a few months after Volcker was appointed Chairman of the Board of Governors of the Federal Reserve System by President Carter, the Fed announced a shift in its strategy from targeting interest rates to targeting *monetary aggregates*, the term used for the Fed's various measures of the money supply. Why the switch?

It may not be possible to reconstruct fully the motivations that are operative in major policy decisions, but clearly in this case Volcker had decided that inflation, in the range of 13 to 14 percent in terms of consumer prices in 1979, had to be stopped. The shift to money targets was a key part of his anti-inflationary policy for two reasons.

First, it helped to establish credibility, a notion important enough to require further comment. Once an inflation is underway, regardless of its original cause, it begins to take on a momentum of its own. A certain inertia sets in that makes the upward movement in prices difficult to stop. This inertia is closely tied to peoples' expectations. If union leaders, for example, think prices will rise, they build into wage demands a premium for expected inflation. They are particularly prone to do this if, in earlier negotiations, they had failed to allow adequately for price increases with the result that wages, in terms of real purchasing power, declined. Wages did, in fact, fall in real terms in selected years in the 1970s and unions adapted by becoming inflation sensitive. Employers, in turn, routinely incorporate higher wage costs into price increases. When people expect inflation they act in such a way as to cause it.

Inflationary expectations are hard to dislodge. It is not enough for the central bank to announce its intention to embark on an anti-inflationary campaign. People have heard statements of intent before. They must begin to believe that the Fed will indeed impose restraint and stay with it for the time necessary to stop the inflation.

It is not clear the degree to which Volcker was intellectually convinced of the correctness of monetarist doctrine. But in any event the shift in targeting was a way to dramatize his commitment to an assault on the inflationary pressure that had been bedeviling the economy for a decade.

There is a second point that may have entered into the deliberations. A tough anti-inflationary policy would certainly result in a rise in interest rates. There are not many economic developments as politically sensitive or more grating on the consciousness of Congressmen. Part of this sensitivity has deep historical roots in the populist movement of the 19th century that was sustained by a vision of money lenders gouging the farmer, the small business owner, and the hardworking man of their just due by exorbitant interest payments. One symbol of this deeply rooted national belief is found in this historical vignette: Harry Truman, whose haberdashery went under in a money crunch in the 1920s, interviewing William McChesney Martin in the Oval Office before appointing him Chairman of the Federal Reserve Board and seeking assurance, almost pleadingly, that, if appointed, he would not raise interest rates. The public's attitude toward the Federal Reserve probably ranges somewhere between tolerance when the Fed is expansionary to anger when the Fed contracts. The Fed is not well cast for a popularity contest. As William McChesney Martin once said, it is the duty of the Fed to take away the punch bowl just when the party gets going.

One way of deflecting criticism of high interest rates in a period of money crunch is to target the money supply instead of interest rates. The Fed can present itself in this approach as quite properly "leaning against the winds of inflation" by exercising discipline in control of the money supply. The rise in rates is an unfortunate by-product, due to the freely exercised decisions of market participants reacting to a long-needed shift in policy. It is a theme that may not play in Peoria, but it is better than nothing.

As implemented, the new policy was not a classic exercise in monetarist strategy. The Fed slowed the growth in money but money control was too uneven to meet the consistency standard that Friedman demands. Monetarists cry foul when the Volcker policy of October 1979 is described as a monetarist experiment much as Keynesians do when the Johnson years are labeled Keynesian. But the results, in terms of the primary objective, are hard to argue with. Clumsy in its execution of the policy or not, the Fed broke the back of the inflation. It did so at a huge cost.

Thought of in terms of the equation of exchange, $MV = PQ$, an anti-inflationary policy imposes a restraint on M in order to control a rise in P. There is, though, an inertia in the inflation process as we have said before. People continue to raise prices and wages even in the face of a monetary crunch. If P continues to rise, when M is reduced or its growth rate constrained, then the effect is borne by Q which represents output. In the initial stages of monetary restraint, the first effect is not to stifle the inflation but to cause a drop in output and a rise in the unemployment rate. Only later do prices respond and inflation abate.

The cost of the victory over inflation was the worst recession since World War II. According to the National Bureau of Economic Research, which dates and measures the business cycle, the decline in real output lasted for 16 months, from July 1981 to November 1982. The unemployment rate rose to almost 11 percent, the highest of the postwar period, and plant utilization fell to about 69 percent of capacity.

One of the dilemmas of economic policy is that we simply do not know how to stop an inflation without causing a recession. There are two ways of confronting this dilemma. Rational expectations theorists simply deny that the dilemma need exist. If the Fed establishes credibility through consistency in its behavior, the public would recognize that the final response to a tightening in the money supply is a stabilizing of the price level. Understanding this they would exercise price and wage restraint instead of delaying the response and causing an unnecessary slowdown in the economy. Unfortunately, this type of reaction has not been the historical experience.

MONEY TARGETS AND FINANCIAL MARKETS

The unemployment of the early 1980s was a result of the Fed's tight monetary policy. The switch from an interest rate to a money target strategy that accompanied the anti-inflationary move had another effect, interesting and perhaps as important as the recession, volatility of interest rates.

When the Federal Reserve chooses between interest rates and the money supply as an operating target, the variable not selected tends to behave erratically. The point can be understood in an intuitive way.

The interest rate and the quantity of money are mutually determined in a supply and demand model. If the price of anything traded is held fixed for some reason, then the quantity exchanged must bear the burden of the adjustment required by some basic shift in demand or supply conditions. There is a long tradition among American manufacturers, for example, of maintaining prices when faced with a fall in sales. There are reasons for this practice, reasons involving such things as uncertainty about how consumers will react to a drop in price. Generally speaking, and recognizing that there are exceptions, manufacturers hold the price line. Since prices do not react to a change in demand, the market adjustment must be borne entirely by output and employment changes. The situation in agriculture, on the other hand, is quite different. Decisionmaking is decentralized among many farmers and output levels cannot be carefully controlled over short-term intervals. Farmers have little choice in bringing crops to market once harvested regardless of the state of demand. The burden of adjustment in this case is borne by price. Crops must come to market. If demand is weak, price is low; if demand is strong, price is high.

In the case of the Federal Reserve's more traditional policy of targeting interest rates, the Fed picked a rate appropriate to the degree of tightness or looseness it wished to maintain. It then held the rate in the chosen range by engaging in open-market sales or purchases of government securities. If a fundamental change in the underlying demand and supply for money occurred, the adjustment response was limited to the quantity of money since the interest rate was temporarily fixed by Federal Reserve action. While the Fed would in time recognize a basic change in underlying conditions and adjust the interest rate target accordingly, the policy left itself open to an erratic behavior of the money supply. It is this weakness of the strategy that Friedman emphasized. When the Fed turned to the quantity of money as the monetary target, however, the situation was reversed. Given a determination by the Fed to stabilize the money supply, any change in the demand for money would affect only interest rates. Under this strategy the quantity of money behaves in a stable way but interest rates tend to be erratic.

It is partly because of the 1979 change in strategy by the Federal Reserve that interest rate volatility observed in the late 1970s and the early 1980s occurred. Managers who were accustomed to stable rates were required to adapt to a quite different financial environment. Few financial decisions were left unaffected. The timing of corporate investment financing became more challenging. Portfolio managers were subjected to greater price risk, for when interest rates fluctuate the prices of debt instruments also move. It is inherent in the nature of the price-yield relationship that the prices of long-term instruments are more sensitive to rate variations than the prices of shorts. Banks, which traditionally held a portfolio of bonds relatively free of price risk because of the stability of interest rates, now found themselves taking large paper losses on their long-term securities. Banks, and other institutions like savings and loan associations, that lend long and borrow short faced the problem that the cost of funds was rising while their income depended on long-term loans made at fixed interest rates.

One way of adjusting to this financial environment is to introduce variable interest rate loans. Hence the innovation in variable rate mortgages and the tying of consumer loans to some base such as the prime rate. Another way of adjusting is to hedge.

One of the more spontaneous developments that takes place when the prices of commodities are erratic in their behavior is the creation of futures markets. In a futures contract one party promises to deliver a commodity at a future date at a price determined now. Futures markets have long existed for farm commodities. One can buy wheat for immediate delivery at the current price in a *spot market* or buy or sell for future delivery at an agreed upon price. Processors of commodities, such as cereal companies, would like to avoid the risk of loss incurred when the price of grains they are holding in inventories falls. Futures markets provide a way of hedging their risk. A firm buys grain in a spot market but sells an equivalent amount in a futures market. If the price of grain falls it takes a loss on grain in storage but gains on the futures contract since it can purchase the grain to be delivered at a price lower than the price agreed on in the futures contract. In a perfect hedge, the loss is perfectly offset by the gain.

When interest rates and the prices of debt instruments began to behave in an erratic way at the end of the 1970s a futures market for financial instruments was created in Chicago where the expertise in futures trading has long existed. Today the largest volume in futures trading is not in wheat, corn, or soybeans but in assets such as bonds and certificates of deposit.

Perhaps most Americans became conscious of these developments during the traumatic market events of October 1987. By that time equity futures contracts were traded on the Chicago exchanges based on the 500 stocks included in the Standard & Poor's Index. One could buy or sell for current delivery at the New York Stock Exchange or in the futures market in Chicago. The practice of dealing in the stock market has, for some time, been fundamentally altered by the use of mathematical models which make buy or sell decisions according to predetermined rules and have been programmed into a computer for rapid execution. The so-called *programmed* buying and selling is a result of the invasion of Wall Street by the *quants* who are admired or detested depending on one's views of the proper way to run an auction market for the nation's assets. These programs can also be adapted for hedging or providing an insurance strategy for a portfolio, a strategy in which outright purchases are balanced by offsetting futures contracts to reduce the price risk. Under such a strategy the two markets, the spot market in New York and the futures market in Chicago, interact.

Much time has been spent since the stock market debacle of October 1987 in debating whether the drop in stock prices was accentuated by programmed trading and by the differences in trading rules in the New York and Chicago exchanges. Whether the market is more unstable because of these developments and whether changes need to be made in the rules of the game is open to debate. But in any event, certain innovations that have taken place in financial transactions in the last decade can be traced to the volatile behavior of interest rates which, in turn, are at least partly the result of the 1979 shift in Federal Reserve strategy.

THE END OF THE EXPERIMENT

In the early 1980s, William Ford, the newly appointed president of the Atlanta Federal Reserve Bank, formed a musical group made up of bank employees to perform at various bank functions as part of an effort to promote team spirit. He himself filled in as vocalist for the combo which he aptly named the *Monetary Aggregates*, after the phrase used by the Fed for the money measures then in vogue as the monetary target. The success of the group has not been recorded for posterity. But in another part of the Fed it became apparent by 1982 that the monetary aggregates adopted by the Volcker Federal Reserve Board were no longer singing in harmony with the behavior of the Gross National Product.

The vital link between money and the Gross National Product is the velocity. If the velocity, V, is reasonably stable, the effect of changes in the money supply, M, on total spending, MV, can be forecast. A stable velocity, or a velocity with predictable behavior, is crucial to monetarism and also to the use of money as a Federal Reserve target. From the end of the second World War to 1982 the velocity behaved in a relatively stable way increasing at an annual rate of about 3 percent. The growth in total spending could be reasonably forecast by adding the percentage increase in the money supply to the 3 percent increase in the turnover rate of money. In 1982 the velocity became more variable in its behavior and started to decline.

Faced with a velocity behavior that had become difficult to read, the Federal Reserve backed off from priority of the money target and adopted a strategy that involves monitoring a number of signals, including a variety of money measures, bank reserves, and interest rates. It is a supreme irony that only a few years after the monetarist policy was adopted the velocity broke a pattern of predictable behavior that had lasted for several decades.

Why did the velocity change in the early 1980s almost as abruptly as the mysterious disappearance of the anchovy catch off the coast of Peru in the early 1970s? The simple answer is that we don't know. A number of possible causes have been examined, including such things as financial deregulation which has caused a change in the way we define money. But after extensive research by a number of economists the reasons for the change in velocity behavior remain fuzzy.

The change in velocity has not only complicated the problem of monetary management; it has also affected the value of monetarism on the market of ideas where economic theories are priced. This decline in the status of monetarism has meant a return from the shadows of Keynesian economics. The value of economic theories partly depends on the success or failures of competing schools of thought. Just as monetarism benefitted from the discomfiture of Keynesian economics caused by the inflation of the later 1960s and the 1970s, so also Keynesian economics has experienced a revival of interest because of the problems of monetarism arising from a misbehaving money turnover rate.

We will return later to the issues over which these two schools of thought have struggled for what Paul Harvey would call "the rest of the story." We interrupt the discussion to take a look in the next chapter at a subject that has moved to a position high on the national agenda but to which neither the Keynesians or the monetarists have given prime attention. This issue is economic growth.

CHAPTER 7

ECONOMIC GROWTH

The late Kenneth Clark, the British art historian whose memorable series entitled *Civilisation* was produced for the British Broadcasting Corporation, wrote a book called *How To Look At A Picture* in which he explained what the trained eye sees when it looks at a masterpiece: the balance, the relationship of the figures, the use of shading, color and form to convey meaning and feeling. If one may switch abruptly from the sublime to the mundane, it is possible to convey visually the behavior of an economy. What is it that an observer should note when tracking the movement of an economy through time as presented in Figure 1?

In the chart the output of the U.S. economy from 1900 to the present, measured by Gross National Product data processed to eliminate inflationary bias, has been plotted as a solid line. This simple, antiseptic diagram summarizes with almost obscene brevity the results of nine decades of the expended energies of a nation, the hours of hard labor and the imagination and inventiveness. Looking at the plotting in a purely technical way, there are two types of movement embedded in the figure. There is, first of all, a wave-like motion whose ups and downs describe the expansions and contractions that take place as an economy goes through periods of prosperity and recession, a movement which is called the *business cycle*. You can use this rule of thumb: since the Great Depression of the 1930s the expansion periods have averaged about three years and contractions one year. The recessions express themselves in human terms as unemployment and lost profits. They have this in common with other bad news; they receive a lot of publicity. Expansions are not usually as well publicized in the news media.

In addition to the cyclical motion, the economy goes through another type of movement over a longer period of time. The cycles

FIGURE 1
Gross National Product, 1982 Dollars

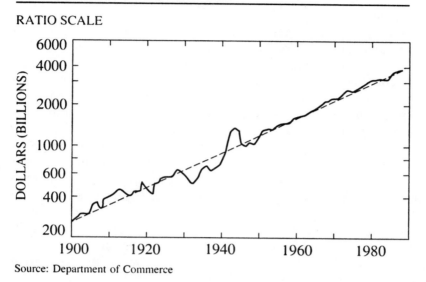

RATIO SCALE

Source: Department of Commerce

follow an upward path indicated in this figure by the dashed straight line. This movement we refer to as *economic growth*. Although the economy turns down periodically (the Great Depression of the 1930s shows up as a massive and prolonged drop on the chart), total output follows, on the average, a persistent growth path.

Economic growth and the business cycle can be thought of in another way. The ability of the economy to turn out goods and services grows over time as production facilities are increased. But over shorter periods, existing plant and equipment are not always fully utilized. In recessions, some of it sits idle. This variation in the use of the production potential is the business cycle, a fluctuation in output around a growing capacity to produce, which is called economic growth.

In his work Keynes was primarily concerned with short-run movements in the economy. This is hardly surprising since the problem he was trying to explain was the short-run collapse of the Great Depression. It is a problem that needed explaining. One of the great ironies of capitalistic systems is that capital equipment capable of producing enormous amounts of goods and accumulated with great sacrifice should stand idle even when people lack the necessities of life and workers go unemployed. We have Keynes's description of the Depression, "the enormous anomaly of unemployment in a world full of wants."

Some of what Keynes did say on the subject of the long-term growth of the economy seems now, over half a century later, rather quaint. There is a fascinating essay that he wrote in 1930 entitled "The Economic Possibilities for Our Grandchildren." In the essay he seems somewhat casual about the problem of achieving economic growth. Reflecting on the enormous increase in output accomplished through the power of science and technology in the century prior to his essay and extending that record into the future, he estimates that "the economic problem," the provision of the material things needed for a good life, may be solved within a hundred years, permitting the human race to turn its attention to more exalted concerns.

The formal model that he developed in *The General Theory* was addressed to the short-run problems of the business cycle. It can be adapted to apply to economic growth and this was done in a technical and formal way by his followers. When the Keynesian economist, Robert Solow, of MIT, won the Nobel Prize in 1987, he was cited specifically for his research related to economic growth. At the practical level, the Kennedy-Johnson tax cut of 1964, one of the first explicit Keynesian-type fiscal policy actions, was partly growth oriented in objective as we have seen in an earlier chapter. Much of the controversy between Keynesians and monetarists has been short run in character, involving such things as the relative short-run effects of monetary and fiscal policy. But the long-run problem of economic growth has now moved to the forefront of the national agenda.

GROWTH

There are two things that can be said about economic growth. The first is that it is a distinctly modern phenomenon. For most of the world's history, mankind produced the same amount of output per person from generation to generation. There were ups and downs, periods of prosperity matched by periods of plague and famine. But for the centuries up to the beginning of the 1700s, there was little change in the standard of living of the average man. The material comfort of an Englishman living at the start of the 18th century was little different from the level enjoyed by a citizen of Rome at the height of development of that ancient civilization. The period of abundance in which we live is part of a thin slice of history.

The breakthrough came with the Industrial Revolution of the 18th and 19th centuries; a fundamental change in the way we produce the things we need, the systematic application of science and technology to the problem of production. With this revolution we begin to see, for the first time, the phenomenon that makes our age unique, a persistent increase in the standard of living.

The second thing that can be said about growth is that the revolution has been unevenly spread. It has moved forward with momentum in the economies of Western Europe, North America, and Japan. In the Third World nations where a majority of the earth's population lives, the revolution is still in its early stages. Since the capacity to produce varies dramatically from country to country, so does the standard of living. The United States stands like a colossus astride the world's economies. With about 5 percent of the world's population, we produce between 20 to 25 percent of the world's output and income.

There are not many objectives that have been assigned as high a priorty by world governments as has economic growth and development. The main reason is that economic growth is the classic solution to poverty. The major way in which poverty has been overcome, in those countries where this has been achieved, is through an increase in the size of the economic pie. Redistribution of income succeeds as a method for relieving poverty only when there is something to redistribute. In some countries total output is so small that the lot of the masses would be improved only marginally even if the pie were cut into different slices. The problem is that there is not enough pie to go around. This is not to say that redistribution is never appropriate. It must sometimes accompany growth if increased prosperity is to be broadly shared and if further polarization of a people into rich and poor is to be avoided. But even in those countries that have been leaders on the growth path, redistribution has not been the major contributor to the relief of poverty. In the United States the proportion of the nation's income controlled by the upper income classes and the lower income classes has hardly changed in the last 50 years. The main way in which poverty has been relieved has been through growth in the size of the economic pie.

There is another gain from growth that is of enormous importance: social relationships are much simpler in an expanding environment. In a stationary economy the only way to improve the position of one group is to take away from another. When the size of the pie is fixed, someone's slice has to get smaller for another's to get larger. We have what is called in the theory of games a *zero-sum game*. One person's gain is at someone else's expense, the sum of gains and losses being zero. Social relationships in such societies are confrontational and competitive. It is winner-take-all; a shoot-out over a poker table in a wild west saloon.

The perspective is quite different when social relationships are looked at from a dynamic point of view. In a growing society the poor can be helped without reducing the standard of living of the upper income classes. Improvement of this type is made with much less social tension compared to the case of redistribution of a fixed bundle of wealth. It has become evident in the last two decades that economic growth produces not only goods but also bads such as pollution of the environment. There has been a huge increase in the awareness of the cost of growth in terms of environmental damage. Policies of controlled growth may be forced on nations as ecological problems and resource scarcities become more intense. But zero-growth policies, which some argued for in the 1960s, are not likely to be adopted. Nations play zero-sum games only if there is no escape.

TECHNOLOGY AND GROWTH

For over 200 years, even before Adam Smith's investigation into the sources of the "wealth of nations," economists have searched for the causes of economic growth. It depends, of course, on the abundance of natural resources, the skill and education of a nation's labor force, and things hard to measure such as the cultural characteristics of a people. But quite clearly at the center of the growth saga stands modern science and technology.

Examples of the marvels of science and technology are within the immediate experience of every person, from the auto we drive and the jet airliner we see passing overhead to the medical advances that save the lives of those we love. Each of these miracles has its own story. Perhaps one of the most dramatic and far-reaching of recent examples of the power of science is the discoveries in microelectronics.

Electronics received enormous stimulus from World War II as did other areas of technology from the aerospace industry to atomic power. Sonar and radar were developed for early detection of submarines and enemy aircraft. The computer was invented to perform the large number of arithmetic computations needed to solve the complicated mathematical equations used in ballistic problems.

The first computers dating as far back as Pascal and Leibniz in the 17th century were mechanical devices with moving gears and wheels. The speed of today's computer requires, instead, the use of electronic circuits. An integral part of a circuit is the relay, an electromagnetic device. When charged with electricity, the magnet closes the circuit; when not charged, the relay springs open. Important for our purposes is the fact that this change in state mimics the logic of computers.

Older vintage calculators designed as a system of gears with teeth to simulate numerical operations could be based on the decimal system with its familiar nine digits and zero. Modern computer logic is based on Boolean algebra, a binary number system using one and zero that can also be thought of as "open" and "closed." Relays, which behave like gates that close and open to direct traffic through a circuit, match in an electrical arrangement the binary choices of Boolean algebra and become, in effect, a logic system on which the modern computer is based. One of the first electronic computers, the Mark I, which was developed at Harvard and began operation in 1943, used electromagnetic relays.

A substitute for the electromagnetic relay is the vacuum tube that an older generation remembers as a standard component in radios and television sets. The vacuum tube can also be operated to have two states, closed or open, on or off, and can, therefore, be used to perform Boolean logic. The vacuum tube has the advantage of being much faster than the electromagnetic relay and the first truly modern electronic computer, the ENIAC, was built with vacuum tubes. The first commercial computer model, the UNIVAC, also of vacuum tube design, was purchased by the U.S. Census Bureau in 1951.

The vacuum tube also has limitations. The ENIAC which had 18,000 vacuum tubes presented a serious cooling problem. The expression *debugging* a computer may have originated with early equipment which was sometimes hampered by moths attracted to the vacuum tubes. It also used large amounts of power. The traditional story, probably apocryphal, is that the lights of Philadelphia dimmed when the ENIAC was first turned on at the University of Pennsylvania.

The transistor, which replaced the vacuum tube, was developed by three scientists at Bell Laboratory—John Bardeen, Walter Brattain, and William Shockley, all of whom received the Nobel Prize in 1956 for what must be rated one of the most important inventions of the 20th century. This solid state gadget, an unpretentious piece of metal a few inches in length with protruding wires, could do the job of the vacuum tube, was more reliable, did not have the heating problem, and required less energy. For a major scientific breakthrough, its introduction to the world was uneventful. A short announcement appeared in *The New York Times* under a "News of Radio" column along with a story of changes in program schedules.

A major advantage of the transistor is that it lends itself to miniaturization. Instead of wiring transistors together on a board by hand, the transistors and connections are imprinted on a tiny chip as an integrated circuit. Miniaturization led in time to the microprocessor, invented in 1970, which is, in effect, a computer on a chip. The invention of the microprocessor made it possible to replace a room full of computing equipment with a sliver of silicon smaller than a contact lens. A microcomputer today has more computing power than the ENIAC, is much faster, more reliable, can sit on a desk, and uses only a fraction of the electricity.

We can add as an aside that just as the microchip avoids the labor intensive process of connecting transistors by hand, the use of satellites and earth stations makes communication possible over enormous distances without the high cost of hardwiring previously needed for transmission between distant points. The most remote villages can be brought into contact with centers of information.

The word revolution is used carelessly in discussions of scientific and social change but when applied to the microprocessor is not an exaggeration. The potential of the microprocessor for use in guidance systems for space rockets and in military hardware was soon recognized. The whole space program would have been impossible without the transistor. But the impact is more pervasive than that. The miniaturization and cost effectiveness of microchip technology has made it possible to bring to the desk of rank and file workers the power of the large main frame computer in the form of the compact personal computer or word processor. Microprocessors are used in digital watches, hand calculators, automotive engines, and microwave ovens. They are the basic components of every piece of electronic equipment. Like basic metals developed in the Industrial Revolution of the 19th century, they are utilized in a wide range of products and effect a qualitative change in design.

Looked at another way, the invention of the microprocessor has made possible the information revolution. We are speaking here not only of the mass of data provided in a computer printout, but also of information in a more subtle sense; for example, signals transmitted in automated systems. Automated equipment not only transmits power (the power to move materials and to shape them), it also monitors machine performance. If a task is not performed according to specification, a device sends a message ordering adjustment of the equipment. These corrective signals can guide a precision cutting tool or halt the firing of the main rockets of a space shuttle in a fraction of a second when a malfunction is detected.

The capacity of machinery run on steam or internal combustion engines to apply enormous amounts of power has been with us since the Industrial Revolution. But something new has been added, an information flow that makes possible automatic control. Information is now as basic to science and technology as such traditional categories as matter and energy. The microprocessor is not just another invention; it has transformed all earlier inventions by adding to them the quality of intelligence.

Breakthroughs, such as the discoveries in microelectronics, are at the leading edge of the growth process. Economists attempt only to understand and monitor the growth phenomenon. Scientists and engineers are agents of growth in the sense that they draw new discoveries from nature that fundamentally change the way we live and the way we provide the material things of life.

INVENTION AND INNOVATION

Inventions by themselves, of course, are not enough. There is a second step. They must be put into production and adapted for markets. The role of commercial exploitation of inventions is a story told by the Harvard economist, Joseph Schumpeter.

Among the most eminent economists of his age, Schumpeter was born in the same year as Keynes, 1883. Born in what is now Czechoslovakia, he came, like Keynes, from a comfortably middle class family; his father a textile manufacturer, his mother the daughter of a physician. His father died when Schumpeter was four years of age and his mother took him to Vienna. Schumpeter had a deep attachment to his mother, a reverent affection felt long after her death, and she was a major influence in his life. After his father's death his mother married a lieutenant general in the Austro-Hungarian army, a rank that gave the family a social status of importance in prewar Vienna. While Keynes was attending Eton, Schumpeter studied at the Theresianum, a distinguished preparatory school reserved mostly for the aristocracy and social elite.

At the University of Vienna he concentrated in law and economics, attending the lectures of such distinguished leaders of the Austrian School as Eugen Böhm-Bawerk, one of the great theorists in the history of economics.

Like Keynes, Schumpeter worked at times in government and business, though his involvement was not as continuous nor did he enjoy the same success in these activist roles. After receiving his doctor of law degree he practiced law in Egypt. He served as minister of finance for a short time in a coalition government in Austria following World War I. He was later president of a bank in Vienna. It failed in 1924 due to adverse economic conditions and his personal financial loss was severe, and he spent the next 10 years paying off his debtors.

In his academic career Schumpeter held a succession of posts in Europe and was a visiting lecturer in Japan and the United States before settling permanently at Harvard in 1932. Devoted to his students, he was an imposing figure in a classroom—a fastidious dresser, elegant in the manner of someone reared and educated in Vienna at the end of the Austro-Hungarian empire. Paul Samuelson, who knew him as a student, wrote in a memorial essay that "with the disappearance of that world, he became completely qualified to play the important sociological role of the alienated stranger." The story has often been repeated that he had three wishes in life—to be a great lover, a great horseman, and a great economist—but that he had been granted only two of the three Which of the two, he apparently never said.

Schumpeter always contended that the important contributions were made during the third decade of a scholar's life. In his case, at least, this was probably true. The book that set the theme for his life's work, *The Theory of Economic Development*, was published in 1912 when he was 29 years of age. It established him as an important thinker. Most of his efforts in the remaining part of his career were devoted to extending and testing empirically the central idea that he developed in his youth.

We can make a sharp, if somewhat exaggerated, distinction between the intellectual focus of Schumpeter and Keynes. As we have said, Keynes's outlook is basically short run. He did not ask what causes an economy to grow over the long pull; rather he asked why an economy at some given moment fails to use fully the productive capacity it already has. To put the matter in another way, he sought out the explanation for the up-and-down movement in the economy which we call the business cycle. Schumpeter is not uninterested in these problems; but his interest arises only in connection with his investigation into another matter. What is it, he asked, that causes a capitalistic economy to expand its capacity to produce over the long run? In a word, what causes economic growth?

In attempting to answer this question Schumpeter focuses, in his *Theory of Economic Development*, on the internal dynamics of a capitalistic economy. He was trying to construct a theory, as he said in the preface to the Japanese edition, "to answer the question how the economic system generates the force which incessantly transforms it." In this concern he has more in common with Marx than he does with Keynes. While he was repelled by the prescriptions of Marxian doctrine for social organization and culture, he was strongly attracted by the broad sweep of Marxist theory and shared with Marx a common interest, the analysis of the forces within a capitalistic system that cause it to develop as it does. In Marx's economics change arises from the class struggle, a struggle conditioned by mutations in the basic modes of production. In the capitalist era, the confrontation in this model is defined by the technology of the Industrial Revolution. In his search for the dynamics of capitalist development, Schumpeter finds another explanation.

In Schumpeter's grand scheme, the source of momentum in a capitalistic system is the urge to innovate and the central figure in the story he tells is the entrepreneur. The entrepreneur is not simply the manager of an existing enterprise. He is an innovator who develops commercially a new product, introduces a new technology, utilizes a new mode of financing, or finds new channels for marketing products. The term *entrepreneur* does not so much describe a person as it does a role that people play. It is a generic term such as *leading actor* with the names on the marquee constantly changing. An entrepreneur may have his moment only once in a business career and then settle into the role of day-to-day management of his creation. A select few innovate over a lifetime. In Schumpeter's theory the entrepreneur is the creative genius of capitalistic development.

Genius has its rewards. For the entrepreneur, it is above-normal profit. Large profit attracts imitators and the innovation on which the profit is based spreads throughout the economy. Investments are made to exploit the profit potential and new industries are born or expanded in a surge of economic growth. Side-by-side with the birth of the new is the death of the old. Older industries and products, faced with new competition, go into decline. The entrepreneur fills a dual role; he initiates what Schumpeter calls a process of *creative destruction*.

In Schumpeter's later writings he extended his theory of economic growth to the problem of the business cycle. In a two-volume epic work he describes the ups-and-downs of the economy in the short run as due to the *swarming* of investment, its concentration in periods of time as imitators rush to get in on new developments. Rising interest rates due to the demand for credit and increasing costs due to pressure on resources cause imbalances in the economy leading eventually to contraction. But the cyclical behavior is a sideshow in the action, a temporary distraction from the main event, the spontaneous, internal drive toward long-term growth.

While Schumpeter and Keynes were contemporaries, their contacts were minimal. Schumpeter enjoyed English society and institutions. He had a lengthy stay in England in 1906 and 1907, when both were in their 20s. "He lived as a fashionable young man in London," one of his Harvard colleagues has written, "visited country houses, and intermingled his social life with occasional visits to Oxford and Cambridge." Keynes was working at the India Office; it is unlikely that they met at the time. At the other end of their lives (Schumpeter survived the British economist by four years) he wrote a memorial essay on Keynes for *The American Economic Review*, the journal of the American Economic Association. He had a gift for the biographical essay as did Keynes. When reading his collection of essays, *Ten Great Economists*, one is reminded of Keynes's *Essays in Biography*. But Keynesian economics had little effect on Schumpeter's work. While the Keynesian revolution was happening at Harvard, Schumpeter stayed aloof from the excitement, for the fact is that he disliked Keynesian economics intensely.

Schumpeter's disaffection followed from the political corollary that emerged from his own theory of economic development. He was not optimistic about the future of capitalism for reasons he explained in *Capitalism, Socialism, and Democracy* which he published in 1942. The very success of capitalism, he argued, breeds social and political resistance. A love-hate relationship develops. Society loves the material prosperity that capitalism provides but is repelled by the cruder manifestations of self-seeking. The thrust of development is hampered by government regulation and high taxes. The emergence of the large corporation also has a constraining effect as bureaucratic management attempts to institutionalize the entrepreneur's innovating genius. Schumpeter is critical of Keynes because he sees Keynesian economics as opening the door for further government involvement.

It is not difficult to understand Schumpeter's hostility. These two great thinkers came from two totally different directions. Influenced by his training in the Austrian School of economics with its firm commitment to market control and, perhaps, by his early life experiences (the chaos of World War I and its aftermath), Schumpeter saw government as a negative force stifling the unlimited growth energy of the economy. Keynes, on the other hand, who thought of capitalism as in the later stages of atrophy, welcomed government action to shore up and reinforce a faltering economy, government action designed and implemented by an elite, educated class in whose judgment he had great confidence. Both Schumpeter and Keynes rejected socialism, in the formal sense of government ownership of the means of production. Both wished to preserve capitalism. Schumpeter wanted to conserve the system by giving full play to the creativity of private initiative and protecting it from government intrusion. Keynes wanted to conserve the system by involving government to supplement and reinforce the private sector.

In any event Schumpeter's basic insight is an important contribution to our understanding of the process of economic growth. The inventions of science and technology are the first step. The implementation of new technology by creative managers is the second. The microelectronics revolution succeeded because the road from Bell Labs in New Jersey led to the development labs and production lines of California's Silicon Valley.

In sketching the key features of economic growth, we have one more step to go—the process of capital accumulation.

CAPITAL ACCUMULATION

One of the most basic prerequisites for economic development is a building up of the nation's capital stock. Production of the goods and services of an advanced economy requires an enormous capital base: factory buildings and equipment, offices and computers, communications systems, and transportation networks. Japan and the United States can each produce more cars than the Soviet Union for the simple reason that they have more automobile factories than the Soviet Union. For an economy to grow, its capital base must be constantly expanded.

Capital accumulation involves more than a simple quantitative increase in productive capacity. It also involves qualitative enhancement. As technological advances take place they are embodied in the design of new capital. A buildup of the capital stock not only provides us with more tools but also with better tools. Capital accumulation is at the heart of the growth process.

In order to build up the stock of capital there must be a temporary tradeoff with the standard of living. In the private sector there are two types of things produced, consumer goods and services and capital goods and services. If the economy is producing at a full employment level, so that total output is as large as possible, then the only way you can produce more capital goods in order to increase the economic growth rate is to produce less consumer goods. Temporary enjoyment must be sacrificed for future abundance.

Put another way, an important element in the growth process is a high level of saving. If the general public does not spend all of its income on consumption but saves a portion, there is a flow of funds to industry through financial institutions for investment in plant and equipment. The higher the level of saving the more resources that can be diverted from consumption to build the capital base. While all of this is perfectly obvious, the diversion of income into investment is a matter of great historical importance. One of the more dramatic examples is the case of the Soviet Union.

From the earliest days of the revolution, highest priority has been given to economic growth in the USSR. The drive to growth has dominated events in Russia. There are several reasons for this preoccupation. For one thing early Soviet leaders, with almost paranoid fixation, saw themselves as encircled and threatened by capitalistic powers. Development of defense capabilities required a strong industrial base.

But there is a more subtle reason. The revolution of 1917 was somewhat unorthodox in terms of Marxist theory. According to Marx a revolution occurs in capitalistic societies when the tensions arising from a concentration of power in the hands of capitalists and the increasing misery of the masses reach a breaking point. This theory of history implies that revolution happens in those countries that are the most capitalistically developed and in which dialectic pressures have reached maximum intensity.

Among the European powers, the least likely candidate for a revolution was Russia. One of the least industrialized countries, 80 percent of the population consisted of peasants. The urban working class which spearheads the revolution in the Marxist scenario was a small minority of the population. When social order broke down in Russia, in the chaos and devastation of World War I, the Communists seized the moment and took control even though the historical preconditions for revolution, in Marxist terms, had not been met. If an urban working class on which to base the revolution did not exist, then one had to be created. Hence the drive to economic growth.

Given the hostility of the Soviets to capitalist nations, there was minimum possibility of augmenting domestic saving through foreign investment. Saving had to come from within. In order to obtain the resources necessary to build the capital stock, domestic consumption had to be restricted. Since the peasants made up the majority of the population, it was the peasants that would have to accept a reduction in the standard of living to permit the accumulation of capital. To extract the surplus production from the peasants, Stalin organized them into collectives where they could be controlled. The totalitarian rule exercised by Stalin and the brutality he inflicted on the Russian people are partly explained in terms of the wrenching of resources from the hands of the peasants to underwrite the industrialization of Russia.

Under Stalin, spending on capital goods, as a percent of the Gross National Product, was about twice the level of investment in the United States and the early performance of the Russian economy was not unimpressive, with an annual growth rate of almost 5 percent for the three decades following the introduction of the first five year plan in 1928. The problem that Gorbachev must deal with is a major slowdown in the growth rate due mainly to rigidities in the Russian system which in the later stages of growth can be paralyzing.

In the western industrialized nations capital accumulation took place, in part, because of an uneven distribution of income that placed a larger percentage in the hands of an upper class that spends less on consumption compared to lower income groups and has, therefore, a higher propensity to generate saving. Capital accumulation also depended on social conventions that encouraged thrift. "The capitalist classes were allowed to call the best part of the cake theirs," Keynes wrote in *The Economic Consequences of the Peace*, "on the tacit underlying condition that they consumed very little of it in practice. The duty of 'saving' became nine tenths of virtue and the growth of the cake the object of true religion."

One of the controversial ideas advanced by Keynes was his challenge of the conventional wisdom on the importance of saving. His concern, as he observed the stagnant condition of the western economies in the 1930s, was that opportunities for profitable investment in the advanced stages of growth would not be sufficient to absorb a large volume of saving. In such an environment, he argued, it is not an appropriate policy to encourage further saving and discourage consumption. It is not surprising when factories stood empty in the economic collapse of the 1930s that someone would question whether we ought to have low levels of consumption in order to add to the capacity that already existed. A number of economists shared Keynes's concerns.

Keynes's views on saving soon became a standard part of the thinking of many economists. It was incorporated into Samuelson's introductory text with an interesting twist, the "paradox of thrift." The argument proceeds along these lines. If investors are willing to use consumer saving for capital projects, then saving performs a useful social function. It permits the diversion of resources into capital goods and enhances the growth rate. If profitable opportunities for investment do not exist, however, then savings lie idle. Not only does saving do nothing for growth, but because of it (since it means less consumption and overall lower sales), the existing stock of capital equipment is underutilized and unemployment appears. Further, and this is the punch line of the paradox of thrift, the act of saving itself can be aborted. If uninvested saving causes aggregate spending to drop, there will be less income to save and saving can actually fall. A decision to save more can result in a society's saving less.

Keynes's challenge to the central role traditionally given to saving not only led to a somewhat startling conclusion; it also had important social and political implications that should be noted. If there is danger of excessive saving in the later stages of an economy's development, as Keynes argued, then the justification of an uneven distribution of income as a way of generating the saving needed for economic growth disappears.

The implication of Keynes's point did not escape attention. Schumpeter, for whom economic growth, and the saving to finance it, was the dominant consideration and who looked upon recessions as only transitory periods of adjustment in a dynamic system, thought of Keynes's "indictment of private thrift" as one of the most significant points in *The General Theory*; "a doctrine that may not actually say but can easily be made to say both that 'who tries to save destroys real capital' and that, '*via* saving, the unequal distribution of income is the ultimate cause of unemployment.' *This* is what the Keynesian Revolution amounts to."

The economic growth problem, the central issue in Schumpeter's work, retains its importance through time. Indeed, one of the most significant facts about the behavior of the U.S. economy for the last decade and a half has been a slowdown in the rate of economic growth.

DECLINE IN THE GROWTH RATE

From the end of World War II through 1973 the economy grew at an average annual rate of 3.7 percent. Since 1973 the economy has grown at about 2.3 percent. A difference of a percentage point or so may not seem important at first sight. But we are speaking of a rate of growth and this involves the power of compound interest where even small changes in the rate make a large difference when spread out through time. An economy that is growing at the pre-1973 growth rate doubles its total output every 19 years. An economy growing at the post-1973 rate doubles its output only every 30 years. This dramatic shift in the behavior of the economy needs careful exploring.

The output of an economy increases for one of three basic reasons. The first is simply growth in population and with it expansion of the labor force. Such growth by itself does not result in improvement in society's economic welfare. New workers produce additional output, but new workers also eat. If job entrants simply match the performance of workers already in the job pool and produce the same average amount, the standard of living of the nation is unchanged. The net addition to total output is absorbed by the addition to population.

A second way in which output can grow is through an increase in the proportion of the population that works. One of the great sociological facts of the late 1960s and the 1970s is the greater participation of women in the labor force. The entry of women in larger numbers has been partially offset by a reduced involvement of males, but, even so, the overall participation rate has increased substantially, from about 59 percent of the population in the mid 1960s to about 65 percent today. If a larger proportion of the population is working, then, of course, total output in the economy grows and the average available per person also goes up.

This increase in output is not without its limitations. It represents a one-time gain. There is a limit to how far the participation rate can rise; when labor force saturation is reached, the potential for further gains from this source vanishes. Growth based on increased participation is also a mixed blessing. A shift in work effort to market activities may reflect a voluntary choice as individuals seek new outlets for expression of their personal talents. But it may also represent a reluctant diversion of effort from other pursuits and a loss of leisure. The number of new jobs created in the American economy in the course of the 1980s has been large compared to the record in Europe. Part of this job expansion has been due to the creation of meaningful activities for new additions to the job market. But another part is simply the mirror image of the increase in the labor force participation rate. There are two ways of looking at the growth in jobs. One way is to point with pride to the creation of new opportunities for entrants into the labor force. Another is to recognize that more members of the family have had to go to work to sustain increases in national output.

The third way in which output can grow is through a rise in output per worker or, in commonly accepted phrasing, an increase in productivity. If each worker is able to produce more then the same population has more goods available and a larger per capita income, and the standard of living goes up.

We have arrived at the crucial element of growth dynamics. Substantial economic progress is based on increases in productivity. With productivity gains, an economy expands; without productivity gains, an economy stagnates.

The slowdown in the economic growth rate since the early 1970s is linked in a critical way with productivity. From the end of World War II through 1973 the average annual increase in productivity was a little under $2^{1}/_{2}$ percent. From 1973 through 1981 the annual increase was a little over one half of one percent. Since 1981 the annual productivity gain has improved somewhat, a little over 1 percent.

Most people may not be familiar with statistical measures such as changes in productivity but they experience directly in their own personal lives what faltering productivity means. The benefit of increased productivity is more income. As workers become more efficient, part of the gain from lower cost is passed on by employers in the form of wage increases. From the end of World War II through 1973, average hourly earnings of nonfarm workers corrected for inflation increased by a little over 2 percent a year. Hourly earnings, adjusted for inflation, have not increased since 1973. The typical worker in nonfarm employment is making less today in hourly pay than he or she made a decade and a half ago.

Why did the growth of productivity, the key to ever-increasing prosperity, slow down? A large amount of work has gone into trying to solve this puzzle. Part of the answer is unknown, as, in fact, part of the reason for the growth of more prosperous periods is also imperfectly understood. A catalogue of reasons that fit into the explanation can be listed, although the relative importance of the various factors is a subject of disagreement.

Almost all researchers point to the slowdown in the growth of the amount of capital available per worker after 1973. The growth in the total amount of capital since that year, while not high, was about at an average level; but since the number of workers entering the labor force increased rapidly in the period, the amount of capital per worker grew at a slower rate. Furthermore, a change in the composition of the labor force, with a larger proportion of women and young workers after the mid 1960s, affected the experience and the amount of training of the workers using the nation's capital resources. Government regulations, particularly those related to protection of the environment and to occupational safety, meant that a proportion of new investment in capital equipment went into such things as scrubbers for smokestacks to reduce air pollution, expenditures that are needed, but, nevertheless, do not lead to greater production of output as usually measured. The rapid rise in energy prices in the early 1970s and again in the latter part of the decade made some of our existing equipment obsolete because of the increased cost of operation. The fact that the productivity slowdown was not limited to the United States, but affected most economies, suggests that the rise in energy prices, a worldwide phenomenon, had a significant impact. The high inflation rates of the 1970s may also have contributed to a slower rate of productivity growth. For one thing inflation creates uncertainty that reduces willingness to invest in capital projects. For another, it has an effect on tax obligations that can influence both the amount of capital investment and its mix in terms of allocation across various industries.

Some researchers have concluded, from data showing a fall in the growth rate of spending on research and development and from data showing a fall in the patents granted to American inventors, that the rate of innovation has slowed down. While the evidence is highly suggestive that innovation has, in fact, been weaker, the argument also exposes something of a mystery. Innovation has been intensive in the computer and electronics industry and yet industries investing in these new developments have not been exempt from a slower growth in productivity. In fact the number of white collar and clerical workers, who would be most affected by office automation, has actually increased as a percentage of the total number of workers. It is possible that there are quality improvements in clerical services and management performance that are not caught by standard output measurement techniques and that the advances in productivity in these activities are not being counted. There is also the possibility that the new technology is not being used efficiently and is simply generating more paper without affecting performance.

Despite the large amount of research done on the productivity puzzle, the complete reasons for the slowdown remain somewhat fuzzy.

THE HISTORICAL PERSPECTIVE

The slowdown in productivity gains over the last decade and a half is disturbing. But it is less so if looked at in terms of the historical record. While recent growth looks anemic compared to earlier post-war performance, it does not look as bad when compared to data over a longer period.

Prior to the recent slowdown there are three major periods that stand out in the international growth record. From about the middle of the 19th century to the start of World War I, there was a major spurt of economic growth as the Industrial Revolution spread among leading nations. For those countries that are now members of the OECD, roughly the nations of Europe, North America, and Japan, total output grew at an average annual rate of about $2^1/2$ percent. Trade among nations grew at a much faster rate than output growth due, in part, to a huge reduction in transportation costs resulting from such innovations as the substitution of steam driven ships for sailing vessels. The bulk of exports was concentrated among the leading nations, but Third World countries were drawn into the growth process through interaction with countries at the leading edge of industrialization. Economic growth for developing countries was then, as it is today, export driven. The decades prior to World War I were a period of world economic boom.

The years from World War I to the end of World War II, a period of two wars and a major depression, were years of international slowdown. Growth for the leading nations was about two thirds to three fourths of the growth prior to World War I. Only a handful of Third World countries grew at the rate necessary to raise per capita income.

The third period, the years after World War II, was the golden age of economic growth. From the end of the war to 1973, total output of the OECD nations grew at about twice the average annual rate of the growth period before World War I. A large part of this growth spurt is explained in terms of a catch up to satisfy pent-up demand and to make up for the delay in innovation caused by the Great Depression and the war. While the performance of our economy and other economies has been disappointing since the early part of the 1970s, it may in large part represent a return to something closer to historic averages. We may have to accept the fact that the performance of the first 25 years after World War II was unique and may not be repeated in the foreseeable future.

A look at the historic record improves our perspective in another way. Much has been made of the fact that the United States has had a smaller rate of growth in the last decade or two than our major trading partners. While it is true that our economy has grown more slowly, this behavior does not represent a fundamental change in our relative performance. For most of the last century, the U.S. economy has had a productivity growth rate below Germany, Japan, and other countries. This may be part of a larger process of convergence that has been observed by economic historians. Countries converge toward a common performance. Nations like the United States that started ahead of the pack find that other economies grow at a faster rate in a catch up process. There is a big spillover from leading nations to other economies of the ingredients that make for economic growth. In a world of free movement of people and ideas, all competitors have access to innovations or learn to imitate. The cost of imitation is not as great as the cost of original invention. With the rapid increase in information as we become a one-world economy and with such institutional developments as the multinational corporation that serves as an instrument of technology transfer, the convergence process may, if anything, become more rapid. Convergence seems to apply to socialist economies as well as market-oriented economies, although to a lesser degree. Only the least developed economies that have little in the way of a technology base to benefit from international advances seem to be immune to the convergence process.

There is a further dimension of the growth problem that has been the subject of intensive debate in recent years. The slowdown in the U.S. growth rate has been closely related by some to a claim that there has been a deterioration in the composition of jobs available to Americans. This deterioration, it is argued, is due to a shift from a manufacturing to a service-producing economy. The change that has taken place in the composition of jobs needs to be looked at carefully and we will return to it in a later chapter. For the moment we turn to one of the problems for which the decade of the 1980s will be remembered, the great federal budget deficit.

CHAPTER 8

THE GREAT FEDERAL DEFICIT

When historians look back at the decade of the 1980s, the economic event that will identify the period, more perhaps than any other, is the massive deficit in our federal budget. How it came about is one of the more fascinating stories of economic policy.

To understand the origin of the deficit one should start with *supply-side economics*, a school of thought with strong influence on policy in the early days of the Reagan administration. If Hollywood were doing the script, the story would begin at a meeting in a Washington restaurant in 1974. According to folklore, it is at this meeting that Arthur Laffer drew on a cocktail napkin for the first time the famous curve that came to bear his name. The event has been recorded for history by Jude Wanniski, then a writer for the editorial page of the *Wall Street Journal*, later to head his own consulting firm, and one of those present. Arthur Laffer is said not to remember the incident. Neither does the third member of the group, Richard Cheney, then in the Ford Administration and now a Congressman from Wyoming. The meeting provides, nevertheless, a starting point for the *Laffer curve* is probably the most well-known feature of supply-side economics.

Part of the reason for the fame of this line drawn on a graph is that it has a quality shared by most economic ideas that attract widespread attention, a simple concept with a powerful message. The Laffer curve shows in a geometric configuration the tax revenues received by the government for various tax rates. There are two rates at which revenues are zero, a zero tax rate and a 100 percent tax rate. At a zero rate there obviously can be no revenue; when government confiscates income at a 100 percent rate, there is little point in people working and tax revenue is also zero. All of this is straightforward enough. The crux of the Laffer curve is what happens in between.

If you start with a low rate and then raise it in a series of steps, government revenue goes up as one would expect. At some point, Laffer points out, higher tax rates dampen private initiative or lead people to engage in unreported activity in an *underground economy.* Reported income and tax revenues fall. When a Laffer curve is presented visually, tax rates are measured along the horizontal axis of a graph and total tax revenue is measured along the vertical. A line that connects the two looks like a hill. As rates are increased one walks up a hillside of increasing revenues. At some tax rate, one reaches the crest and then walks down the hill of decreasing government receipts. The tax authority has reached the limit in its power to command resources.

The basic assertion of a Laffer curve is irrefutable. There must, indeed, be some tax rate so high as to kill initiative and cause economic activity and government income to decline. This is an obvious but trivial observation. The critical issue is where we are at the present moment in terms of the Laffer curve. What is the rate, in the real world of tax administration, at which the decline in revenue occurs? The implication that caught public attention in the early 1980s is that we are indeed on the *perverse side* of the Laffer curve where an increase in taxes causes revenues to fall.

When Arthur Laffer came forward with the Laffer curve, it was not his first appearance on the public stage. There was a previous billing.

In President Nixon's budget message presented to Congress in early 1971 there was an economic forecast that predicted a Gross National Product of $1,065 billion. This *ten-sixty-five* forecast that presumed a nine percent jump in the nominal GNP and almost 7 percent in real terms, was widely regarded as unduly optimistic. It is interesting to read after two decades the views of a group of distinguished economists assembled by *Time* magazine to comment on the administration forecast. Included in the group were Walter Heller, who had served as Chairman of the Council of Economic Advisers under Kennedy and Johnson, Beryl Sprinkle, later to be Chairman under President Reagan, and Alan Greenspan, Chairman of the Council under President Ford and later appointed by President Reagan as Chairman of the Board of Governors of the Federal Reserve. *Time*'s "Board of Economists" agreed that the administration forecast was overly optimistic. The GNP forecast of this group averaged around $1,050 billion. *Time* reported that at a hearing before the Joint Economic Committee, at which representatives of the administration testified, one member of the Committee, commenting on the wishful thinking of the forecast said that it "reminded him of a remark by an anthropologist friend: 'The Zuñis realized that the rain dance didn't bring the rain, but it made the tribe feel better.'"

It turned out that the forecast came not from President Nixon's Council of Economic advisers, whose members viewed it with skepticism, but from the Office of Management and Budget which was headed at the time by George Shultz, who was later to hold, among other distinguished positions, the office of Secretary of State. Shultz had come to Washington from his position as Dean of the University of Chicago Graduate School of Business. Newsmen traced the forecast to a young economist also from Chicago whom Shultz had brought to his staff, Arthur Laffer. The model that he used for the forecast was made up of only a handful of equations with the money supply as the dominant explanatory variable, a design feature offensive to the Keynesians of the day but one on which monetarists insist. While the emphasis on money satisfied those of monetarist persuasion, the model failed to provide for a lagged effect of money supply changes, a lag central to Friedman's work and that of his disciples. Laffer managed to irritate the hierarchies of both of the two major competing schools of thought and, as a young man of only 30, he took a lot of criticism. His forecast turned out in the end to be more on target than that of his critics, but the attention span of the media is typically brief and so it was in this case. Laffer soon dropped from the news and eventually returned to Chicago. Some people have strong recuperative powers. In the early 1980s Laffer, now a professor at the University of Southern California, reappeared on the scene as the guru of supply-side economics.

To say that supply-side economics began with the Laffer curve would oversimplify the matter, for the relationship that Laffer emphasized is the most dramatic part, but only part, of a larger body of doctrine.

SUPPLY-SIDE ECONOMICS

Keynesian economics can be described as demand-side economics. Keynes's concern was with an economy operating at less than potential and the problem is insufficient demand. People are not buying what the economy has the capacity to produce and productive resources lie idle. To put the matter in another way, Keynesian economics is basically concerned with the short-run behavior of the economy over the course of the business cycle.

Supply-side economics, in the broadest sense of the term, focuses on a different problem: how can we increase the productive capabilities of the economy? The *supply-side* label, again in the broadest sense, can be thought of as simply another name for the type of analysis that Schumpeter emphasized, the theory of long-term economic growth. Understood in this way supply-side economics is, as one would have concluded from the previous chapter, one of the most venerable and traditional areas of analysis in the history of economic thought. It also has great relevance for the moment for our own country and especially for Third World nations for whom economic development is the pressing economic issue. In one sense, all economists are supply-side economists.

When we use the phrase *supply-side economics* to describe the economic strategy of the Reagan Presidency, however, we are thinking of economic growth theory with a particular twist. The supply-side economics developed by a small group of economists and espoused by the administration emphasizes the effect of taxes on economic growth and its adherents interpret the effects of fiscal decisions in a way different from Keynesian economists. The first impact of a tax cut, according to Keynesians, is an increase in aggregate demand in response to an increase in disposable income. Increased spending by consumers causes the economy to move toward full utilization of existing resources. Keynesians, such as those on Kennedy's Council of Economic Advisers in the 1960s, also point to a supply-side effect due to the stimulus to investment that comes with higher rates of capacity utilization and due also to the increase in after-tax profitability of investment outlays that results when a tax cut is properly formulated. Supply-side economists emphasize the supply-side consequences of a tax reduction almost exclusively and concentrate on the effects on incentives in a broader way.

The stimulus to growth is explained in terms of microeconomic analysis, the theory of individual behavior, and comes from the effect of a tax cut on relative prices. For example, a cut in taxes increases the after-tax wage, the price of labor. If we assume that workers react to wage incentives, and economic theory would suggest that they do, the supply of labor is stimulated by the increase in after-tax earnings. A tax cut also means that the after-tax interest rate is raised. Savers are motivated to increase their saving, presumably, by the promise of a higher return. Increased saving permits the diversion of resources from consumer goods to investment in plant and equipment, an addition to the capital base that enhances economic growth. The principal difference between supply-siders and Keynesians, then, is that the latter emphasize the effect of a tax cut on current spending and short-run production, while the former emphasize the effect on long-run output potential. It is worthwhile pursuing the matter a little further to appreciate fully the difference between the two.

One of the theorems that follows from the basic Keynesian paradigm is that a tax cut is less stimulating to the economy than a direct increase in government spending for goods and services. The reasoning is as follows. In a Keynesian model fiscal stimulus has an amplified effect on the economy. An increase in government spending causes income to rise by that amount, but there is a further increase in income as consumers who benefit from the government spending also make purchases. These increased consumer outlays represent further income for still other consumers who, in turn, add to the spending stream. An initial stimulus from increased government outlays leads to successive rounds of purchases with a final impact on Gross National Product larger than the original stimulus. In the formal terms of economists, fiscal policy has a *multiplier* effect.

A multiplier effect can be initiated by a tax reduction as well as by an increase in government spending. A tax cut, by increasing disposable income, causes the public to spend more on consumption. This stimulus leads, just like an increase in government purchases, to successive rounds of additional consumer spending. The reason why the overall expansion due to a tax cut is less than the expansion initiated by government spending is related to the tendency of consumers to save at least part of an increase in income, including an increase due to a tax cut. To use a numerical example, if government spending for goods and services is increased by $10 billion, the full $10 billion is pumped into the economy to start the multiplier effect. If taxes are cut by $10 billion, a portion is saved and only part is spent. The original stimulus due to the tax cut that starts off the multiplier process is less than in the government spending case and the total expansionary effect is also less.

Supply-side economists, who share in common, perhaps more than anything else, a deeply committed belief in the impotency of government, react strongly to this line of reasoning. They argue that an increase in government purchases, while temporarily stimulating the system, competes with the private sector and ultimately dampens economic growth. A cut in taxes, on the other hand, diverts resources to the private sector, increases incentives, and stimulates a long-run increase in productive capacity. In the final analysis, a tax cut does more for the economy than an increase in government outlays. Supply-siders argue that Keynesians confuse the issue by concentrating on a purely transitory phenomenon. The two schools of thought, the Keynesians and the supply-siders, approach the problem from two quite different directions.

In their emphasis on tax reductions, the critical rate to supply-siders is the marginal tax rate. To see the full point, a word of explanation is needed. The marginal tax rate is the rate that applies to incremental income. Every taxpayer faces the marginal tax rate each April as the last step in the traumatic process of filling out an income tax form. After sifting through the mass of paper spread out on the diningroom table—the check stubs, the interest statement from the mortgage holder, the scraps of paper with half legible notations retrieved from the bottom of a sock drawer—and working through the successive steps on the form, you eventually get to the punch line, the amount of tax owed. Locating the taxable income in the proper table, the taxpayer is told that he or she owes some specific dollar amount plus a certain percent for all income over a certain level. The percent that applies to this last increment of income is the marginal tax rate.

In economic theory decisions are always made at the margin. Human beings are poised, at any moment in time, on the edge of making new decisions. In deciding whether to produce and sell an additional amount of output, the seller compares the additional, or marginal, revenue that accrues to the firm with the additional cost of bringing the output to market. If the incremental revenue exceeds the additional cost, the firm adds to its profit by selling more. A worker offered the chance to work overtime may at some point decide that it's not worthwhile, meaning that the additional income is not sufficient reward to make up for the loss of leisure and time with their family. Decisions are made at the margin.

Supply-siders see taxation as a tool to affect motivation. If one wants to influence behavior in the marketplace through government fiscal action, the crucial tax is the marginal tax rate. Supply-siders cite particularly the high marginal rates that applied to the top income brackets in the 1970s, arguing that if they were lowered so that individuals could keep a fair part of each additional dollar earned, an explosion of energy would be released.

The good things that happen in the supply-side model when taxes are cut include an increase in labor supply, a higher saving rate, more investment in capital goods, larger productivity gains, and a faster rate of economic growth. The increased capacity of the economy to meet the demand for goods, due to enlargement of the capital base, dampens inflationary pressure. For the government's budget position, there is also a happy conclusion. On the perverse side of the Laffer curve, government revenues drop if tax rates are increased, but a counterpart to the curve's logic is that government revenues rise when tax rates are reduced. After an initial deficit due to the tax cut, the budget moves toward balance as incentives take hold and tax revenues share in the general prosperity.

THE SUPPLY-SIDERS

It is always difficult to classify economists into different schools of thought. Even when close in basic beliefs they differ strongly in matters of detail. Economists are like fingerprints; there are no two exactly alike. Few accept all of any reigning orthodoxy. In his later days Marx was so unhappy with doctrine advanced in his name that he protested "I am not a Marxist."

Supply-side economists are like other economists; they have sharp differences of opinion on specific issues. But it is still possible to identify a set of individuals, who, one way or another, were closely associated with what came to be known in the Reagan era as supply-side economics.

There are, of course, Arthur Laffer and Jude Wanniski. Wanniski is one of the more visible and ebullient members of the group. A self-educated economist, he made up in ceaseless energy for what he lacked in formal training. His book, *How the World Works,* was written to explain supply-side economics to the general public and, if not the bible, is one of the more often cited books of the movement. Wanniski's position on the staff of the editorial page of the *Wall Street Journal* provided him with a forum for influencing opinion. More important was his role in converting Robert Bartley, who was in charge of the editorial page, to supply-side views. The unique version of supply-side economics that we are discussing here was not much debated in the pages of the professional journals in which economists usually communicate. The most important original source for the ideas of the truly committed supply-siders who became attached to the Reagan administration is the editorial pages of the *Wall Street Journal.*

Paul Craig Roberts, a University of Virginia trained economist, joined the staff of Congressman Jack Kemp of New York in 1975. Congressman Kemp, influenced by various members of the supply-side group, became the most dedicated adherent of supply-side economics among elected public officials. He cosponsored in 1977 with Senator William Roth the Kemp-Roth bill that provided for a 30 percent cut in taxes spread over three years, a piece of legislation that was the forerunner of the 1981 tax cut that was the centerpiece of the Reagan economic program. After playing an important role in developing the Kemp-Roth bill, Roberts left his work in Congress and joined the staff of the *Journal* as associate editor and columnist where he played a key role in advancing the ideas of supply-side economics. He later joined the Reagan administration as Assistant Secretary of the Treasury for Economic Policy.

Also included in the cast of this policy play was Norman Ture, a Washington economic consultant who developed an econometric model with supply-side effects included that was used by Roberts to support the case for the tax cut of Kemp-Roth. Ture later served in the Reagan administration as an Undersecretary of the Treasury for economic and tax affairs. George Gilder, while not an economist, wrote a widely read book entitled *Wealth and Poverty* which is a modern restatement of the free market economics of Adam Smith and is generally supportive of the economic philosophy of supply-side economics. President Reagan is reported to have recommended the book to friends and members of his administration. Irving Kristol, New York intellectual and founder and editor of *The Public Interest*, in which occasional articles by supply-siders appeared, was generally supportive. Martin Anderson, who came to the scene from Stanford's Hoover Institution and served in the White House as director of Reagan's Office of Policy Development, was one of the more important members of the group in terms of participation in the policy decisions of the administration. He has left his contribution to the record, an insider's account of the supply-side movement in his book, *Revolution*. Robert Mundell, a distinguished member of the faculty at Columbia University, had an indirect impact through his influence on members of the supply-side group, particularly Arthur Laffer—a colleague at Chicago for a period of time—and Jude Wanniski with whom he had contact when both were in New York.

And then there is David Stockman. Out of the Midwest, Stockman attended Harvard Divinity School after finishing his undergraduate studies at Michigan State University. While a student there he was a live-in baby-sitter in the household of Senator Daniel Moynihan, then a member of the Harvard faculty. Stockman went to Washington in 1970 to beome an aide to Congressman John Anderson of Illinois. He was later to play the Anderson role in practice sessions with candidate Ronald Reagan as he prepared for his debate with Stockman's former employer during the 1980 Presidential campaign. Elected to Congress from Michigan in 1976, he developed a reputation for ability, partly through a quality possessed by others who have managed to become influential members of Congress—the tenacity required to master the intricacies of the federal budget. Through his contact with Reagan in the mock Anderson debates and because of his known expertise in the minutiae of the budget, he captured a plum appointment in the administration for influencing economic policy, the directorship of the Office of Management and Budget.

When economists cluster in groups, they tend to do so with intensity. There is emotional allegiance to ideas and those who share them, as well as intellectual commitment. Schumpeter's description of Keynesian economists of an earlier vintage would apply just as well to other groups. "A Keynesian school formed itself, not a school in the loose sense in which some historians of economics speak of a French, German, Italian school, but a genuine one which is a sociological entity, namely, a group that professes allegiance to One Master and One Doctrine, and has its inner circle, its propagandists, its watchwords, its esoteric and its popular doctrine." Perhaps it is the softness of economic science that makes it difficult to eliminate all but one of competing theories even after decades of debate, that lends to economic discourse a shrill tone that might lead outside observers to conclude that for many economists those who disagree are not only wrong but wicked. The more vociferous of supply-side economists seemed to be operating in their heyday at an even more elevated level of intensity, harsh in their condemnation of the opposition, in constant alertness for any deviation of the committed from doctrinal purity. Most economists form schools. The Hollywood script writer might write supply-siders into the story line as forming a gang, wearing black leather jackets, and riding into Washington on Harley-Davidson motorcycles.

Supply-siders share an interest with others who concentrated on supply-side issues in the 1960s and 1970s. A number of economists urged a rollback in the amount of business regulation to free up the decision process and encourage price and quality competition and entrepreneurial inventiveness. Others examined such issues as the effect of minimum wage laws on the labor supply and the impact of social security on saving behavior. The tax cut of the Kennedy administration was Keynesian in its attempt to stimulate aggregate demand; but the package also included a significant reduction in the top marginal tax rate on personal income and tax cuts for business aimed at increasing investment in plant and equipment and were supply-side in purpose. Even the simplest of formal Keynesian models also had built into them a feedback mechanism whereby part of a tax cut was recaptured for government out of the increased incomes generated by a tax cut stimulus. Supply-side economists share credit for a revival of interest in the microeconomic implications of fiscal actions. The fact that some of the standard econometric forecasting models now include a supply-side component among their equations is an example of their influence.

Perhaps the best insight into supply-side economics is to note that its weakness is found in its exaggeration of claims. From a theoretical point of view, you would expect a reduction in tax rates to have a stimulating effect on work habits, saving, and investment. The practical and crucial question involves the size and timing of these effects and on these matters there were, and still are, unresolved ambiguities. The problem with supply-side economics is hyperbole or, as Herbert Stein, Chairman of the Council of Economic Advisers under President Nixon, has written, "the extreme notion that marginal rates of taxation are a lever capable of moving the world."

THE REAGAN 1981 TAX BILL

The man who played the leading role in this script did not ride into Washington on a motorcycle. He rode into town on his faithful horse, wearing a white hat and with ideas of his own. How much of the narrowly-defined supply-side canon Ronald Reagan accepted or understood is not clear. It is well known that his management style as President was to delegate details to subordinates. Those who worked closely with him describe him as passive in approach, reacting to proposals rather than originating them. In any event, his mind-set is different from that of the intellectuals on leave from their think tanks who were advising him on economic policy. Professionally trained economists abstract from details to build models that describe with minute distinctions fundamental economic relationships. Most presidents don't think in this way. President Reagan, in particular, we are told, thinks in terms of anecdotes and of specific situations he has personally encountered and uses to form ideas with general application. Learning the inside story on Reagan's thoughts about supply-side economics will not be easy, for the advisers who tell it are not immune from the very human temptation to claim him as a dedicated convert in order to cloak their own ideas with the prestige of the Reagan Presidency.

This much seems certain. Reagan had as his central political position an imperative of reducing the presence of government in the socio-economic environment. You control government the same way you control a teenager—to use one of his favorite analogies— by taking away the child's *allowance*. Governments spend all you make available and the way to reduce the presence of government in the economy and society is to cut taxes and reduce revenue. A tax cut not only brings benefit to the individual taxpayer but also serves as a technique of government control. He also had, from personal experience, a clear understanding of the burden of high marginal tax rates. While a successful movie actor in Hollywood, he cut back on the number of movies he made a year because the high marginal rates imposed on large incomes in the 1940s and 1950s meant that the personal benefit from working more months of the year was, in terms of spendable, after-tax income, quite low. Punitive taxes, he knew, can destroy initiative. He also came from a state where taxes had recently become a hot political issue. Proposition 13, a referendum on limiting property taxes, had passed in mid-1978 in California by a 2 to 1 margin and is frequently associated in popular discussion with a taxpayers' revolution. His thinking, in broad terms, was consistent with some of the assertions of supply-side economics.

Apparently President Reagan was drafted as a formal member of the supply-side club by Congressman Jack Kemp. Kemp was a candidate in the presidential campaign of 1980. While it appeared unlikely that he would succeed in getting the nomination, his political support would help candidate Reagan in his contest with George Bush. Kemp was willing to give his endorsement but, in time-honored political tradition, for something in return: Reagan's adoption of the Kemp-Roth proposal for a 30 percent tax reduction over three years. The reaction of the Reagan camp to the Kemp offer seems, as told by insider Martin Anderson, somewhat casual. "When Reagan and his political advisers heard the terms of the deal," he writes, "they shrugged and essentially said, 'Why not?' Reagan had already indicated support for a series of annual tax rate reductions as a part of his comprehensive economic plan. Why not give Jack Kemp's political future a boost by endorsing the Kemp-Roth tax proposal?"

The President's 1981 tax legislation, as finally passed by Congress, was an amended version of the Kemp-Roth bill, but a close facsimile. Instead of a 10 percent cut in personal income taxes for three succeeding years, the Economic Recovery Tax Act provided for a 5 percent cut in the first year and a 10 percent cut in the following two years. An important benefit to business came in the form of accelerated depreciation allowances that permitted businesses to write off capital investments more rapidly. These provisions were widely viewed as quite generous and some of the benefits were rescinded in the Tax Equity and Fiscal Responsibility Act of 1982. Other parts of the 1981 legislation included a reduction in the top tax rate for investment income and capital gains and provided incentives for saving in the Individual Retirement Accounts.

Even if Ronald Reagan had not been elected President, some form of tax cut would almost certainly have been enacted in the early part of the 1980s because of *bracket creep*. When a country with a progressive income tax system has a healthy economic growth rate, personal incomes rise and people move up the tax brackets. The average tax rate that applies to the nation's income increases. Inflation accelerates the bracket creep. People are taxed on their nominal income with all the inflationary bias left in. Even if employees only receive a wage or salary increase sufficient to cover the rise in the cost of living so that real income is unchanged, they still move up to the next tax bracket since nominal income is higher and the average tax rate that applies increases. Congress made some adjustments in taxes by lowering rates or liberalizing exemptions and deductions to make up for the bracket creep caused by inflation of the 1970s but not enough to compensate fully.

Inflation also leads to higher taxes for business. If depreciation is determined, for example, on the basis of original historical cost of buildings and equipment, depreciation cost is understated since capital goods must be replaced at inflated prices. Given this understatement of cost, taxable earnings are higher and so are taxes, all because of the inflation.

Tax adjustments would most likely have been proposed by another President but not by the amount of the Reagan cut. The 1981 tax cut represented the largest decrease in taxes in our nation's history. In one stroke Reagan cut back the government's allowance.

If the country were operating on the perverse side of the Laffer curve, a cut in taxes would not result in a fall in tax revenues. In fact, revenues would increase. In planning for the 1981 tax cut the administration did not make the assertion that a simple Laffer curve type of result could be expected. Those involved in the design of policy strategy realized that the tax cut would have to be accompanied by a decrease in government outlays if large deficits were to be avoided. The problem was where to cut and how to get the body politic to accept them.

To get a realistic understanding of the potential for cutting federal outlays, several things should be noted. First of all, the composition of the budget has undergone a fundamental change in the decades since World War II. Direct spending by government agencies, for example, accounts for a smaller part of the budget than before. While total federal outlays have increased, the federal government's claim on goods and services from the nation's Gross National Product has actually declined. In President Eisenhower's last term, 1956–1960, for example, federal purchases of goods and services were 14 percent of the GNP and a third again larger than purchases by state and local governments. Twenty years later, in the four years before Reagan assumed office, 1976–1980, federal outlays for the nation's output averaged less than 8 percent of the Gross National Product and were a third smaller than purchases by state and local government. Over two thirds of the total expenditures on goods and services in the latter period were for national defense.

The dramatic change in the federal budget has been its conversion into a giant transfer machine, drawing in large sums of money in the form of taxes and distributing them to individuals and organizations in a wide variety of programs. If cutbacks in outlays are to be made then, obviously, transfers have to be curtailed. When voters think in terms of reducing transfers, they probably think first of cutting the welfare components of government transfers. While welfare programs can of course be cut—they were in fact pared back in 1981— they are not large enough to provide the cuts necessary to make up for the loss of revenues from a large tax reduction such as the one initiated by the legislation of 1981. Means-tested programs, including welfare and Medicaid, which are directed at the lower income classes, account for a little over 7 percent of federal outlays. Social Security and Medicare, which apply to the general population, on the other hand, are 28 percent of federal spending. Social Security outlays are large enough to make a difference in reducing federal expenditures. The nation has made a decision, however, through a series of legislative enactments over the last half century, to provide security for the elderly. Unlike programs aimed at the lower income groups, Social Security has a large political constituency and, for all practical purposes, has been removed from the list of items eligible for retrenchment. The programs that could make a difference cannot be cut and the programs that can be cut are not large enough to make a difference.

The problem of reducing federal expenditures is also complicated by the fact that a large part of the budget involves fixed commitments. This is a problem familiar to anyone who has tried to economize on a family budget. A fairly high proportion of a family's income is claimed off the top by obligations that have to be met—the monthly mortgage payment, utility bills, food, and routine medical care. What is left over represents a relatively small proportion of the family's monthly income. The federal government is in the same position. A large part of total outlays are mandated by law. *Entitlements* have been created to which all citizens who meet certain conditions specified by the original legislation have an automatic claim. To reduce these would require a basic redrafting of the law, a lengthy process that gives ample time for organization of significant political opposition. Other types of outlays, such as the payment of interest on the public debt, cannot be avoided under any circumstances. The discretionary part of the budget is relatively small. Currently, nondefense discretionary spending is only 16 percent of total outlays.

Whatever success the administration had in reducing transfers and nondefense discretionary outlays would have been at least partially offset by the major increase in defense spending required by the priority assigned by the President to national preparedness. After the Vietnam War, spending on defense was deemphasized and declined as a percent of Gross National Product. It fell steadily over the 1970s, starting to rise again at the end of the Carter administration. In this period of reduced defense allocations, outlays were directed more at operating costs, payroll, and maintenance. A general feeling developed over the 1970s that a higher level of expenditures was necessary. Carter requested in his last budget proposal before leaving office a substantial increase in defense outlays. Reagan asked for an increase in real terms—after the adjustment for inflation—almost twice the percentage increase requested by Carter. The Reagan proposal had a heavy emphasis on new weapons systems and involved the largest increase in defense spending in peacetime history.

SPENDING CUTS AND THE BUDGET PROCESS

President Reagan got about half of the spending cuts he requested, more than most would have thought possible. The drive to get the reductions was led by the new director of the Office of Management and Budget, David Stockman.

The process in place when Reagan came into office and still in place today is based on the Congressional Budget and Impoundment Control Act of 1974. This legislation is in the spirit of budget reform actions that take place periodically in our history. The budget represents in capsulized form the basic priorities of the nation. It is not surprising in a country as large as the United States, with a heterogeneous population and with constitutional provision for the sharing of budget responsibility between Congress and the President, if the inevitable tradeoffs in reaching a consensus about priorities are aesthetically unsatisfying in their final form. Democracy in action is not always a thing of beauty. Budget reform is an attempt to impose discipline on the participants in the process who have been given an impossible task.

The immediate cause of the 1974 budget reform was the impoundment of funds by President Nixon. Nixon is not the first president to *impound* or refuse to spend, funds appropriated by Congress for specific purposes, but the Nixon impoundments were more numerous than those of other presidents and forced a mini-crisis on the constitutional issue of congressional and executive authority. The executive-legislative conflict over budget control was actually larger than the impoundment issue; it was also part of the Watergate affair. One of the proposed articles of impeachment considered by the House Judiciary Committee in the proceedings against President Nixon—a proposal not included in the final set—involved a charge of abuse of budget authority in connection with the incursion into Cambodia during the Vietnam War.

The 1974 legislation occasioned by the Nixon use of impoundment imposes constraints on the President's authority to "defer," that is, delay, or "rescind," that is, cancel, projects for which funds have been appropriated by Congress. The purpose of the act, though, was not only impoundment control but also budget reform. A general consensus had built up in Congress that some of its budget procedures were outmoded and that modification was necessary. The 1974 legislation reflected the two purposes, to limit the President's ability to block the use of funds and to force Congress to proceed with budget decisions in a more rational manner.

The budgeting process begins in January of each year when the President presents his budget message to Congress which has the ultimate authority for taxing and spending. Prior to the Budget Act the various parts of the President's budget were assigned to the appropriate committees and brought back separately to the legislative bodies for action. At no point did Congress look at the total package to determine whether or not it represented the priorities that Congress intended or examine the implications of the budget totals for the overall economy. The 1974 Act provided a procedure whereby the budget is viewed as an entity. The bill required Congress to approve by May 15 of each year a budget resolution that specifies the level of total spending, the expected tax revenues, and the size of the surplus or deficit. This resolution provided the basic guidelines for the various committees dealing with specific appropriations and tax matters. Its intent was to force the committees, with long-established prerogatives jealously guarded by members with established seniority, to conform to constraints imposed by the overall will of Congress. A second budget resolution affirming or modifying the spending and revenue levels of the first resolution was required by September 15.

To facilitate the process, the Act provided for new organizational arrangements, among them the establishment of a budget committee in both the House and the Senate. It also created the Congressional Budget Office, the counterpart to the Office of Management and Budget which provides the President with the technical expertise necessary for budget decisions. The purpose of the Congressional Budget Office is to supply Congress with objective, nonpartisan research on budget issues. It is charged to provide Congress each year with an analysis of the President's budget as well as budget projections for the next five fiscal years.

The preparation of these budget projections is no simple matter for in order to make spending and revenue estimates it is first necessary to make an economic forecast. Revenues depend on the level of national income. In a period of prosperity revenues are high; in a recession, revenues are low. Certain government outlays, such as unemployment compensation, also behave cyclically. An economic forecast is a prerequisite for revenue and spending estimates. The budget presented by the President to Congress also requires an economic forecast. The forecast of the Congressional Budget Office provides a measure against which the President's forecast can be compared.

These are the procedures established by the 1974 legislation that the Reagan administration faced as it came into office with total commitment to gain control of the federal budget. Through the ingenuity of David Stockman, legislation originally designed to limit Presidential budget authority was converted for use in implementing the Reagan fiscal revolution.

One little-understood procedure provided for in the 1974 Act is known as *reconciliation*, a step in the process designed for removing inconsistencies in the final House and Senate budget packages. Reconciliation was intended, in the original legislation, to come after the appropriating committees had completed action on budget details within their jurisdiction and as the second budget resolution was being finalized. In practice reconciliation was not used for the first four years after the new budget process became operative, mainly because insufficient time was allowed in the schedule for the work to be completed by the start of the fiscal year. In 1980, the year before Reagan assumed office, the reconciliation step was moved up to go with the first budget resolution. Stockman saw reconciliation, placed in this new time slot, as a vehicle for packaging spending cuts in one large omnibus bill with instructions to the appropriating committees to report back spending cuts conforming with the overall budget resolution. The reconciliation was pushed through the Senate by a Republican majority carried into office by the Reagan landslide and through the House by a disciplined Republican minority that joined forces with conservative, Democratic "Boll Weevils." The result of this strategy was a budget coup acomplished in a few days with about 250 members of the House and Senate feverishly working in committees to grind out 600 pages of detail in what became the budget package. Senator Moynihan, in commenting on the cuts heavily concentrated on social programs, is quoted as saying: "We have undone thirty years of social legislation in three days."

THE BUDGET DEFICIT

By mid-1981 the economic policy that George Bush had branded in the heat of the Republican primary as *voodoo economics* and that Senate Majority Leader Howard Baker called, at the time of the passage of 1981 legislation a *riverboat gamble* was in place.

The economic forecast that came with the budget program came to be known as the *Rosy Scenario*. When Reagan was inaugurated the country was in the early stages of an economic recovery from the mini-recession that had occurred in the first six months of 1980. The Administration forecast projected continued expansion in 1981, a 4 to 5 percent annual growth in real output for 1982 through 1984 and beyond, a halving of the inflation rate to 6 percent, and a balanced budget by 1984. Most economic forecasters predicted continued recovery from the recession of 1980, but the administration forecast for real GNP growth required a healthy dose of optimism. Economic growth over the 1970s had averaged a little under 3 percent on an annual basis.

The major problem with the forecast is that it lacked internal consistency. The economists who advised the Reagan Presidency represented a wider range of strongly held opinion than is true of most administrations. In the Treasury there were supply-siders Norman Ture and Paul Craig Roberts and monetarist Beryl Sprinkel. The Secretary of the Treasury, Donald Regan, had come from the world of finance, head of Merrill Lynch, and presumably had no strongly based theoretical economic position. David Stockman, Director of the Office of Management and Budget, was a supply-sider but with a habit of judgment tempered by pragmatism. His commitment to the faith would soon be challenged following publication of an article by William Greider based on a series of interviews with Stockman and published in the *Atlantic Monthly*. The Council of Economic Advisers was chaired by Murray Weidenbaum, a mainstream economist from Washington University in St. Louis. Monetarists were represented on the Coucnil by Jerry Jordan who was known for his work on a monetarist-based econometric model done while a member of the research staff of the St. Louis Federal Reserve Bank. Working in the White House itself as an adviser was supply-side economist Martin Anderson.

The supply-siders expected a surge in Gross National Product as a result of the tax cuts. Monetarists emphasized the importance of monetary restraint to stop the inflation that had averaged over 12 percent in 1980. How the economy could be expected to expand at a fairly rapid rate—an expansion needed to generate the income and tax revenues to move the budget toward balance—in the face of a restrictive monetary policy was not clear. David Stockman, in his account of the period, describes the *Rosy Scenario* as an attempt to satisfy through a statistical compromise a variety of positions.

The spending reductions obtained in the Stockman blitzkrieg were not enough to make up for the decrease in revenue due to the tax cut. But with a little luck in the performance of the economy, the gargantuan deficits that were incurred in the succeeding years might have been avoided. An abundance of tax revenues requires a healthy and expanding economy. What the administration got was the worst recession since World War II.

While the official forecast for Gross National Product may have been unduly optimistic, the Reagan economists cannot be faulted for not foreseeing the recession that began in July 1981 and continued for 16 months until November 1982. Most economists missed the drop in GNP by a wide mark. In October of 1981, the consensus of the *Blue Chip Economic Indicators*, a widely used compilation of the predictions of 50 of the major forecasters in the country, anticipated an increase in real GNP of over 2 percent for 1982. The GNP actually dropped by $2^{1}/2$ percent, a total forecasting error of almost 5 percentage points.

The recession caused a shortfall in revenues and an increase in unemployment compensation payments triggered by the rise in the unemployment rate to its highest level since World War II. Instead of balancing the budget by 1984 as the Rosy Scenario had predicted, there was a deficit of $185 billion.

One part of the administration forecast turned out to be less optimistic than the actual outcome. The inflation rate dropped faster than expected; the rise in consumer prices in 1982 fell below 4 percent. While the drop in the inflation rate was due primarily to the actions of the Federal Reserve, Reagan, to whom Milton Friedman had long been an informal adviser, supported the Fed's anti-inflation policy and shares in the credit. Some administration advisers were suspicious of the Federal Reserve—operating out of reach, immune to influence because of the autonomy granted by law—and eventually became dissatisfied with the monetary actions. Supply-side economists, in particular, protested the restraint which they viewed as excessive and as stifling the expansion that they expected to follow the tax cuts.

It is ironic that the one positive development of the period, the drop in the inflation rate, aggravated the deficit problem. Inflation subjects taxpayers to bracket creep; they pay more taxes. The taxpayer's loss is the government's gain; inflation is a boon to federal revenues. Administration revenue forecasts were incorrect not only because of the drop in income due to the recession but also because the inflation rate slowed by more than expected. The major success story of the early 1980s turned out to have an unhappy ending in its impact on the budget.

The deficits that followed in dreary succession over the fiscal years of the 1980s were the largest in our peacetime history. Budget deficits have been the rule rather than the exception since World War II. We have had only one surplus in the last 25 years. It is generally recognized because of Keynes's influence that deficits are not necessarily bad and may be appropriate at certain points in the business cycle. The cost of liberation from the orthodoxy of classical public finance may be, in practice, a bias toward deficit budgets. The deficits of the 1960s averaged on an annual basis a little under 1 percent of the Gross National Product. In the 1970s they averaged a little over 2 percent of the GNP. The deficits of the Reagan years, however, are of a different order of magnitude. Over Reagan's term of office, they averaged over 4 percent annually. In fiscal year 1983 the deficit reached a high of over 6 percent of the Gross National Product.

As Lord Keynes, Baron of Tilton, contemplates the current U.S. deficit from the distant place where deceased economists reside, he must be muttering to himself, "that's not what I meant at all."

Budget deficits add each year, of course, to our total national deficit. When the administration took office the federal debt was a little over $900 billion. Because of the large deficits the debt more than doubled over the two terms of the Reagan Presidency. You can measure the burden of the debt for countries the same way you assess the problem of family debt; compare the debt to income or, in the case of nations, the Gross National Product. While the nation's outstanding debt grew over the period since World War II, it grew more slowly over the first three and a half decades than the Gross National Product so that the debt, relative to GNP, declined. Immediately after World War II, the debt was larger than the Gross National Product. Over the 1950s, 1960s, and 1970s, the debt held by the public fell as a percentage of GNP reaching a low of 24 percent in 1974. It hovered in this range until the 1980s when it began to rise reaching a level of 43 percent of the Gross National Product.

A debt rising at this rate is a matter of concern. The 1985 economic outlook prepared by the Congressional Budget Office had a rather fascinating discussion of the conditions under which the debt would become explosive, that is, the conditions necessary for the debt-to-GNP ratio to increase without limit. If, in a melt-down scenario, the debt as a percent of Gross National Product got large enough, it would take the entire GNP just to pay the interest. The

CBO concluded that the conditions for movement in the direction of an explosive increase did not exist at the moment. The conclusion was not as important as the fact that the question was even asked. The question itself suggests the fragile state of federal finances.

To be a serious problem the debt does not have to become so large that it gets completely out of control. Long before that, accumulating deficits raise interest charges that must be paid and increase the problem of moving the budget toward balance. Like a family trapped with credit card payments, the Treasury is committed to large carrying costs in service of the public debt. In the 1960s and the first part of the 1970s interest payments were about 7 percent of total government spending. They rose over the latter part of the 1970s both because the debt grew and because interest rates were higher. They reached about 10 percent of budget outlays the year Reagan took office. They now are at a level of about 14 percent.

There is a feedback mechanism at work in the dynamics of the public debt. Deficits lead to more debt, more debt means higher interest payments, and higher interest payments lead to a larger deficit. An unending spiral is started that can only be halted by an increase in taxes or a cutback in noninterest outlays. As the fixed commitment of interest payments becomes a larger part of the budget the available choices for cutting expenditures shrinks. Just as the interest paid by a family heavily indebted with consumer loans represents funds that could have been used in some other way, so also federal outlays in interest payments force a tradeoff with other types of public spending. The tradeoffs are not small in size. Interest payments are now almost twice as large as outlays for means tested programs, basically welfare and Medicaid, over one and a half times as large as Medicare reimbursements, and over 8 times as large as unemployment compensation payments. As the tradeoffs get tighter, the freedom to avoid tax increases is reduced.

EFFECTS OF THE DEFICIT

One of the arguments traditionally advanced as to why government deficits are undesirable is based on the so-called *crowd-out effect*. If the government goes to the market to finance a deficit, it crowds out private borrowers by forcing up interest rates and reduces investment and the rate of capital formation. With a lower rate of capital accumulation, the economic growth rate is reduced. It is in this sense that it is often said that the deficits are mortgaging the standard of living of our children.

Interest rates have been at historically high levels in the 1980s, partly because of the federal deficit. To interpret the economic implications of interest rate changes correctly it is necessary to distinguish between the nominal, or quoted rate, and the *real* rate. The real rate is the quoted rate corrected for inflationary bias and the rate that more accurately measures the cost of capital. Nominal rates less the actual inflation rate for short-term Treasury securities were mostly between 1 and 2 percent in the 1960s. They were lower in the 1970s, becoming negative in some years as lenders failed to allow properly for inflation. In the first half of the 1980s real rates were generally above 4 percent.

It is not easy to determine, however, the precise effect of the federal deficit on investment and there is not a clear consensus among economists on the crowding-out issue. There are a number of reasons why the impact of the deficit on private capital accumulation may be muted.

If investment spending, first of all, is not sensitive to changes in interest rates, then an increase in rates would have a modest effect on capital spending. Accumulated empirical evidence suggests that investment does react to increases in real rates and that deficits do crowd out capital accumulation in the private sector. The negative effect of high, after-tax real rates on investment can be dampened if part of the tax cuts that lead to a deficit are in the form of accelerated depreciation or investment tax credits for business, as was indeed the case with the 1981 legislation. These incentive-oriented tax changes lower the after-tax rate and offset the before-tax increase in interest charges.

It is also possible that savers are sensitive to interest rate changes and that higher rates stimulate an increase in saving large enough to dampen the rise in the cost of capital. The possibility of large response by savers is increased if capital flows freely in international markets and is responsive to higher rates. National credit needs are then partially offset by the inflow of foreign money.

One argument that deficits do not matter is based on the *Ricardo equivalence theorem,* which was resurrected by Robert Barro, now a Harvard economist. David Ricardo, who wrote in the early part of the 19th century, is a towering figure in the history of economics. He, along with Robert Malthus, author of the famous *Essay on Population*, is responsible for the pessimistic predictions of early economists that caused Thomas Carlyle to brand economics *the dismal science*. Keynes described in a charming essay the lifelong friendship of Malthus and Ricardo, and their continuing debate on economic issues carried on through a stream of correspondence. They present an interesting contrast in personalities.

Malthus served for a time as an ordained minister in the Church of England after graduating from Cambridge, but spent most of his life as a professor of history and economics at East India College, which was set up by the East India Company to train its managers. His essay on population developed from a long discussion with his father about a book written by William Godwin, the father-in-law of the poet Percy Bysshe Shelley. Godwin's daughter, and Shelley's wife, Mary Godwin Shelley, is the author of one of the more famous Gothic novels written in 18th and 19th century England, *Frankenstein*, a story brought to 20th century movie goers in all its graphic horror, courtesy of Hollywood and the actor Boris Karloff. Malthus's essay, first published anonymously in 1798, went through seven editions. It had a major influence on Ricardo who, in his model, described population growth as pressing against productive capacity until wages are forced down to a subsistence level. It is this subsistence theory that Marx later brands the *iron law of wages*.

In sharp contrast to Malthus, who was educated in the conventional manner of the day, Ricardo ended his formal training at the age of 14 and joined his father's investment firm as an apprentice. At the age of 22, he went into business for himself; at 42, he retired a wealthy man. Keynes tells in his essay how Ricardo cut his friend in on issues of government securities during the Napoleonic War. Ricardo was a member of the syndicate that did the underwriting. The cautious Malthus lost his nerve before the battle of Waterloo and wrote Ricardo to close out his position. To Malthus's chagrin, Ricardo, the cool-headed speculator, stayed in the market to reap, as he reported in a letter to Malthus, "as great an advantage as ever I expect or wish to make by a rise." As Keynes tells this story, his admiration for the stock broker-economist is obvious.

Ricardo happened on Adam Smith's *Wealth of Nations* at the age of 27 while on a vacation, bored and looking for something to read. He became fascinated with the subject of economics and a decade later started writing on issues of public debate. He was 47 when his classic piece, the *Principles of Political Economy and Taxation*, appeared in its first edition in 1817. Anyone comparing Adam Smith's famous *Wealth of Nations*, written by the Scottish professor at the University of Glasgow, with the treatise by Ricardo, the practical, successful businessman, is in for a surprise. Smith's book is a tome filled with practical examples from industry and trade that embellish the theoretical portions of the book. Ricardo's, on the other hand, is a thin treatise done in the manner of the severe abstractions of modern economic theory.

Robert Barro, along with others, has applied a line of reasoning used by Ricardo in some of his early 19th century writings to the current problem of the federal deficit. Ricardo argued that financing government outlays by taxes or by the issuing of debt are equivalent. Rational people would recognize that a deficit financed by borrowing must eventually be paid for by taxes. They therefore increase their saving to allow for the future tax obligations. The higher level of saving prevents interest rates from rising and crowding-out private borrowers in credit markets.

The Ricardo equivalence theorem holds only under certain conditions. The behavior of the older generation, who could realistically expect to avoid the future taxes, for example, is presumed to be influenced by benevolent concern for their descendants. They increase their saving to protect wealth left for their heirs. Intergenerational transfers such as investment in education and bequests do, of course, take place so that the presumption of concern for one's progeny is sensible enough. To the degree that one generation does not choose to protect a future inheritance, however, or perhaps is uncertain of the way in which the burden of future taxes will be distributed, it may accept the apparent windfall and respond to a decrease in taxes by increasing its own consumption. In which case, there is a crowd-out effect.

What can we say about the effect of the deficit on investment in the 1980s, the period in which we are interested? Despite the rise in real interest rates to historically high levels, the negative effect on net private domestic investment was not as dramatic as one might have expected. Following World War II, net domestic investment ranged from an average of 7^1/2 percent of the Gross National Product in the 1950s to just under 7 percent in the 1970s. From 1981, Reagan's first year in office, to 1987, a period which included the worst recession since World War II, net investment averaged a little under 5 percent of Gross National Product. A rough assessment would suggest that there was crowd-out, but that it was dampened by the investment tax credits and accelerated depreciation provisions of the 1981 legislation that diluted the after-tax effect of high market interest rates.

One should not interpret this conclusion that the budgets of the 1980s have had a limited impact on domestic investment as suggesting that the economic effects of the deficit are of minor importance. They are not. For one thing, even though the crowd-out was moderate, the deficits heightened the degree of uncertainty that usually exists about the future course of interest rates and the value of financial securities and contributed to a certain fragility that has been characteristic of financial markets in the 1980s. The stock market crash in October 1987 was not due solely to the large federal deficits, but they contributed, directly or indirectly, to this sobering experience. But there is another and more important effect of the deficits. The negative impact on investment was also limited by the inflow of foreign funds. This inflow, attracted by high interest rates, had the effect of shifting the crowd-out from the domestic economy to our foreign trade balances with adverse consequences for U.S. exporters and import competing industries. The major effect of the deficit has been indirect in the form of feedback from the foreign trade sector. This is a large part of the deficit story, and we will explore it in detail in the next chapter.

THE DEFICIT, AFTERMATH

It is a well-known axiom among historians of the American Presidency that our newly elected chiefs of state have a fleeting moment to leave their mark on history. Fresh from an election victory, they are first met by a receptive attitude from Congress, an attitude that soon shifts to resistance to presidential initiatives. In his first year, President Reagan got most of what he wanted in tax reductions, all the increases in military spending—with some downward adjustment in appropriations in later fiscal years—and about half of the targeted spending cuts. After this first year, he was left with a budget gridlock.

The tax cuts were hardly in place before it became evident that we were in for a succession of massive deficits and that something needed to be done. Obviously, two alternatives were available, increase taxes or cut spending. There were some small increases in taxes, *revenue enhancements*, as for example in the Tax Equity and Fiscal Responsibility Act of 1982, but short of enough to make a significant difference. A popular president then removed from the political agenda, for all practical purposes, a tax increase sufficient to move the budget toward balance. Both the President and Congress were unwilling to propose cuts in categories of nondefense spending, such as Social Security and Medicare, that are large enough to make a difference. The limited options that remained were further reduced by the yearly increase in interest payments that followed the rapid accumulation of debt.

Faced with a breakdown in the decision making process, Congress resorted to an interesting invention; it automated the budget mechanism through the Gramm-Rudman-Hollings Act of 1985.

Gramm-Rudman should not be confused with the tax reform law of 1986 that was designed to leave total tax revenues unchanged but to rearrange the distribution of the tax burden. Three years in development and a sweeping change in the tax code, the 1986 legislation was designed to correct distortions in the tax laws and reduce the influence of tax provisions on investment choices and the allocation of resources to different uses. The 1986 Act is widely admired but, it should be repeated, was designed to be revenue neutral.

It was the intention of the original Gramm-Rudman Act to provide a schedule for the gradual reduction of the deficits. They were to be cut by a specific amount each year until balance was reached in 1991. If the deficit ceilings were exceeded and Congress and the President could not agree on actions to trim the deficits to the prescribed level, a mechanism was automatically triggered to cut spending—an action described in the law as *sequestering*. The original law was declared to be unconstitutional because the procedures for administration of the Act were said by the Court to violate the constitutional separation of powers between the legislative and executive branches of government. In its new form, the Act revised the schedule for meeting the deficit targets and extended the target year for reaching budget balance.

During the Reagan years, Gramm-Rudman had a modest effect, at best, in moving the nation toward a solution to the deficit problem. Although the Act has the potential to force Congress and the President to make difficult choices, this unpleasant result can be avoided through the use of the proverbial "blue smoke and mirrors." Creative accounting, optimistic budget and economic forecasts, and the selling of government assets make it possible to meet the Gramm-Rudman requirements without making unpopular decisions. It may, nevertheless, be a useful legislative device. One of the most pressing policy tasks of the 1990s will be to bring the budget under some reasonable degree of control.

President Reagan is widely recognized as the most conservative president since Herbert Hoover. The results of administration policy are in sharp contrast to the orginal expectations. One of his major goals was to cut federal spending. Federal outlays were almost 23 percent of the Gross National Product when he came into office; when he left they were slightly higher, although the composition of outlays was significantly altered away from social welfare programs and toward defense spending and interest payments. The federal deficits incurred were far above the historic peacetime experience.

Supply-side economics, with which the administration was closely associated, offered an alternative to Keynesian fiscal policy. Most Keynesians had come to realize by the time Reagan came into office that the fiscal tool is not as effective an instrument for stabilizing the economy as they first thought. One of the major problems is the awkwardness of the legislative decision making process. The lag time in making revenue and spending decisions is too long for the budget to be used efficiently as a counterbalance to variations in spending in the private sector, even assuming one could correctly forecast the behavior of the economy over future quarters and prescribe the proper amounts of budget deficit or surplus.

The supply-siders intended to rehabilitate the use of the budget for policy purposes but with a different focus. The emphasis was not on stimulating aggregate demand to move the economy to full utilization of resources and full employment. The purpose of tax cuts was to motivate people to work harder, to save more, and to invest in new capital projects. The objective was not short-run stimulation of the economy but long-term expansion of the productive capabilities of the nation.

The results of the supply-side policies contrast sharply with what was promised. There is no evidence that the labor supply increased as a result of the tax cuts. Personal saving did not go up as a percent of disposable income; it dropped significantly below the saving rate of the 1970s. Public dissaving in the form of federal deficits absorbed a large part of available credit. Investment spending as a percent of GNP was lower than in the three previous decades.

The happy event of the 1980s is the sustained recovery from the trough of the 1981–1982 recession. A reasonable observer would find it hard to classify this longest peacetime expansion in history as a supply-side happening. It has all the signs of an old fashioned Keynesian episode, an expansion led by consumer demand stimulated by a massive tax cut. History may conclude that supply-side economics only turned out in the end to be Keynesianism on steroids.

CHAPTER 9

ECONOMIC POLICY AND INTERNATIONAL MARKETS

When the Dow Jones Industrial Average stepped off the edge of a cliff on October 19, 1987 and dropped 500 points, the effect was felt around the world. For the major stock markets, connected by electronic hookup, move in rhythm with the sun from London to New York to Tokyo and back again across Asia to the European continent. The domino effect of Black Monday is only one episode in a big story of recent decades, the increased linkage among nations both in exchange of goods and services and in trade in financial assets.

Other industrialized nations, such as Great Britain, have long depended on international markets for a large part of their economic well-being. The United States has traditionally been a more self-contained economy, but in recent years we have become more immersed in foreign trade. When John Kennedy died in 1963 our exports plus imports were 10 percent of the nation's Gross National Product. They are now a little over twice that percentage of the GNP. What we do in the production and marketing of goods affects other nations to a greater extent than before. What other nations do touches each American family as we have discovered with some consternation in the decades of the 1970s and 1980s. Because of increased involvement in international economic activity, our economic policy decisions must be made with greater awareness of their international implications.

It is also in the international trade and financial market that the major effects of our budget deficits discussed in the last chapter are to be found.

The day-to-day activities of most Americans provide little background experience for understanding international trade and financial arrangements. We lack the intuitive feel for foreign transactions that we develop through contacts in domestic markets. To understand the impact of world economic events on our country, particularly in the last decade, we need to begin by taking a look at the inner workings of the international financial mechanism.

When people trade in a domestic economy there is one price that has to be determined, the price of products in terms of the domestic currency. International transactions are complicated by the fact that there is a second price, the price of the domestic currency in terms of the currency of the trading partner. We call this second price the *exchange rate*. When many nations trade, a system has to be established for determining the ratio at which currencies exchange for one another. One of the best ways to understand the system now in place in international financial markets, and also to develop a feeling for the periodic crises that are reported in the news media, is to look at the historical developments that led us to where we are today.

THE GOLD STANDARD

Modern financial arrangements begin with the gold standard which in its purest form governed international trade relations from the latter part of the 19th century to World War I. Gold has always had an almost mystic appeal throughout history for people of all cultures. It not only has its own unique beauty; since it does not rust, it has a certain permanence not shared by other metals such as iron. This eternal quality must explain at least part of gold's attraction to human beings for whom life is short and most things transitory. Its universal acceptability made it particularly suitable as a form of money starting with early civilizations.

Gold also has another quality that makes it useful as a medium of exchange. Since it is valuable relative to weight, it has a low transportation cost. When gold was money, a large amount of purchasing power could be carried in a pouch in the palm of the hand. Other commodities that were used as money lacked this convenient property.

There is an incident told in a fascinating book by Forbes Wilson, *The Conquest of Copper Mountain*, that illustrates the importance of a money's portability. In the 1930s a mountain of ore was discovered deep in the jungles of New Guinea by a Dutch geologist, the largest above-ground deposit of copper ever found. Because of its inaccessibility no attempt was made at the time to explore its commercial potential. An expedition was organized in the early 1960s to visit the site, take samples, and investigate the possibility of mining the ore. Wilson's book tells the story of the expedition. The investigating team hired local natives to carry supplies and equipment. The natives to whom paper money meant nothing were given ax blades as payment. It took 10 percent of the bearers hired to carry the supplies simply to carry the payroll of ax heads.

When gold was introduced as a monetary standard in the economies of the modern era, the rules of the game were relatively simple. To be on a gold standard participating nations must do two things: define the value of their currencies in terms of gold and agree to buy and sell gold at the Treasury at the official price. When these two commitments are made, the value of currencies relative to one another is automatically determined. Since currencies are defined in terms of a common thing, gold, they become defined in terms of one another.

Suppose, for example, that the United States defined gold as worth $35 an ounce; or to put the relationship in an equivalent way, $1 is worth $1/35$ of an ounce of gold. If the British define the pound as equal to $3/35$ of an ounce of gold, the relationship of the pound and the dollar is automatically determined at $3 to the pound.

Under a gold standard holders of dollars and pounds trade currencies at an exchange rate determined by the official prices. They do this in foreign exchange markets operated by banks and other dealers in currencies. The rate in foreign exchange markets must match the official price or otherwise participants ship gold among the treasuries. We should have said *almost match* since the exchange rate can deviate from the official price by a small amount because of the cost of transporting gold.

Suppose that it cost 3 cents to ship $3/35$ of an ounce of gold. An American wishing to acquire a pound could buy the gold from the U.S. Treasury for $3, ship it to Britain for 3 cents, and obtain a pound for a total outlay of $3.03. The American would never pay more than $3.03 for a pound since one could be had for this price by shipping gold. The British citizen, on the other hand, would be unwilling to trade a pound for less than $2.97 since he or she could obtain at least this much by buying $3/35$ of an ounce of gold at the British Treasury for one pound and shipping it at a cost of 3 cents for a net return of $2.97. These rates, $3.03 and $2.97, define the limits of fluctuation from the official price and are called, in the lingo of the gold standard, *the gold points.*

The constraint on variation in the exchange rate under the gold standard is one of its most attractive features. Businesses operating in international trade must necessarily run the normal risk of those engaged in enterprise. If exchange rates are also subject to wide fluctuations, further risk is encountered since investors have no assurance about the terms under which profits made in a foreign currency can be repatriated to the domestic money. Stability of the exchange rate is a property preserved for a time in international arrangements, as we shall see, after the gold standard had become a part of history. It is also one, in a period of erratic exchange rates, to which many look back with nostalgia.

There is a second effect of the gold standard much emphasized by 19th century economists. It imposed a discipline on trading nations in the form of an automatic adjustment process known as *the price specie-flow mechanism.* This mechanism was identified as early as 1750 by the philosopher and economist David Hume and it worked in the following way. The positioning of the exchange rate within the boundaries of the gold points depends on the relative supply and demand for a nation's currency. This supply and demand for a nation's currency in turn depends on the supply and demand for a nation's goods. If there is a strong American desire for British goods, for example, there would also be a strong demand for the British pound and the price, in dollars, would be bid up to $3.03, the higher of the two gold points. If the American desire for British goods is weak, then the British pound would not be in demand and Americans could obtain it for a price at the lower boundary of the gold points, $2.97.

The competitiveness of a nation's products today is multidimensional depending on such things as design, quality, service, delivery arrangements, and the price in terms of the domestic currency. In the era of the gold standard when trade was in basic commodities and simple manufactured goods, a nation's competitiveness was determined mainly by price. A country undergoing inflation would find that rising prices reduced the demand for its goods and caused a drop in the value of its money relative to other currencies in foreign exchange markets. When a nation became noncompetitive, the exchange rate would press against the gold point. Instead of trading currencies outside the boundary of the gold points, market participants would ship gold. The noncompetitive nation experienced a drain on its gold supply.

The price specie-flow mechanism provided an automatic check to limit the outward flow of gold and to restore a nation to a competitive position. In the period we are describing, gold constituted the basic money supply. It circulated freely in the domestic economy and internationally. When gold flowed out of a country, the nation's money supply would shrink. The decrease in money would cause a downward adjustment in prices according to the quantity theory that states that the price level is determined by the amount of money in circulation. The nation's competitiveness was automatically restored by the gold flow. At the same time, the country gaining gold experienced an increase in money supply and an upward pressure on prices. Its competitiveness was weakened. The gold standard, in summary, forced a two-way adjustment to move trading partners toward one another to restore a basic equilibrium in their trade relations.

This equilibrating process was not painless. Prices were more flexible in a downward direction in the 19th century than they are today. But even then prices could be sluggish in reacting to a drop in the money supply, particularly as wage and price rigidity became more of a part of the institutional system. Part of the adjustment required by the loss of gold had to be borne by decreases in output and a slowing of general economic activity rather than by a drop in the price level. A country experienced recession and unemployment. It was common to refer to such episodes as *going through the wringer of deflation*.

For cases where the necessary retrenchment was simply unacceptable, the gold standard provided an escape, like the *deus ex machina* of a Greek tragedy. The device by which the gods rescued the nation in peril was devaluation. Devaluation required the simplest of adjustments, an increase in the price of gold in terms of the nation's currency. In our previous example, the United States had defined the dollar to be worth $1/35$ of an ounce of gold and the British had defined the pound to be worth $3/35$ of an ounce of gold. The two currencies exchanged, therefore, for $3 to the pound.

Suppose that the United States, under pressure in foreign exchange markets, devalues by increasing the price of gold from $35 to $70 an ounce. This has the effect of changing the value of a dollar from $1/35$ to $1/70$ an ounce of gold. If the official price of the pound remains unchanged, then the pound retains its value of $3/35$ of an ounce of gold, or to make it more easily comparable with the new American price, $6/70$ of an ounce of gold. With the dollar now at $1/70$ of an ounce of gold and the pound at $6/70$ of an ounce of gold, the official exchange rate changed from $3 to the pound to $6. Almost by magic, American goods have become more competitive. An American product priced at $3 cost the British one pound before the devaluation. It can now be bought for half a pound. On the other hand, British products become more expensive to Americans. A good priced at one pound that would cost Americans $3 under the old exchange rate now costs $6. Through the simple device of manipulating the official price of gold, the Americans become more competitive, the British less so, and equilibrium is restored.

Devaluations were always times of great drama, the denouement of a crisis for a nation's currency. In its execution, devaluation required a good deal of finesse. Decisions were made in great secrecy. A conviction among participants in international financial markets that a nation intended to reduce the value of its currency would trip a massive selloff causing further depreciation of its standing in foreign exchange markets. Not only the timing but also the amount of the increase in gold price was carefully considered. The size of the devaluation had to be large enough to convince speculators that a second devaluation would not be required, but not so large as to invite retaliatory devaluation by trading partners.

There was a certain stigma attached to lowering the value of one's currency by devaluation, an admission of national weakness and in practice great powers resorted to such an extreme solution infrequently. Capital movements permitted nations to finance an excess of imports up to some point and monetary restraint caused by the outflow of gold prevented deterioration in the trade balance from getting too far out of hand.

Later theories of the gold standard had a more sophisticated explanation of the corrective process than that provided by Hume's price specie-flow mechanism. But the essential character of this monetary regime remained. It was an automatic adjustment mechanism.

As such, it extended to the international scene Adam Smith's invisible hand of control. According to the complete scenario, adjustments in relative prices cause resources to be allocated for use in a domestic economy in an optimum way according to choices freely expressed in a decentralized market system. Price adjustments also regulate trade in the international economy, with gold movements automatically preventing lasting disequilibrium in trade patterns.

Under the system the proper role of government is one of laissez faire. Officials avoid interference in the international economy just as they abstain from intervening in domestic trade. An action to which they would more likely be tempted is intervention by the central bank. Banks, of course, existed under the gold standard but with this difference: their reserves consisted of the precious metal. A loss of gold, tripped by a drop in the value of the currency that caused the exchange rate to press against the gold point, reduced the reserve holdings of banks and with it their ability to create money. It would be possible to avoid the monetary consequences of a gold outflow by some neutralizing action by the central bank. But the gold standard was more than a mechanical arrangement; it provided a code of conduct. Banks were expected to play the rules of the gold game. The hardships due to deflation only enhanced the credibility of the system. Pain is frequently associated with virtue.

The odds against the reestablishment of a gold standard are overwhelming for the simple reason that modern governments are unwilling to turn over the management of a nation's affairs to an impersonal international mechanism. Remnants of the gold standard that survived after World War I came apart during the Great Depression as the severity of worldwide unemployment made the consequences of the system unacceptable. During World War II emergency arrangements were implemented for international transactions. As the nations turned to the business of reconstruction after the war, they put in place a substitute for the gold standard.

BRETTON WOODS

The international conference that was held at Bretton Woods, New Hampshire in 1944 to set up a new international arrangement was, to a large degree, an Anglo-American affair. Germany, Italy, and Japan, all of whom were to become important players in the economic game in the postwar period, did not participate in the creation of the system for obvious reasons. France, which was still under occupation at the time of the meeting, was represented only by a government in exile that played a minor role. The two great powers present were Britain and the United States. Keynes was the leading figure of the British team and was one of the architects of the postwar plan. He was also active in the early stages of implementing the system. The meeting he was attending in Savannah when his final illness began was the first meeting of the Board of Governors of the International Monetary Fund, the institution created to administer the new arrangement.

The Anglo-American alliance that dominated the meeting was not one of coequal partners. The United States was at a peak of economic influence while Britain was in dire economic straits, with its immediate future heavily dependent on U.S. loans. One commentator has written that "it is unlikely that there will ever be another world conference in which American power is so preponderant." The American plan, rather than the plan Keynes preferred, prevailed in the end.

Keynes gave top priority in his thinking to management of the domestic economy for purposes of maintaining full employment. He wanted in the postwar period an international arrangement that would permit a government to pursue stability of the domestic economy as its prime goal with minimum international constraints. The system that was created did not allow the members as much independence in managing their affairs as he would have liked. But pragmatism was part of his personality makeup and he was quite capable of compromising over even substantive details. He supported the plan that was finally agreed upon and encouraged its acceptance at home.

The plan adopted at the conference retained one of the essential features of the gold standard, the stability of exchange rates. Under the plan gold was not allowed to move freely so that gold movements could no longer serve to contain fluctuations within the limits of the gold points. A similar result was obtained, however, in another way. Under the Articles of Agreement of the International Monetary Fund, the governing document of the new system, the United States agreed to redeem all dollars presented to the Treasury by official sources at a price of $35 an ounce. Since the dollar was linked to gold in a precise way, it became a substitute for the precious metal.

The dollar was the anchor that provided stability for the system. Other participating nations defined their currencies in terms of gold and the dollar and as a consequence in terms of one another. Except for the United States, nations were no longer required to redeem their currencies in gold or to allow its free movement. They agreed, however, to maintain the value of their currencies within 1 percent on either side of the official price by a *pegging* operation; that is, by buying and selling their currencies to prevent variations in the free market price from exceeding the accepted boundaries. When exchange rate movements made it necessary for them to purchase their currencies, they drew upon their *foreign reserves* which consisted of gold, the dollar, and to some extent the British pound.

There was no automatic corrective under the Bretton Woods arrangement. If a nation became less competitive and had to intervene too often in foreign exchange markets to maintain the value of its currency, it ran the danger of exhausting its foreign reserves. Borrowing from the International Monetary Fund provided relief. Since funds available to the IMF were limited and rules governing loans restrictive, the industrialized nations occasionally formed pools to support one of their members whose precarious position threatened to destabilize the entire system. A nation could not borrow indefinitely and sooner or later had to impose its own discipline. If inflation were causing the problem, restrictive monetary and fiscal policies would have to be used to dampen price increases, policies inevitably accompanied by a recession and an increase in unemployment. The Bretton Woods arrangement could not prevent the need for discipline with undesirable side effects. It did make it possible for a nation to buy time and impose a restrictive policy with some measure of deliberation. If a situation became totally unmanageable, Bretton Woods permitted the ultimate *out* of devaluation that permitted a nation to start over again at a new official rate that could more realistically be defended.

WHY BRETTON WOODS FAILED

The monetary system set in place at Bretton Woods had a long run. Despite occasional crises, it was a successful arrangement for 25 years and one that coincided with the postwar golden age of international economic growth. It succeeded because of a unique set of historical conditions and eventually failed because these conditions no longer existed.

The international prosperity enjoyed by the community of nations after the war was due partly to the opportunities at that point in history. The collapse of investment spending during the Great Depression in the 1930s and the low priority given to private capital accumulation during the war years set the stage for an investment boom after the war was over. This catch-up expansion thrived in a relatively stable political and economic environment due in large part to U.S. leadership. Political stability was provided by the guarantee of western security through U.S. military superiority. Economic stability was enhanced by a sound dollar, a result of a relatively constant price level. American espousal of free-trade doctrine insured unhampered operation of comparative advantage in world trade relations and in this environment of expanding trade and rapid economic growth the monetary arrangement negotiated at Bretton Woods worked reasonably well.

The continuation of this success depended critically on the benevolent hegemony of the United States. In the 1960s strains appeared in this leader relationship that ultimately made the Bretton Woods arrangement no longer workable.

To begin with, the pivotal position of the dollar could probably not be sustained indefinitely. The system provided, it will be recalled, for the free exchange of dollars into gold by the U.S. Treasury upon request through official foreign channels. The major currencies were, in turn, convertible in terms of dollars and of each other. A key to the system was the soundness of the dollar and the guaranteed link between the dollar and gold.

It was suggested, as early as the latter part of the 1950s, that use of a key national currency for international reserves involved a built-in destabilizer in the world monetary system. The problem arose from the need to expand international reserves to accommodate the growth in world trade. The world gold supply did not grow at a rate sufficient to meet this need. The problem with the use of gold as money is that it is frequently in short supply. Most of the gold that has been mined from the beginning of antiquity has been preserved. Keynes's statement that you could transport all of it on one modern liner is probably still true. Given the shortage of gold, increases in world liquidity had to come from larger holdings of dollars. Greater availability of dollars implied continuing deficits in the U.S. balance of payments, but continued U.S. deficits tended to create doubts about the stability of the dollar and the ability of the United States to honor its commitment to redeem dollars for gold for a fixed price. If the United States did not run deficits other nations lacked the reserves to finance expansion of trade. If the United States did run deficits the dollar would eventually be in jeopardy.

Keynes understood the problem associated with the use of a national currency as international money. An arrangement for which he argued provided for the creation of an institution somewhat like a world central bank with the power to create an international money, called in the Keynes Plan *the bancor*. A remnant of the idea was resurrected in the 1970s when the IMF was authorized to create a means of international settlement called by the awkward name *special drawing rights*.

The pressure exerted on a currency when it plays the central role in the international financial system is the reason the Japanese have taken steps in the past to prevent the yen from becoming an international currency.

The burden placed on the dollar by its use as an international money was further complicated by other developments. The cost of insuring world political stability through maintenance of a large military establishment and through the extension of foreign aid became, at some point, oppressive. The American involvement in Vietnam, in particular, produced serious economic stress. An abrupt increase in military spending under the Johnson administration in the mid-1960s, superimposed on an existing ambitious domestic program without a compensatory tax increase, initiated a period of inflation that lasted, with a varying degree of intensity, into the early 1980s.

The United States fell to some degree into a trap inherent in the dominant currency arrangement. While the United States bore the cost of leadership, it also enjoyed the unique privilege of being able to create at will currency units that had international acceptability. The system was built on the implicit assumption that the United States would not abuse the privilege. But the temptation to meet domestic and foreign obligations by the inflationary creation of dollars, instead of by hard decisions in allocating national resources, was an inherent part of the system.

The inflation of the latter part of the 1960s seriously compromised the international position of the dollar. Given the rise in the prices of American goods, the dollar became overvalued relative to gold and other key currencies. Since the dollar would now buy less in terms of U.S. products, foreigners were reluctant to pay the same price for the dollar as they had before.

CLOSING OF THE GOLD WINDOW, 1971

By the early 1970s it was quite clear that a formal change was called for in the dollar relationship to gold in effect since Bretton Woods. The problem lay in getting agreement for the adjustment from trading nations since a change in the basic par value of the dollar had implications far beyond the effects of a devaluation of one of the other major currencies. For one thing the dollar represented the basic unit of account in terms of which contracts in world trade had long been stated and it was the common denominator by which other currencies were measured. There was a further problem. Devaluation of the dollar would improve U.S. competitiveness by making the dollar cheaper in terms of foreign currencies. Some nations were reluctant to accept this favorable shift in the terms of trade for the world's leading exporter. In the end an orderly arrangement for devaluation was not worked out. Faced with increasingly intense attacks by speculators who expected the dollar to be devalued, the United States acted unilaterally. On August 15, 1971 President Nixon announced the "closing of the gold window." The United States would no longer redeem dollars in gold.

In part the announcement simply recognized a condition that had existed for some time. Although prior to this the United States stood ready to redeem dollars in a technical sense, in a more practical sense it could no longer fulfill its commitment. The fact that the country had lost gold in substantial amounts and that foreign-held short-term liabilities now exceeded the gold reserve was not necessarily an unmanageable state of affairs. It had not been uncommon during Britain's years of leadership in world finance in the 19th and early 20th century for outstanding claims to be three times the amount of reserve holdings. International as well as domestic bankers can work on a system of fractional reserves. But the U.S. position had become unmanageable. The number of dollars outstanding exceeded the U.S. gold reserves by tenfold. The United States would not have been able to deliver if even some of those holding dollars exercised their claim to gold, an action that in a legal sense they had the right to do. That they did not do so was in large part a matter of self-interest. All nations had a stake in the stability of the international financial arrangement and a run on U.S. gold reserves would have thrown the system into chaos.

Although the gold window was in reality at least partially closed prior to 1971 by a gentleman's agreement not to raid the U.S. Treasury, the official ending of dollar redemptions by the Nixon administration fundamentally altered the role of the dollar and the system of which it was the centerpiece. With its value no longer determined by a guaranteed relationship to gold, the dollar was allowed to find its value in terms of the free interplay of supply and demand as these reflected the relative competitiveness and productivity of the U.S. economy in international markets. Torn loose from its moorings, the dollar began to *float*.

In cutting the dollar loose from gold, the Nixon administration had in effect put the ball in its trading partners' court. They were now presented with an accomplished fact. If the major nations wished to end the float and return to a system of fixed exchange rates they would have to accept a formal devaluation of the dollar.

There was a certain urgency attached to reconstructing the old system, an urgency arising from a strong preference for the stable exchange rates of the Bretton Woods system and the gold standard before it. A number of economists, of whom Milton Friedman was one, had begun to challenge the desirability of fixed rates long before the dollar devaluation of the 1970s. These economists had argued that the system should be replaced by a system of floating exchange rates. Under this floating system a nation would refrain from influencing the value of its currency and allow it to seek its own level. A currency would reflect on a day-to-day basis the value that suppliers and those demanding the currency assigned it in free markets.

Under floating rates it would not be necessary for governments to adopt restrictive monetary and fiscal policies to restore a nation's competitiveness. Foreign exchange markets would apply the corrective. If a country became less competitive because of a rise in the domestic price level, a fall in the value of the currency would restore the nation's trade position. With an inflation, products would cost more in terms of domestic prices, and foreign purchasers would be discouraged from purchase. But a fall in the exchange rate, a more favorable price to foreigners for the domestic currency, would compensate for the inflation and restore the nation to its competitive condition. Under the system of pegged rates, exchange rates are stable, but the economy fluctuates. It makes more sense, it was argued, to let exchange rates fluctuate and keep the economy stable.

The arguments for a floating system were not persuasive in the view of the major governments. Committed to a historic tradition of fixed rates, they attempted to return to the Bretton Woods arrangement of adjustable pegs following the U.S. closing of the gold window. Two attempts to put the system back together were made, one in late 1971 and the other in early 1973. The attempted revisions involved two key items: a redefinition of currency values—devaluations of the various currencies as seemed appropriate—and a broadening of the range of accepted variation in their value. Both attempts at reconstruction failed and nations reverted to the floating exchange system we have today. The transition to float was not a conscious, deliberate decision. The world powers were simply unable to put the Humpty Dumpty of Bretton Woods back together again.

We will come back to the story of how the new system has worked out. But we return first to the subject matter of our last chapter, for the floating exchange rates inherited from our past history have provided the financial environment in which the effects of our budget imbalance have played themselves out in international markets.

THE TWO DEFICITS

The sequence of events set into motion in the world economy by the large federal deficits of the 1980s can now be described briefly. It starts with the Treasury borrowing necessary to finance the large deficits that followed the tax cuts of 1981. This dominant federal presence in the nation's credit markets exerted an upward pressure on interest rates. As the differential between rates in American markets and in markets abroad widened, foreign funds were attracted to the United States. In order to purchase U.S. financial instruments, holders of marks, yens, and pounds had first to convert them into dollars. The increased demand for our currency due to the inflow of capital caused a rise in its value in foreign exchange markets. The appreciation of the dollar made our exports more expensive for buyers abroad and imports from other countries cheaper in the American market. The deficit in our federal budget was converted, through movements in interest and foreign exchange rates, into a second deficit, a deficit in our balance of trade.

Our trade balance in goods and services was positive for the first 25 years after World War II, with the exception of relatively small annual deficits on three occasions. That is, we sold more abroad than we bought from other nations. With increased foreign competition in the 1970s, particularly from Japan and the countries on the rim of the Pacific Basin, our trade balance was negative in five of the ten years of the decade of the 1970s. The deficit reached a high of $15 billion in 1978. Positive in the first two years of the 1980s, due in part to the lower demand for imports because of the 1980–1981 recession, the trade account again turned negative in 1982 as the value of the dollar increased on foreign exchange markets. The trade deficit rose at an alarming rate over the succeeding years to reach a level of over $160 billion in 1987.

The effect on American industry was uneven. Some industries are impacted more by events in international markets than others. American barbers in New York City, for example, do not compete with barbers in Tokyo. The transportation cost—the cost of flying to Tokyo for a haircut or in the reverse direction—is so large compared to the value of the service that haircuts fall among items classified as *untradables*. Generally speaking, services are not as much affected by international competition as are hard goods. The brunt of the decline in U.S. exports and the competition from foreign imports was borne most heavily by the smokestack industries of the Midwest, by American farmers, and by import-sensitive industries such as textiles and apparel. The expansion in the American economy that began in November 1982, following the recession of 1981–1982, was somewhat schizophrenic. The country developed a split personality with some regions enjoying prosperity, while others, particularly those with heavy employment in manufacturing and agriculture and more vulnerable to the effects of the appreciation of the dollar, were in the equivalent of a recession.

Financial movements in the international economy are the flip side of trade in goods and services. If a nation runs a trade deficit by importing more goods and services than it exports, it must borrow the money to cover the difference between its spending and its income. As trade deficits accumulated in the 1980s, so also did our national indebtedness. During the 19th century the United States was a debtor nation, a typical position for young, developing economies. As one of the new powers on the international scene after World War I, we moved to the status of a creditor nation, exporting more goods and services than we were importing, lending to other nations, and accumulating investment claims that generated a stream of annual interest payments in service of the debt. With the massive capital inflows of the 1980s triggered by the deficit in our balance of trade, the nation became in 1985—once more and for the first time in over 70 years—a debtor nation.

The imbalance in our trade patterns has not been without its positive side. The accumulation of debt permits a nation, just like a family living off credit cards, to enjoy temporarily a consumption binge. We not only consumed the output of our own economy, we also enjoyed the surplus output of other economies—the cars, the electronic gadgets, and the goods and services purchased in travel abroad. The lower cost of foreign imports, due to the appreciation of the dollar, dampened inflationary pressures so that we enjoyed the best of both worlds, abundance of products and a more stable price level. The inflow of foreign funds also kept interest rates from rising as much as they normally would in response to heavy Treasury financing.

There is also a negative side. While the retarding effect of government borrowing on domestic investment was lessened by the inflow of foreign funds, the crowd-out was simply shifted to the nation's export and import competing industries that suffered a drop in production levels and rising unemployment. As our standard of living was temporarily augmented by imported consumer goods, dollars were accumulating in foreign hands. At some point the credit cards must be paid off. Holders of dollars want to redeem them eventually for American assets and output.

One can look at the skyline of any major city in the United States and see office towers now owned by Japanese investors. These properties make good examples of the *buying of America* much deplored in popular discussions. The concern is probably overstated, for investment in real properties across international lines is a healthy sign of the movement of capital toward its best return and, in any event, foreign holdings in the United States remain relatively small. We ourselves have long held substantial ownership in foreign properties, an ownership that citizens of other countries often find disturbing. But the acquisition of skyscrapers by the Japanese is a symptom of the type of transactions set into motion by the appreciation of the dollar.

Sales are always two-way deals. What did we get for these office towers? You can also look at the busy expressways of our major cities and see thousands of Toyotas, Datsuns, and Hondas speed by every hour. It was cars for skyscrapers. The Japanese and other foreigners have accumulated vast amounts of dollars as we went on a consumption binge in the 1980s. It would be naive to expect them to want nothing in return. When you trade marbles on the playground, you have to give your agates to get your favorite rollers.

As our trade position moves toward balance in the future and we export more goods abroad than we import, our standard of living will be generally affected. There is a dynamic element in the behavior of the trade imbalance just as there is in the case of the federal budget deficit. To achieve balance with exports equal to imports will not be enough. Dollar claims in the hands of foreigners must be serviced by interest payments. Just to hold our external debt constant, it will not be sufficient to export just enough to pay for current imports. We will need to run for some time into the future a surplus large enough to cover our interest commitments.

THE DOLLAR'S LONG ASCENT

The rise in the value of the dollar lasted from 1980 to the early part of 1985. Precisely how much it had risen by the time it reached its crest is not easy to say because of measurement problems. Changes in currency values are tracked by indexes designed for this purpose. There are a number of them available differing in such details as whether inflation rates are taken into account and whether the comparison is made in terms of one national currency or against an average of a basket of currencies. If a multilateral index is used, the result depends on precisely what countries are included in the index and the method used for weighting the various currencies in terms of the nations' relative importance in trade volume. The choice of index involves some degree of arbitrary judgment and it is impossible to define changes in the value of a currency unambiguously, but all indexes show a sharp rise in the value of the dollar over the period 1980–1985. A trade-weighted index prepared by the Federal Reserve to measure variations in the value of the dollar as against the value of the currencies of 10 major industrial countries is frequently used for comparison. Over the period in question, the dollar rose almost 40 percent in terms of this index. The effect of such a change on U.S. competitiveness is immediately apparent, equivalent to placing a 40 percent charge on U.S. exports and a 40 percent subsidy on foreign imports.

That the dollar rose in value during the early part of the 1980s, even during the 1981–1982 recession, is not surprising. Several factors contributed to the appreciation. The large inflow of foreign capital increased the demand for dollars. In addition to the temptingly high interest rates caused by federal borrowing, the benefits for investment incorporated into the 1981 tax legislation also made the United States attractive for foreign funds. The outlook for lower inflation in the U.S. compared to the expected inflation rates of trading partners added further appeal for investors abroad. The appreciation can be explained in terms of so-called *fundamentals* typically used to explain the level of exchange rates.

Why the appreciation of the dollar continued as long as it did to the beginning of 1985 is, however, something of a mystery. An accumulation of changes that gradually took place in the basic, underlying factors should have been expected to slow the appreciation down and cause a leveling off. Around the middle of 1982 the Federal Reserve eased back on the tight money policy initiated in late 1979. Interest rates went into a decline and the spread between U.S. and foreign rates narrowed. The effect of the higher valued dollar on U.S. trade in goods and services began to be felt in 1982 with exports falling below imports in that year. The relatively weaker demand for American goods and services would ordinarily be a reason for a decline in the dollar in foreign exchange markets. But the dollar continued to rise.

Economists are still not in agreement as to why the dollar did not reverse itself earlier than it did. The search for an explanation brings us back to the budget deficit. Large deficits cause currencies to appreciate. The outlook for the persistence of large deficits was a reasonable expectation in 1983 and 1984 and the dollar continued to appreciate as people acted on these expectations. Currencies not only represent a means of settlement in market exchanges; they also represent financial assets just as stocks and bonds do. The price people are willing to pay for them depends, in part, on judgments about their prices in the future. As in the stock market, so also in the foreign exchange market, expectations play an important role and in ways that we do not completely understand.

There is something unsettling about the failure of broadly accepted theories to explain current events convincingly. If we do not know why something has happened in the past, we also lack the ability to forecast, with some confidence, what to expect in the future. Introducing the element of anticipation about the U.S. deficit helps to explain the appreciation of the dollar beyond a time that seemed consistent with the underlying fundamentals, but it doesn't help to relieve the anxiety about the future, for speculative behavior based on expectations can suddenly reverse itself.

A general belief that the dollar would soon have to come down — a belief that strengthened as the trade deficit continued to worsen — was combined with anxiety over whether it would be a hard or soft landing. If the dollar began to drop in free flight as foreigners suddenly became unwilling to hold further amounts in their portfolios, the effect could be disturbing. A flight of foreign funds could cause interest rates to rise as available credit was reduced and tilt the economy into recession.

THE DECLINE OF THE DOLLAR

The possibility of an unhappy ending to the long rise of the dollar led to pressures for some type of government intervention in foreign exchange markets and this brings us back to the performance of the floating exchange rate system.

This system into which we stumbled for lack of ability to sustain a fixed rate regime has never been popular with policymakers, even less popular in Europe than in the United States. In practice the swings in exchange rates have been larger and more frequent than advocates of flexible exchange rates in the 1970s expected. Short-run volatility involving movements within a month or less has been considerable. Business has learned to live with these short-term variations through the use of a number of management techniques. It is the wide movements sustained over a period of several years that have caused particular concern. The prolonged rise of the dollar led to a conviction on the part of some economists and policymakers that the dollar was *overvalued*, meaning that its value could no longer be explained in terms of understandable and basic influences and that the dollar had as it were taken off on its own.

The commitment of the Reagan administration to free market solutions in the domestic economy was in this period extended with consistency to foreign exchange markets. In the early days of the dollar's rise, the administration refrained from intervening to slow the increase in value. After Donald Regan, Secretary of the Treasury, and James Baker, White House Chief of Staff, switched roles in the administration's organizational structure in early 1985, there was a sharp reversal of policy. When Baker took over as Secretary of the Treasury, he arrived at the height of the dollar's problems. American industries had been hit hard by foreign competition both abroad and at home and he soon shifted the United States into a more activist posture, motivated at least in part by a desire to dampen the rising clamor for protectionist legislation.

The new direction in policy was dramatized by a surprise meeting of the so-called Group of Five (the United States, England, France, Japan, and West Germany) at the Plaza Hotel in New York in the fall of 1985. The result of the meeting was an agreement to intervene in foreign exchange markets to exert downward pressure on the dollar. The accord marked a movement from the spirit of the floating exchange rate to the spirit of intervention contained in the arrangements of Bretton Woods. In his State of the Union message in early 1986, President Reagan was explicit in his endorsement of the policy. "We must never again permit wild currency swings to cripple our farmers and other exporters," and he suggested the possibility of an international conference to reinstitute something along the lines of the fixed rate arrangements that had collapsed during the Nixon administration in 1974. The President's proposal for a formal conference received a cool reaction from the other industrialized nations and was quietly dropped later in the year, but efforts to initiate a less ambitious type of international cooperation continued.

There are two ways in which nations can affect exchange rates through policy actions. First, they can do so through pegging operations, the buying and selling of currencies in the open market to affect their prices. A more basic effort involves a coordination of policies to affect underlying conditions that cause exchange rates to move as they do, for example, differences in economic growth rates. *International policy coordination*, a phrase referring to both types of action, became the buzz word. At the economic summit meeting in Tokyo in the spring of 1986 the Group of Seven—the Group of Five plus Canada and Italy—agreed to annual meetings of finance ministers to monitor the compatibility of the nations' policies including such things as rates of economic growth. The rhetoric was stronger than the action and produced little more than continued pressure by the United States on West Germany and Japan to stimulate their economies in order to provide a more favorable market for American exports. A commitment to common intervention in foreign exchange markets to affect the price of the dollar was reaffirmed and extended, however, in the Louvre accord in early 1987, an agreement to intervene when necessary to maintain the dollar within an unofficial and secret trading range. It is an arrangement with considerable flexibility. The range to be defended can be changed freely at the option of the participating nations and without public notice. The agreement was not, however, simply a matter of rhetoric. By far the larger portion of the dollars added to foreign reserves in 1987 represented funds acquired by central banks from interventions in support of the U.S. currency.

Whether the trading nations ever choose to abandon the floating exchange rate system is impossible to forecast. There are some who find the movements of the dollar during the 1980s disturbing and would like to return to the security of a fixed rate regime. There is already some adherence to stable rates in today's economies. About three dozen nations peg their currencies to the dollar; others peg to major currencies such as the German mark and the Japanese yen.

The members of the European Community are committed, with the exception of Britain, to stability among their currencies through an arrangement that requires intervention on a reciprocal basis when two currencies get out of alignment.

By far the majority of world trade takes place, however, under a system of floating rates and the problems associated with fixed rates are so formidable as to make a return to this system unlikely. Exchange rates depend on such basic fundamentals as the economic growth experience of the various countries, changes in productivity, and their relative inflation rates. These basics can vary significantly even over relatively short periods of time. When such changes do take place, the prevailing exchange rate is no longer appropriate and pressures come into play to move it to another level. Under a fixed rate regime nations are required to defend their currencies by buying in the open market to maintain the rate within the designated band. The change in basic conditions may make this defense impossible; at some point nations run out of reserves to support a currency's value. The problem is typically aggravated by the actions of speculators who sell expecting the currency to drop. Under such conditions the risk to speculators is minimal. If the currency does fall, they win; if it does not, they are only out the transactions cost of moving from one currency to another. At some point the official price is no longer defensible and a change in the official price, a devaluation, becomes necessary.

The move to devaluation is usually accompanied with a great deal of stress and the action is delayed beyond what conditions would suggest as timely. Nations must also guess at the rate that the market would support. While economic theory suggests that there must be an equilibrium rate toward which market forces move a currency, our understanding of these forces is too incomplete for us to know precisely what that rate is at any given moment. A fixed rate regime involves enormous problems. The European Monetary System, the most ambitious attempt to maintain stable rates since the emergence of the floating rate system, has experienced periodic tensions over the last decade as national currencies have resisted being squeezed within an official band when their economies moved in directions inconsistent with the official currency definitions. The nations of the world got into the floating exchange rate system in the first place simply because of their inability to manage the exchange rates of a large number of countries each with sharp differences in inflation rates and in the relevant measures of the performance of their economies.

The floating rate regime, on the other hand, has the advantage of automatic and frequent adjustments in exchange rates to allow for economies constantly in transition. It is difficult to imagine how the western nations would have adapted to the external shocks of the 1970s, such as the dramatic increase in energy prices, on a fixed rate system. Under the flexible rate system the adjustments were made reasonably well. Floating rates do not dissipate the effect of shocks completely or prevent the effects of unwise policies from transmitting themselves among the world's trading partners. They do have a capacity for absorbing a large part of the disturbing influence of outside events.

What we will probably have in the future is a floating system with periodic return to episodes of intervention when key currencies, particulary the dollar, undergo large movements unsettling to international economic relationships. There seems to be sentiment accumulating among nations for more stability. The success in achieving it will be uneven. Reserves available to move currencies in different directions are small relative to the volume of daily transactions on foreign exchange markets. The evidence seems to suggest that if intervention is combined with announcement of a policy change that has credibility, it can influence the relative values of currencies but for the most part only for short periods. There is in the end no good substitute for disciplined management of economic policy to avoid disturbances in international financial markets.

But we have gotten ahead of the story. While the nations were busily engaged in discussion of plans to stop the rise of the dollar, the dollar reversed its course. The fact is that the dollar had already started its decline in March 1985 before the more activist position was adopted, though it took some time to recognize that a depreciation of the dollar was indeed under way.

THE J-CURVE

Since there was a rather widespread conviction that the dollar had overshot the mark in its ascent to the heights reached in early 1985, the drop in value was not a surprise. There was concern on the part of U.S. policymakers that the drop in value not turn into a free fall. The decline, once begun, was orderly but steady. By the early part of 1988 the dollar had completely wiped out the appreciation that took place from 1980 to 1985; it had fallen to the same level from which it had started its upward journey.

Once it was clear that the dollar had gone into a decline, observers of the international scene waited for the second shoe to drop, the improvement in the U.S. trade position. They had a longer time to wait than expected.

Improvement in the balance of trade following the depreciation of a currency has traditionally been explained in terms of what is called the *J-curve* theory. The theory says that a nation's trade position worsens before it gets better after a decline in currency value. The main reason is that changes in the relative prices of merchandise resulting from the change in currency values are rapid but quantities of exports and imports adjust slowly. In our case, the total value of imports rose since in the initial stages of the adjustment process the level of import quantities was unchanged, but the cost in dollars went up. At the same time, export quantities did not increase in response to the cheaper dollar for some time. Since the larger outlays for imports were not offset by increased income from exports, the total trade position temporarily deteriorated. According to the usual pattern of the J-curve, once the change in relative prices makes itself felt in terms of quantities of goods exchanged, the trade position begins to improve. The downward movement on the descending part of the *J* ends and movement up the ascending part of the letter begins with an increase in the value of exports over imports. Improvement is normally expected to take place within a year; in the case of the dollar it actually did not begin to show until well into 1987.

There are a number of reasons advanced for the delay in the J-curve effect. Following depreciation, imported goods would normally become more expensive for Americans since they must now give more dollars for each unit of foreign currency. Exporters abroad cushioned the effect by lowering the price in terms of their own currency and accepting narrower profit margins. These margins had been generous during the period of the high-valued dollar and could be cut to keep price competitive. Some foreign exporters, such as the Japanese, attach more importance to market share than do American firms and are willing to accept profit reduction in order to maintain footholds in foreign markets. Furthermore the U.S. economy continued its expansion during the period following the dollar decline, while the economies of our trading partners advanced in a sluggish fashion. The demand for foreign imports continued to remain high, while the demand for American goods was moderate. Finally, the fall in the value of our currency was overstated by some of the more frequently used indexes. Some indexes include only the major industrialized nations for purposes of comparison. While the dollar fell appreciably against these currencies, it rose against others not included in the indexes, such as the currencies of Latin American countries that had undergone devaluation. In addition, some of the countries along the rim of the Pacific Basin pegged their currencies to the dollar and followed it in its downward movement leaving the relative competitiveness of products unchanged. Three years after the peaking of the U.S. dollar in early 1985, the Taiwan dollar had risen substantially against the U.S. dollar but only by half as much as had the Japanese yen; the Korean won, the Singapore dollar, and the Hong Kong dollar rose by only small amounts or not at all.

Trade patterns cannot resist the effects of a depreciating currency indefinitely and in 1987 signs of improvement in the U.S. trade position finally appeared. Our trade balance is the difference between our exports and our imports. While the net balance has not yet turned positive, there are definite signs of better performance. Exports have boomed and except for Latin America gains have been widespread geographically to western Europe, Japan, and other Asian nations. The effect of the export improvement has been most pronounced on manufacturing. Most damaged by the rise in the value of the dollar, it has the most to gain from the depreciation. As exporters of manufactured goods become convinced that the improvement in trade has permanence and begin to add to plant capacity, larger exports have a feedback effect on the capital goods industry. The lengthy expansion of the 1980s was led in the first four or five years by consumption spending and the service industries. Starting in 1987 the expansion entered a new and more balanced phase with manufacturing again assuming a leading role.

While exports have built up momentum, imports continue to remain high. Part of the reason is the more competitive pricing by foreign producers. Another is the lag in the change in consumption habits. It may be that Americans are willing to pay a higher price for what they view as higher quality foreign products. In a word, the consumer is hung up on imports. For real gains to be made against the trade deficit, however, imports will have to fall below exports.

THE LONG-RUN SOLUTION

How and when the deficit in the balance of trade will finally resolve itself is, of course, unknown. What is known is that such a large deficit will require a turnaround so large that the task of carrying it out will last well into the 1990s. The dollar will have its ups and downs; the path followed by currencies is never smooth. How far the dollar will have to fall has been a matter of intense debate.

Some have argued that the dollar has fallen more than necessary. This position is based on the *purchasing power parity* theory which states that the appropriate relationship between two currencies such as the yen and the dollar is reached when the price of some product in dollars is the same in the United States and Japan. On this basis the dollar became undervalued by mid-1986 when it fell below its purchasing power parity with the yen.

Others have argued that parity judgments can be misleading. A traveler may think that the dollar and the yen are not correctly aligned if the cost of a night's lodging in a Tokyo hotel is more than the cost of a night's lodging in New York. But the comparative cost of hotel rooms can be misleading, for hotel rooms are among the *untradables*. They do not compete in international markets. Those who are skeptical of the purchasing power parity argument are of the opinion that if trade deficits are too large, specifically too large to be financed by private capital flows, then the dollar must still have too high a value. The governments should not by joint action prevent it from dropping further as they did in 1987 and 1988. Some would argue that a return of the dollar to its value when the roller coaster ride started in 1981 is not enough to restore balance in our foreign trade. Further depreciation, at least eventually, may be required.

Whatever the appropriate level of the dollar, restoring the trade balance will not be easy. For the world has changed and the economic environment as we move into the 1990s is not the same as it was at the beginning of the decade. Among these differences is a change in the capacity of the economies of Latin America to absorb U.S. goods.

These nations, which together make up one of our major markets, are nations struggling with massive external debts. Of the 15 Third World countries usually listed as *heavily indebted*, 10 are from Latin America.

It is a traditional role of a developing economy to be a debtor nation. Third World countries lack the output levels required to finance the investment necessary for economic development. The standard of living is already too low to permit the transfer of resources from use for consumer goods to the accumulation of capital equipment. The classic solution for escaping from the trap of poverty is the importing of capital funds from the developed economies whose output levels produce a surplus sufficient for foreign investment. This increase in the capital base of developing economies is then used to generate an increase in output that can be exported to earn the funds to service the loans. Debt can be accumulated in increasing amounts for decades as long as it is reasonably related to productive capacity and the ability to export to external markets. Such a reasonable relationship does not exist in the case of the Latin American countries.

The problems of Third World countries in managing their external debt was aggravated by a series of events originating in the late 1970s and early 1980s among the economically developed nations. The central banks of the major nations, including the United States, tightened credit in the late 1970s as an anti-inflationary policy. The effect on developing countries was an increase in charges that had to be paid to service their debt. The U.S. federal deficit extended the upward pressure on rates. Americans are sometimes unaware of the impact that our actions have on other countries. The sheer size of the U.S. economy means that changes in policy can have enormous effects in world markets. Not only did the increase in interest rates caused by Treasury borrowing to finance the federal deficit raise the cost of servicing Latin debts, but the appreciation of the dollar, in which these debts are denominated, also made interest payments and payment of principal more expensive. Their net interest payments almost tripled between 1979 and 1984.

Another complicating problem for the indebted nations was the slowdown in the economies of the industrialized countries in the early 1980s. Growth in the developing nations has been tied historically to expansion in the developed economies that provide the markets for Third World goods. Exports of the indebted economies increased about $2^1/2$ percent a year during the 1970s. They slowed in 1980 and decreased in 1981 and 1982.

The large accumulated debt of the Latin American countries and other nations forced a switch in traditional economic roles. Instead of importing capital the indebted nations were forced to become net exporters of capital in order to service their mammoth obligations. Instead of funds moving from the developed economies to the underdeveloped, they now had to move in the opposite direction from the underdeveloped to the industrialized nations. To earn the funds to cover their obligations, the indebted nations have to move their trade balances toward surplus; that is, export more than they import.

Such a turnaround is not accomplished without discipline. The government must bring its budget under control and consumers must reduce spending to generate the saving needed to service the external debt. If saving is not sufficient, domestic investment projects must be canceled to free up funds. The cutbacks in investment have important implications for long-term economic growth. Imports must also be reduced and monetary restraint must be imposed to stabilize the price level to maintain competitiveness.

The indebted nations moved into a surplus in balance of trade in 1983 but progress in managing the external debt has been slow. Total debt service costs were around 40 percent of exports at the start of the 1980s and are about the same today. The success that has been achieved has imposed a severe price. For Latin America the 1980s will remain as a bad memory. Economic growth has been in the neighborhood of 1 percent and per capita income is below what it was at the start of the decade. This weak economic performance has created a fragile political environment for governments attempting to put into place more democratic processes.

These Third World debts have also created problems for the United States. They are part of the reason for the fragility of the American banking system in the 1980s as major American banks have had to deal with large batches of loans with questionable performance records. A rash of defaults in the early part of the decade would have raised serious questions about the solvency of some institutions. Although the banks have begun to get better control over these shaky assets through negotiated debt restructuring and increases in loan loss reserves, for some these loans still make up a bothersome proportion of primary capital.

Perhaps more important, the debt of Latin American nations has complicated our problem of moving to a trade surplus. We cannot expect them to meet their commitments to American banks and at the same time to absorb freely the output of U.S. manufacturers. The overall effect of Third World debt has been to change a U.S. trade surplus with Latin America in 1981 to a trade deficit today.

At the same time Latin America has become a weaker market for U.S. exports, the newly developed countries of Asia have become stronger competitors for our export industries in world markets and for import competing industries at home. Our trade deficit with the Four Tigers of the Orient—Hong Kong, Singapore, South Korea, and Taiwan—is now about 20 percent of our total trade deficit and if it continues to grow will soon equal our deficit with Japan. These are powerful competitors whose export-led growth supported by heavy capital investment has already lifted the per capita income of some of them close to the European level.

The Europe with which our economy will interface will also be different from the Europe at the start of the 1980s. In some ways what happens in Europe in the 1990s will be the mirror image of what happens in the United States as we attempt to reverse our balance of trade. The appreciation of the dollar had a distorting effect on the mix of the U.S. economy in the 1980s as export and import competing firms, particularly in manufacturing, were hindered by a high-valued dollar. Export industries in Europe, in nations such as West Germany, on the other hand flourished. With the decline of the dollar and the rise of the German mark, these roles will be reversed. As the external market for German goods is less favorable, a restructuring of industry with less reliance on exports will have to take place, similar to that experienced in the United States during the period of the appreciating dollar. Such a realignment has already begun in Japan with a new emphasis on domestic markets. The need for restructuring comes at a time when unemployment rates in Europe, for a variety of reasons, have been at historic highs. The U.S. balance of trade with Western Europe shifted in Europe's favor in 1983. The nations will now surrender markets reluctantly and can be expected to provide stiff resistance.

The game will also be played in a different ball park. The 12 nations of the European Community are committed to eliminating commercial and financial trade barriers among themselves by the end of 1992. This freeing up of trade among the participating nations includes elimination of stifling bureaucratic requirements. For example, it has been reported that a truck driver transporting goods across the European Community has had to sign 150 forms in the course of his trip. Already the number of forms required has been reduced to one. If all goes as planned this freeing of markets should have a major impact on this trading block.

Early in the *Wealth of Nations* Adam Smith discusses the importance of specialization, which he called *the division of labor*, for the economic growth of a nation. It is in this chapter that he describes the assembly line type of production that he observed in his famous pin factory example, in which the work of producing a pin was broken down into the separate tasks of drawing the wire, cutting it, grinding it, and fastening the head. In all, he tells us, there were 18 distinct operations. In a world without zippers the pin was an important fastener. An economist recently checked on the present status of pin *manufactories* in the United Kingdom and found that there are only two firms today employing a total of 50 workers, with pin output only 10 percent or less of their total production. Adam Smith estimated that the factories he observed produced 4,800 pins per worker a day and he marveled at the efficiency of an assembly line. One of the firms still producing today turns out 800,000 pins per worker a day. Smith would not have been surprised at the power of increased specialization combined with technology.

Smith had the insight to see that for factories capable of turning out a large volume of goods to be able to operate, there has to be large markets capable of absorbing the output. "The division of labour," he wrote in one of his more often quoted statements, "is limited by the extent of the market." The reason why the United States grew to be an economy of such enormous power is not only because of its vast amounts of resources and a social environment with relatively few obstructions to innovation, but also because the Founding Fathers inserted into the Constitution the provision that there should be no barriers to interstate commerce. This provision led to the creation of a giant internal market free of impediments to trade and commerce without restrictions to the movement of capital and labor. Large markets have a profound feedback effect on technology and the organization of production and make it possible to approach optimum conditions of efficiency.

The removal of barriers to commerce and the movement of resources across national lines will create in Europe, with a population of 325 million people, a super internal market for goods. A realignment of firms through mergers and acquisitions, including consolidation of banks and other financial institutions, is expected in a shuffle to adapt production and distribution facilities to this new market. This stimulus to European economies should make them more formidable competitors even if a concern of some observers turns out to be ill-founded. This concern is that the removal of internal barriers to trade will be matched by trade impediments to those outside the community.

THE FEDERAL DEFICIT, ONE MORE TIME

The solution to the trade deficit problem will have to include, as one of the most basic requirements, a movement toward a balanced federal budget. The twin deficits of the budget and trade are intimately linked and will have to be solved together. If we shrink the trade deficit, we reduce the inflow of foreign capital. Unless the demand of the Treasury for funds is also reduced, then interest rates move upward with a retarding effect on overall economic expansion.

The large federal deficit has not only strongly limited fiscal policy as a stabilization tool, it has also complicated the conduct of monetary policy. The traditional objective of central banks has always been to prevent inflation. Our concern for full employment in the postwar years—with varying degrees of commitment—gave our central bank a second target, one that is not always compatible with the price stabilization goal. The imbalance in our foreign trade position has added another concern, the international movement of capital and the behavior of the dollar. It is not possible for our central bank to manage all of these problems simultaneously. An export-led boom in manufacturing stimulated by a more competitive dollar, for example, creates the danger of inflation as industries begin to approach capacity levels of output. These inflationary concerns cause the Federal Reserve to tighten up and exert upper pressure on interest rates. Higher interest rates, in turn, attract foreign capital in larger amounts and cause an appreciation of the dollar. As the dollar rises in value the momentum in moving toward a trade balance is broken.

We do not live in a simple world. Keynes would have understood. He himself, a half century ago, wrestled with the fundamental problem of reconciling the domestic and international performance of the British economy. The details are somewhat different, but the basic issues remain the same.

CHAPTER 10

THE QUALITY
OF ECONOMIC LIFE

Alfred Marshall, mentioned previously, is one of the towering figures in the history of economics. His *Principles of Economics*, published in 1890, summarized, reshaped, and extended the work of a century of scholars who came before him. A large part of modern economics has its origin in Marshall. His book is a classic that went through nine editions and influenced generations of economists.

Marshall was also Keynes's teacher at Cambridge. The two make for an interesting contrast. Keynes was a scholar, Marshall's greatest student, but also a sophisticated man of the world. A man of enormous self-confidence and charm who led a dual life, Keynes was accepted for his original and powerful intellect by the business and government establishment, yet at ease with the nonconformists of Bloomsbury. Marshall, on the other hand, lived out his life mostly in the confines of Cambridge, painfully unsure of himself at times, a cautious writer continually delaying publication of his work, and a healthy man acting as if on the verge of becoming an invalid.

Marshall's first interests as a student were mathematics and science. He later developed an interest in ethics and turned to economics after coming face-to-face with poverty on visits to the slums of London. At one time he was a candidate for the ministry. Though he abandoned his plan for ordination, he was, says Keynes in his memoir on Marshall, a missionary all his life with an intense interest in the conditions of the working class. For the ultimate purpose of the study of economics was, in his mind, the betterment of mankind. Keynes relates how Marshall kept on the mantel in his room a small oil painting of a destitute man. He called it his "patron saint" and when tempted to become self-absorbed in theoretical abstraction, the portrait of the man with the gaunt face was there to remind him that the ultimate purpose of economics is the service of humanity.

Keynes was influenced by Marshall's social consciousness and his interest in economics also led in the end to the social implications of economic performance. In the concluding chapter of *The General Theory*, there are two major faults of the economy of his day that he emphasizes: the widespread unemployment with which his book is mainly concerned and what he judged to be the *inequitable* distribution of income and wealth.

In our survey of the controversies in the evolution of economic policy over the postwar period, we have been preoccupied with the abstractions with which economists must work if they are to make sense of what they see around them. But for most individuals, ideas like the velocity of money and equilibrium of exchange rates are foreign to their daily experience. Theirs is a world of immediate, day-to-day happenings, sometimes rewarding and sometimes threatening: a world of job opportunities and of job displacement, of gains in take-home pay and of income stagnation, of comfortable housing and a growing class of homeless, a world of prosperity and of welfare recipients. The world of daily human concern is a world that Marshall and Keynes understood. The face of poverty has not changed since the beginning of civilization, only a few details in the lines and the profile. It is a world to which we turn in this chapter as we take a look at problems currently on the national agenda and of pressing interest to most Americans. If Marshall and Keynes were here today, what would they see?

THE STATE OF THE ECONOMY

Looked at from one point of view, the American economy is in robust health. The increase in new jobs over the course of the last two decades is high by U.S. standards and by far the best performance among the major industrialized nations. While the number of jobs in the United States has grown by about 30 percent since early before the 1970s, employment in Japan has grown by about a third of the U.S. rate and in the nations that make up the European Community employment has not grown at all. At the end of 1982 the United States began the longest economic expansion since World War II. The rapid rate of job creation since the 1981–1982 recession is reflected in the unemployment rate that dropped to just above 5 percent in 1988, its lowest level since 1974.

Despite the buoyancy in the economy, there is in the air, as we approach the decade of the 1990s, a general concern about the economic future. Part of the anxiety can be traced back to the problem of the foreign trade deficit discussed in the last chapter. The loss of markets due to the appreciation of the dollar over the 1981– 1985 period aggravated an already growing national concern about a deterioration in U.S. competitiveness. The general theme has been that we are losing out in manufacturing to other nations and shifting to service jobs where the quality of opportunity is less. The ritual expression is that we are becoming a nation of people frying each other's hamburgers and taking in each other's laundry.

This anxiety has been capsulized in the phrase *the deindustrialization of America*, which is the title of a widely discussed book first published in 1982. The conviction that we are losing in the foreign trade race also led in the 1980s to a call for government involvement in forming an *industrial policy*, a phrase that describes a combination of activities—depending on who is filling in the details—ranging from enhancement of research and development to formation of a federal entity for providing investment funds for promising ventures. Walter Mondale is reported to have read a copy of the page proofs of Robert Reich's *The Next American Frontier*, published in 1983 and one of the more intensively discussed proposals for an industrial policy, and to have commented to aides that "this is the Democratic economic platform for the presidential race of 1984." Interest in industrial policy lapsed into oblivion with Reagan's election victory. Yet a fear remains that well paying jobs are being lost because of foreign competition and that the middle-income class that has traditionally filled these jobs is disappearing, leaving the social structure divided between a class of high-income recipients and a class of low-income workers employed in low-paying service jobs.

SHIFTS IN THE U.S. ECONOMY

Is the United States, in fact, being deindustrialized? A large amount of research has been done in an attempt to answer this question. A survey by the Boston Federal Reserve Bank recently summarized 26 key studies that have been published on the subject. As is often the case in a soft science like economics, the results of the research are not unambiguous. Some facts are agreed upon. Some matters are unresolved; it has not been possible to reach precise conclusions from the data available. In still other cases, conflicting results have been obtained depending on the method of analysis, the data sources used, the way in which numbers are adjusted to eliminate bias, and the time period covered. Obviously the question about the condition of U.S. industry is of major importance. It is also one that is hotly debated. After all the research effort, what do we know about the present state of the U.S. economy?

Looked at from one point of view, the widespread belief that the U.S. is losing its manufacturing base is not supported by the facts. Manufacturing output has been a relatively constant proportion of the real Gross National Product, in the neighborhood of 21 percent, since World War II. It is true that services have increased as part of GNP, from 59 percent to 68 percent, but the gain has not been at the expense of manufacturing. Manufacturing is part of a larger grouping of industries engaged in the production of *commodities*. The commodities category includes, in addition to manufacturing, agriculture, mining, and construction. Agriculture, mining, and construction have decreased as a proportion of the Gross National Product since World War II, but manufacturing has not.

The perception that the nation is being *deindustrialized* is due, in part, to the short-run view taken in forming the judgment. The sharp appreciation of the dollar in the 1980s did indeed create problems for manufacturing, an industry more vulnerable to international competition than services. The plight of some highly visible manufacturing industries bunched in the country's industrialized heartland dramatized the issue. There were other episodes besides the appreciation of the dollar that created difficulties for specific industries. The sudden rise in the price of oil in the 1970s, for example, left the U.S. with its fleet of gas guzzling passenger cars vulnerable to foreign imports. The sluggishness of American producers in responding to a drastically altered market created an opening for the smaller, more fuel efficient cars produced in Europe and Japan and set the stage for an enduring market penetration through exposure of the American public to an attractive substitute.

Though American manufacturing has been hit by the disadvantage of a high-valued dollar and external shocks such as the rise in energy prices, the data suggest that manufacturing, in the aggregate, while subject to short-run ups and downs, has, nevertheless, held its own.

The constancy of manufacturing output is one part of the story. Looked at from another point of view, a fundamental and significant change has taken place in our economy. While manufacturing has maintained its percentage contribution to the Gross National Product, jobs in manufacturing have declined as a percent of total employment and the proportion of workers in services has increased. Employment in the production of all commodities, including agriculture, mining, and construction as well as manufacturing, has dropped in the period since World War II from 46 percent of workers to 28 percent. Manufacturing employment, by itself, has fallen from 27 percent of total workers to 19 percent. At the same time that workers making hard goods fell as a percent of the total, employment in service industries rose from 54 percent of all workers to 72 percent.

The reason for the seemingly contradictory development that manufacturing output has remained the same proportion of the GNP despite the fact that worker in manufacturing have declined as a percent of the total is that advances in productivity, output per worker, have been greater in manufacturing than in services. A smaller percentage of workers can produce the same percentage of output.

HOURLY EARNINGS AND INCOME

The shift of employment toward services has coincided with another major and disturbing event, the fact that the average hourly earnings of American workers, adjusted for inflation, have not increased since the early 1970s. If nonwage benefits such as health insurance are added in, total compensation has increased by a modest amount but far short of the improvements experienced prior to the early 1970s.

Changes in hourly earnings give us one way of measuring the money dimension of the quality of economic opportunity. Another is family income. Census data show that median family income adjusted for inflation has also not changed since the early 1970s. There are problems with the census numbers. When adjustments are made for changes in the size of the American family and other factors, average family income has grown but at a much slower rate than in the earlier postwar period. The fact that average family income has increased, though modestly, while workers' earnings have not, is explained by the higher rate of labor force participation. One-worker families have now become two-worker families.

The implications of 15 years of constant real hourly earnings and a slow increase in family income following 25 postwar years of rapid increase in earnings and income are, of course, enormous. Advances in the standard of living, which are the ultimate measure of economic performance and were steady, predictable, and large in the postwar period, became stalled in the 1970s and in the 1980s. The slowing of improvements in the standard of living is the result of the slowing of the rate of economic growth, the subject of a previous chapter.

It is interesting to compare the experience of national wage stagnation with the ordeal of unemployment in terms of its effects on economic well-being and the way it enters into public consciousness. Unemployment, the more traditional failure of market economies, is like a sharp blow, immediate in its impact—the separation of a person from the national income stream and a demoralizing sense of not belonging. It is a problem of high visibility and one with which the general public can easily identify. The ending of wage gains is more of a slow and creeping paralysis. Unlike a major drop in business activity, income stagnation is what one observer has described as "a kind of quiet depression." Only gradually do people realize that improvements in living standards are harder to come by. It is not easy to tell whether a failure of income to grow is only a temporary pause, a normal experience in the progression of economic events, or a persistent loss of momentum. The signals that the market sends out blur the perception. Nominal increases in income continue. There are more dollars in the pay envelope. But the increase in pay is matched by an increase in the general price level and it takes time to realize that what really counts, the purchasing power of the pay envelope, has remained unchanged.

With unemployment, in a word, the social problem is immediately evident. With wage stagnation, the problem is only gradually recognized and the reasons for the slowdown, which are subtle and deeply embedded in the complicated workings of the economy, are not readily understood. People are left with a vague sense of discontent and the frustration of not knowing who is to blame

The dissatisfaction resulting from slow income growth has been aggravated by large cost increases in specific items that vitally affect the sense of well-being. Americans have traditionally attached importance to home ownership. High interest rates and the increase in the price of domestic dwellings, above the average of other goods included in inflation indexes, have made housing outlays a larger proportion of the incomes that are themselves increasing at a sluggish rate. Families that bought homes in the early 1970s, before real estate prices skyrocketed and before interest charges rose to a level that makes the cost of servicing a mortgage prohibitive to many, were left in the favorable position of low monthly payments and accumulated capital gains. The younger generation, faced with the prospect of high mortgage costs, finds the American dream of owning a home of doubtful fulfillment. It has been pointed out that a 30-year old man in 1973 paid 21 percent of his monthly earnings in carrying charges for a medium-priced home; in 1983, a 30-year old man paid 44 percent of his monthly earnings to finance the same quality home.

Like the cost of housing, the cost of a college education, another item above average in importance to American families, has been escalating. A college degree has been a standard way for advancing up the economic and social scale in the postwar period. The cost of getting on this escalator is becoming harder to manage.

The sluggish rate of increase in wages and incomes has been offset to some degree in the 1980s by the cut in taxes that increased the amount of take-home pay. This relief was partly financed by the inflow of foreign funds that have been used to help cover the federal deficit created by the tax cut. American families have reacted on their own to the historic break in the trend of increasing income and to the increasing pressure on the family budget in ways that have important implications for the economy and our society. At the start of the 1970s a little over 40 percent of women worked. As we enter the 1990s, just under 60 percent are employed. The increased activity of women in the job market is partly due to a changed view of the role of women in society. It is also due to an effort to maintain the family's standard of living. Families have also resisted the effect of slow income growth by cutting their rate of saving from disposable income in an effort to maintain consumption. They have also borrowed against future income by buying on credit, to the extent that consumer debt, relative to income, has been at historic highs. Both actions, the reduction in the saving rate and the increase in consumer credit, affect the funds available for investment in our capital base.

THE CAUSES OF STAGNANT WAGES

Is there a connection between the failure of wages to rise over the last 15 years and the shift of employment from manufacturing to services? Some observers think there is. Manufacturing pays better than the service industries, the argument goes, and the move to services has held American wages down.

In examining the effect of the switch to service employment, it is useful to start off by freeing ourselves of some misconceptions. When we think of *services* we may think of an occupation such as domestic service. By far the larger part of employment in services is included in industries such as transportation, communications, utilities, and finance. A movement to service may not mean lower pay; there are high earning occupations included in service industries as well as in manufacturing. The pilot of an L-1011 jetliner, who operates with some of the most sophisticated technology available, for example, is counted in published data as working in a service industry. Again, movement from manufacturing to service employment may have no effect on earnings at all. A manufacturing firm may decide to reduce the size of its in-house legal department and hire an outside law firm to take care of its legal matters. If a displaced lawyer joins the law firm that has been retained by the corporation, the lawyer moves from manufacturing to a service industry, though the job duties and, presumably, the salary are unchanged.

Employment in communications and utilities, both in *services*, has remained the same, as a percent of total employment, over the postwar period. Jobs in wholesale trade and also in retail where hamburger cooks are counted have increased a modest amount, while those in transportation have had a small loss in share. Some of the biggest increases in service employment have been in business services, which include accounting and computing firms, and health services. The *personal services* category, which includes those who take in other peoples' laundry, has actually decreased over the postwar period both in terms of share of total output and share of total employment. Much of the job shifting has not been toward unskilled activities; it has been toward those requiring specialized skills.

But what about the overall effect of the shift to services? There are several points about which there is no dispute. Wages are lower in services on the average than in manufacturing. This difference is at least partly due to lower increases in output per worker in the service industries compared to manufacturing. Productivity has increased in the postwar period at 1.6 percent a year in services versus an annual gain in manufacturing of 2.7 percent. Not every service industry has lagged manufacturing. Communications and utilities, for example, have grown more rapidly in output per worker than manufacturing. But, generally speaking, productivity gains are larger in manufacturing industries. This is not an unimportant detail. Wages tend to rise with increases in worker efficiency. If workers produce more per hour, unit labor costs decline, and employees can be paid a higher wage.

Why productivity gains have been lower in services than in manufacturing is something of a mystery. One of the determinants of productivity, for example, is the amount of capital available per worker. Services have not suffered from a shortage of capital. Four of the seven industries included in services by the census have more capital available per worker than manufacturing. But productivity gains have been smaller in services in general and the fact is that real hourly earnings are lower than in manufacturing.

In addition to the fact that service jobs tend to pay less, it also has been observed by a number of researchers that low-paying jobs have increased as a percentage of new full-time jobs. There has also been some loss in the proportion of total income received by those in the middle of the income distribution traditionally occupied by blue collar workers in well-paying manufacturing jobs, though the loss in the middle has been due to movement toward higher income levels as well as toward lower. Both of these facts are consistent with the shift of employment from manufacturing to services.

Some researchers, however, reject the view that average earnings are lower because the demand for people to fill the higher paying jobs in manufacturing is less. Rather they explain the phenomenon in terms of a change in the makeup of labor supplied to the market. The proportion of teenagers in the labor force increased over the 1970s and 1980s. Since the years of experience and skill levels of these workers is limited, average pay is lower. New low-paying jobs are concentrated heavily among the young. Once this group develops more advanced job skills, it is argued, patterns that have been observed in the labor market will reverse themselves. There also seems to be some evidence that there is a higher skill level and education requirement for well-paying service jobs compared to well-paying, blue collar jobs in manufacturing.

Other labor market analysts, particularly some associated with the Department of Labor, take an agnostic view. They are not really sure what is happening. The deep recession in the early 1980s and the foreign trade deficit due to the rise in the value of the dollar may have caused temporary maladjustments that will, in time, be corrected.

The attempt to identify the cause of poor hourly earnings performance is not an idle exercise. If the shift away from manufacturing is the basic influence at work, then a case for some kind of government involvement in an industrial policy designed to strengthen the manufacturing sector is more easily made. If the supply of labor is the problem, if more limited skills are being brought to the market by a contingent of young workers, then strengthening of education and training would be a more appropriate policy, if any action at all were needed. If the agnostic view is correct, a wait-and-see attitude is called for.

No one explanation seems to provide the entire reason for the deterioration in job quality. A prudent conclusion would seem to be that changes in the industrial structure and in the age composition of the labor force explain part of the less favorable job options, but we do not know the size of the effect.

INDUSTRY SHIFTS: THE LONG-RUN VIEW

There is much to be gained by stepping back from this problem of a decline in job quality and a change in industrial structure and getting the advantage of the long-run perspective. The shift of employment in the United States out of manufacturing due to productivity gains has been going on for more than a century. The same pattern of movement can be observed in other nations.

Basically the shift to services should be viewed as a positive development. Large gains in productivity in manufacturing make more goods available at a lower cost. In response people increase their purchase of manufactured products. How much more they consume depends on choices freely exercised in the marketplace. The pattern for all of the industrialized nations has been that part of the increased capacity to produce, due to the gains in productivity in manufacturing, is used for more hard goods, but part is also directed toward services for which the demand is quite elastic in the upper stages of the economic development process. Instead of more manufactured products, people choose travel, education, health care, and even government services. Efficiency in manufacturing makes it possible for people to have the services that they associate with a higher standard of living. A shift in the labor force to a different type of industrial structure is necessary to accommodate changing consumption patterns. Shifts in employment among activities are part of the dynamics of economic growth.

Even more dramatic than the fall in manufacturing employment has been the decline in agriculture. It is fundamental to the growth process that the most basic industries be made efficient. If one farm worker can feed 35 other workers, which is roughly the case in the United States today, you transfer labor from producing the basic necessities to production of things with higher social value. For the industrialized nations, the shift from agriculture has been a long and continuous process with a highly visible movement of population from the rural to the urban area. If this shift is not managed successfully through improvements in farming methods, agriculture becomes a drag on the growth process. This is the case in the Soviet Union where 20 percent of their workers are employed in agriculture compared to less than 3 percent in the United States.

As individual manufacturing industries mature and the products they produce become more standardized, they tend to migrate to areas with abundant and low-priced labor. This happens both within the country, such as the movement of the textile and apparel industries in the United States from the north to the south starting in the 1890s, and across country lines from industrialized nations to developing economies.

Today this pattern of geographical relocation of industry takes on a more sophisticated form sometimes described as *networking*. In networking, a corporation spins off parts of its activities and retains the parts giving it a competitive edge and having the highest profit potential. It may retain the functions of new product design and development, for example, but contract out production to low-wage locations, either within the United States or abroad. The corporation then markets the output. Almost all of General Electric's electronic products are made in Asia. Although the VCR was invented in the United States, none are produced in America. Any number of other examples of corporate *outsourcing* could be cited. Networking is almost unlimited in its uses. Any part of corporate activity, from product design through final marketing, can be subcontracted to specialist firms, including some abroad.

Pessimists are concerned that in networking you end up with what *Business Week* has called a *hollow corporation*, a shell that owns no production facilities and makes its contribution simply by drawing together all of the assorted activities involved in placing a final product in the hands of the consumer. They also question whether service industries can prosper if manufacturing declines in importance because of the linkage between the two. Manufacturing firms buy a variety of legal, financial, engineering, and other services. *Business Week* recently observed that "General Motors Corporation's largest single supplier is not a steelmaker or a tire manufacturer but Blue Cross/Blue Shield." Some analysts question whether you can have a strong service sector without a strong industrial base.

Optimists view the corporation in its networking arrangements as creatively transferring low-profit activities to locations at a lower stage of economic development and retaining for itself high-profit activities that draw on expertise in high technology, well-established market channels and name recognition, and proven capability in market placement and market penetration. They also point out that the data available on the linkage of industries since World War II do not show that the impact of manufacturing on the rest of the economy has decreased.

In the economically advanced nations, maturing industries and lower-level functions that migrate to other locations must be replaced by new industries and new activities to compensate for the loss of the old. This renewal requires creativity at the cutting edge of science and technology combined with innovative management and an educated, skilled, and adaptable work force. It must also take place while other leading nations are attempting to maintain their economic momentum. Along with the United States, Japan has shifted some types of production to *offshore* facilities and is absorbed in the effort to capture the high tech markets. The battle of Detroit to maintain its position with consumers has been replaced with the battle of Silicon Valley in the struggle for leadership in microelectronics. The need for renewal is one of the major challenges facing the United States today.

One of the favorite topics of economists and historians in recent years has been an analysis of the *British disease*. Britain, the first of the industrialized nations, lost industry steadily to new competitors such as Germany and the United States starting as early as the latter part of the 19th century. Its decline as a great industrial power is due to its inability to compensate for the loss of mature industries with the creation of new ones. But why did it fail to achieve this renewal? The study of the decline of nations is less than an exact science, but at least some contributing factors to the failure of the British to adapt can be cited. The lack of a strong scientific and technological base in a society that insisted on educating its elite in the classical languages is probably a factor. The attitude that business is not a socially acceptable career for the graduates of British universities is another. At the other end of the social spectrum, restrictive labor practices, enforced by a labor movement that failed to adapt its goals to changing economic conditions, prevented the restructuring of manufacturing processes required for industries facing intense competition from low-wage labor abroad.

Whatever the source of Britain's problems in maintaining a competitive position, the dynamics of economic change force all advanced nations to continually adapt. Change is part of the process of "creative destruction" described by Schumpeter. Old industries die and new industries are born; workers are displaced and new work opportunities are created. Great economic powers are challenged by rising nations who are ready for their moment in history.

The process of adjustment after World War II was eased by worldwide economic expansion. The United States was in a particularly favorable position, faced with a seller's market as Western Europe and Japan recovered from the destruction of the world conflict. When the growth process slowed down for most nations around 1973, adjustment became more difficult.

The most important ingredients for maintaining the good economic life are continuing advances in technology and rapid increases in productivity. The economic problem, in its most elemental form, gets down to one basic fact. Over the long pull you cannot have more goods to distribute and consume than your economy is able to efficiently design, develop, and produce. The most basic cause of the decline in job quality is the slowdown in productivity gains starting in the early 1970s. Increases in real hourly earnings and family income require a steady rate of improvement in output per worker.

WHAT GOVERNMENT CAN DO

The question naturally arises as to whether government can make a contribution to more rapid advances in technology and productivity. The Japanese government is involved in channeling investment funds in specific directions of development and arranging and supporting joint ventures among Japanese corporations at the cutting edge of technology. This had led to interest in experimentation in industrial policy in the United States.

In a sense, our country already has an industrial policy in the form of innumerable tax provisions and regulations that affect the direction of investment and the distribution of American industry within the United States and abroad. This mishmash of accumulated legislative enactments sometimes enhances economic growth and sometimes retards it. The removal of undesirable disincentives for investment and changes in regulatory practices that clutter up the industrial landscape and impede creative innovation are obviously appropriate.

If we mean, though, by industrial policy a government effort to identify the *winners* in the growth game and to subsidize their activities through grants and loans, a majority of economists, regardless of political persuasions, are skeptical about the prospects for success. The economic growth process is an extremely complicated phenomenon. We cannot say with precision how various factors will contribute to growth in the future. We are not even entirely sure of what caused our successes in the past. Industries that *win* are frequently long shots and hard to pick at the beginning of the game. Admirers of Japanese success point to the role of the Ministry of International Trade and Industry (MITI) in working with business and financial institutions to develop Japan's competitiveness in international markets. What is not often pointed out is its failures in foresight. It tried, for example, to keep Honda out of the automobile industry.

There are broad-based activities of government that are clearly helpful. Education is fundamental to the growth process and support of education has been a traditional government function. The types of skills we develop are also important. In Japan they give high priority to graduating PhD's in science and technology. The United States is becoming a world leader in the training of lawyers. An increase in funding of research and development, particularly for universities, is another government initiative that has wide support. The removal of unnecessary barriers to joint efforts by corporations in high-risk and high-cost ventures is also a possible contribution.

There is one policy position on which economists agree almost unanimously. A strong sentiment favoring protectionism surfaced in the United States in the 1980s as the pressures of competition became greater. Looking at the U.S. experience from the broad historic view makes it easier to see that our problems are basically not due to policies adopted by other countries that require retaliatory action on our part. Such actions are regarded by trade specialists as a mistake. The vast majority of economists have absorbed the doctrine of Adam Smith that tariffs and other blocks to trade have the effect of reducing world output by preventing the exercise of comparative advantage among trading partners. They are also self-defeating. A protectionist policy simply shifts the burden of competitive adjustment. A quota or tariff on imports may help one industry in our country, but countermeasures adopted by trading partners may have a dampening effect on another industry. In the end, both nations are less successful.

If there is one subject on which the economics profession and public opinion are in sharp disagreement, it is the matter of free trade. Protectionist sentiment lies just below the surface of the collective consciousness and is easily aroused whenever foreign competition is perceived as a danger. Alan Blinder, a leading Keynesian of the younger generation, has recently enunciated "Murphy's law of economic policy" which states that "Economists have the least influence on policy where they know the most and are most agreed; they have the most influence on policy where they know the least and disagree most vehemently." The general public is willing to tolerate experiments in Keynesian fiscal and monetarist monetary policy about which economists have sharp differences of opinion. The public does not accept an undiluted commitment to free trade policy even though 95 percent of economists think protectionism unwise.

The difference is understandable. As is generally the case in unregulated markets, the benefits of free trade are enjoyed by society as a whole, but the cost in terms of plant closings, job displacement, and loss of capital is borne by individual workers and stockholders. Limited experimentation by the federal government in job retraining for workers and grants and low interest loans to impacted firms have been attempted to ease the cost of adjustment to competition in the past. But in practical terms the straightforward alternative for those affected by foreign trade is to seek protection from Congress. Adam Smith said that one of the most instinctive types of human behavior is "to truck and barter and exchange one thing for another." He could have added that the second most instinctive behavior is to seek protection when the forces of creative destruction become too painful.

INCOME DISTRIBUTION

We have been talking up to this point about the behavior of the average earnings of workers and about the changes in the average income of American families. A complementary problem, the distribution of income around the averages, is also a vital issue in the public consciousness. Who gets the income generated by national economic activity? How many rich, how many poor, and how many in between; and how has the pattern changed through time?

The method used by the census to present the nation's income distribution is to divide families into quintiles and show the before-tax income received by the top 20 percent on down to the lowest 20 percent. At the present time, the top 20 percent of American families get 45 percent of the nation's income. The bottom 20 percent get 5 percent. If census data are adjusted for taxes and for receipts such as Medicare and Medicaid benefits, the degree of inequality is reduced somewhat.

What the distribution of income should be in a nation is, of course, a matter of political and moral judgment. For whatever it is worth, income distribution in the United States is more uneven than it is for some of our close international competitors, such as West Germany and Japan.

Few of us have a good feel for how income is divided, how other families live. We are seldom exposed directly to poverty, for example. Are there poor people in the United States? They're here, we just don't see them. We see people who are poor, but in some casual contact, a clerk in a store or a janitor in a building. We do not look into the stark face of poverty in its own environment and see for ourselves the lack of food, clothing, and housing and the other goods and services that give variety to life. Most of us do not even have an accurate sense of where we ourselves fit in the income distribution. Most American families living in a prosperous suburb think of themselves as being in the middle-income bracket. They are probably not. In 1987 an annual family income of $52,900 was enough to put you in the upper 20 percent income bracket. An income of $86,300 put you in the top 5 percent of all American families.

A family with an annual income of $14,450 or less in 1987 fell into the bottom 20 percent of all families. Is this poor? It is quite common for us to judge our own state of well-being by comparing ourselves to others. Our perception of how prosperous we are depends on what we see around us. In part, at least, poverty is a relative thing. If being in the lowest fifth of the income distribution is our definition of poverty, then 20 percent of our nation's families is always poor.

The Social Security Administration made an attempt in the early 1960s to define poverty in an absolute sense; that is to determine the income necessary to provide a family with the minimum amount of goods and services acceptable in our society. It goes without saying that deciding on that basket of goods is partly a matter of judgment, but it is possible to calculate a rough figure that approximates the reality within a narrow range. In 1963 the poverty line for a family of four was set at $3,200.

One of the ways that Lyndon Johnson attempted to establish his own identity as President, following the tragic death of President Kennedy in November 1963, was to announce, in his *Economic Report* issued to Congress in January 1964, his famous *war on poverty*. After that the idea of a poverty threshold became a commonly accepted point of reference. In 1964, 19 percent of American families were below the poverty threshold. The proportion of families in poverty fell over the 1960s and early 1970s, reaching a low of almost 11 percent in 1973. Since then it has risen again, going above 15 percent in 1983. According to official data, 13^{1}/$_{2}$ percent of American families are now poor. The cutoff point is $11,611 for a family of four.

It is ironic that only a wealthy nation can afford a war on poverty. The major underdeveloped nations of the world are dealing with mass deprivation that will yield only to large and steady increases in the total national output. Only the developed economies, which have brought prosperity to most of their citizens through a long history of economic growth, can afford a program to assist the families that, for whatever reason, do not participate in the general prosperity.

THE DYNAMICS OF THE INCOME DISTRIBUTION

One of the more interesting and surprising things about the income distribution in the United States is that it has been relatively constant since World War II. One would have thought that with the many changes that have taken place over the last four decades, particularly the increase in government programs to help those at the lower income levels, that the income distribution of the country would have been significantly altered. The fact is that it has not. The top 20 percent received 43 percent of nation's income in 1947 and receives 44 percent today. The bottom 20 percent received 5 percent in 1947 and receives a little under 5 percent today. Except for a tilt in the direction of more equality in the 1960s, another tilt in the direction of less equality in the 1970s, followed by a somewhat sharper movement toward inequality in the 1980s, the income distribution has been relatively steady. The same pattern of stability also holds for other developed economies. Obviously there have been offsetting forces at work that have left the distribution relatively unchanged.

Family income *derived from earnings* is more unequally distributed today than in previous periods. The main reason for this is a two-way change in the number of workers in families. Over the last two decades families with more than one worker have increased; families without any workers have also increased. The increase in the number of more than one worker families is mainly due to the entry of women into the labor force in large numbers. The increase in families with no workers is due to the rise in the number of elderly and in the number of families headed by women. The effect of these two changes is to widen the distribution of income derived from work effort.

The reason why the income distribution is relatively unchanged, despite the increase in the inequality of earned income is, of course, that unearned income has compensated for the earned income shift. Social Security payments have provided income for the elderly and welfare payments have provided income for the families headed by women. The degree of compensation in the two cases, however, has been quite different.

There has been a policy decision on the part of our nation to make adequate provision for the material well-being of the aged. The program that began with the Social Security Act of 1935 has been expanded through time. Medicare was added in 1965 and retirement benefits have been raised in a series of periodic adjustments. The most important change occurred in 1972 when the benefits were increased by 20 percent and indexed for inflation. The indexing was, apparently, an effort to eliminate the periodic political pressure to increase benefits. These legislative enactments came, by unfortunate coincidence, at the same time that the economic growth rate dropped and inflation began to be a national problem. Both developments made financing the increase in benefits more of a challenge than originally thought. The economic slowdown caused social security tax receipts to grow more slowly; inflation caused benefits, now adjusted automatically, to rise. In addition to the indexing to protect payments from the erosion of inflation, the benefits formula is also adjusted to account for the increase in real wages in the economy due to economic growth.

Because of the increase in benefits and in the proportion of the elderly who are covered, the Social Security program has played an important role in lifting senior citizens above the poverty line. It is estimated that about one half of the elderly would fall below the poverty threshold without it. The 1985 *Economic Report of the President* pointed out that by 1983 the before-tax average income of elderly families was, on a per capita basis, equal to the income of nonelderly families.

The places in the poverty group vacated by the elderly over the last two decades were taken over by families headed by single women. In 1967 40 percent of those in poverty were elderly and 7 percent were women with a child under the age of six. By 1984 only 20 percent of the poverty group consisted of the elderly and 13 percent was made up of women with a child under six years of age. Single women with dependent children over the age of six also have added to the poverty group.

The main government program that provides assistance to such families is the Aid to Families with Dependent Children, which is what is usually meant when people refer to the *welfare program* and which was enacted into law at the same time as Social Security. It was originally thought that it would remain a limited effort to aid states in providing assistance to widows and orphans. It has expanded over time into a program that is a major source of income for families headed by women.

The public attitude toward the welfare program is dramatically different from the attitude toward Social Security. Social Security is thought of as something that has been earned through years of contribution and has no social stigma attached to it. If there is one point of agreement about welfare, on the other hand, it is that it is liked by practically no one. From the viewpoint of the general public, it clashes with some of the most widely accepted of American values, the work ethic and the independence and stability of the family. For recipients, the requirements to prove eligibility and the process of administration are degrading. These are sentiments that Keynes and Marshall would have understood, for modern programs of help for the needy have their historic roots in the English poor laws that go back to 1601 under Queen Elizabeth when a public social welfare policy was first established. Over four centuries the basic tension in welfare programs has not changed fundamentally, a sentiment of humanitarian concern mixed with begrudging reluctance.

The administrative arrangements for the AFDC program reflect this ambivalent attitude. Unlike Social Security, which is federally financed and has uniform national benefits for all participants and nationwide standards for eligibility, Aid to Families with Dependent Children is financed jointly by the federal and state governments but is administered by the states, with benefits determined at the state level. Monthly payments differ dramatically. The highest payment by a state to a single woman with two children is over six times as large as the lowest amount paid by a state. Unlike the Social Security payments, welfare benefits are not indexed. The states, which have had their own budgeting problems in the 1970s and 1980s, have not adjusted benefits to compensate fully for inflation, with the result that real welfare benefits have declined since the early 1970s. They have done so at a time when the number of families headed by women with children has increased, so that although the elderly have improved their income position, families headed by women with children have continued to hover around the poverty threshold since the early 1970s. Almost half of single mothers with children fall below the poverty line today, a percentage almost unchanged from the early 1970s. A fifth of the female-headed families have less than one half the income needed to exit from the poverty group. The concentration of poverty among families headed by women has come to be labeled the *feminization of poverty*.

In the 1980s a new twist was added to the welfare debate. The idea that welfare might actually do more harm than good by creating a culture dependent on welfare was advanced by Charles Murray in his 1984 book, *Losing Ground*. Murray pointed out that more money was spent on means-tested programs over the 1970s and 1980s but the number of families in poverty actually increased. His book is widely referred to in debates about how much welfare dependence there is and whether parents pass on dependency to their children.

The availability of data necessary to reach conclusions about the issues Murray raised has been a problem. To answer questions about length of time on welfare and the behavior of children of welfare parents, one has to track a group of people over one or two decades. Longitudinal studies are now available but some key issues are as yet unresolved. In some cases there are conflicting or inconclusive results. In others the conclusion depends on how one interprets the findings. For example, one study tracked 15 years of behavior of roughly 700 people, who at one time or another were on welfare, and found that 30 percent were recipients for one or two years, 40 percent for three to seven years and 30 percent for eight years or longer. One could conclude from these numbers that only 30 percent had long-term dependence (defined as eight years or longer), that welfare is not addictive, and that it provides assistance for what is basically a transitory event. One could also conclude that 70 percent had long-term dependence (defined as three years or longer), and that welfare is basically a long-term matter. The conclusion would depend on the length of time that the observer considers to be long term, three years or eight years.

The claim that children of welfare recipients themselves become welfare recipients has not been tested enough for the results to be completely conclusive. One study has shown that while daughters of heavily dependent welfare parents were more likely to become heavily dependent on welfare than daughters of nonwelfare families, still only one in five from the sample became heavily dependent in later life. Even in these cases it is impossible to separate out the effect of welfare in encouraging dependence from environmental influences, such as education and family stability, that also affect the behavior of welfare children.

THE MATTER OF ECONOMIC JUSTICE

The national dialogue over the issue of the social safety net has been complicated by the slow rate of growth in the economy and in family income since the early 1970s. When the economic pie is expanding at a healthy rate, most of the population is better off even if the distribution of income remains unchanged. There are some in society that do not share in the general prosperity, particularly those that do not have a working member in the family. Even a job is not necessarily a means to material comfort. If we take the total of all heads of households in 1984 who were of working age, in good health, and without young children, and therefore normally expected to work, 21 percent of men and 45 percent of women had weekly earnings so low that even if they worked 52 weeks out of the year, they could not earn what is necessary to move a family of four above the poverty threshold. But even families that cannot benefit from prosperous times directly by activity in the job market are more likely to benefit indirectly in a period of rapid economic growth through more generous public assistance. To repeat John Kennedy's analogy, "a rising tide lifts all boats."

The rich have a vested interest in emphasizing the importance of growth as a solution to poverty since it costs them less than an expanded welfare program. The poor, on the other hand, have the impatience of the hungry. They cannot wait for tomorrow; their needs are immediate and they press their case for assistance and a redivision of the pie. In a world where workable solutions must be found, political leaders must walk the line between the two remedies for poverty, growth and redistribution. It has to be recognized that social welfare programs can be expanded to the point that the tax burden needed to pay for them stifles initiative and reduces the growth rate. A society can be strangled by its own safety net. At the same time programs to help the unfortunate are not necessarily inconsistent with growth and are, to some degree, complementary. Even beyond humanitarian considerations, they are the price paid to relieve social tensions and provide the stability necessary for initiatives leading to growth to take place.

The slower growth that the United States has experienced since the early 1970s has made the problem of resolving issues of equity more difficult. The rate of economic growth affects political sentiment. In conditions of prosperity, the majority are more willing to accept expansion of social welfare programs. In a period of slow growth and less rapid increase in national resources, financing the aid for the less fortunate of society becomes more of a strain and political resistance increases. This is reflected in a turning of political sentiment to the more conservative side of the political spectrum, a movement that has occurred over the last decade both in the United States and some of the countries of Europe. The shift in political sentiment occurs at the same time that the needs of the poor become greater. The tension between the need for efficiency and growth in the economy and the demands of distributive justice becomes more difficult to manage.

Keynes once wrote that capitalism is probably more efficient than any other economic system for achieving our economic objectives. The trick is to be as efficient as possible "without offending our notions of a satisfactory way of life." It is a social objective not easily satisfied.

CHAPTER 11

WHO KILLED
JOHN MAYNARD KEYNES?

We started this book with a chapter entitled "The Death of Keynes." Is Keynes really dead? Does Keynesian economics no longer have relevance for modern economies and, if not, what killed it off as a viable model for national policy?

There are no easy answers to these questions. The debate about the usefulness of Keynes's work is almost as intense now as when it was first introduced. There are still sharp differences of opinion among economists, differences that measure how far we still have to go in settling the conflicts that have dominated the evolution of economic policy over the last 50 years.

Richard Nixon was once quoted in the early 1970s as saying, "We are all Keynesians now." Milton Friedman later agreed with the statement, but with a critical addition on which he insisted, "and none of us are Keynesians anymore." Friedman's pithy summary provides a basis for examining the legacy of Keynes. Some of what Keynes wrote survives in its influence and some does not. The problem is to decide which is which.

THE BASIC KEYNESIAN PROPOSITIONS

We have seen that one of the central beliefs that Keynes advanced was that an economy may not tend toward full employment and may require some form of government compensatory action to bring it to this desired level of activity. After decades of debate, economists still do not agree on this key issue.

The New Classical economics, in a revival of the classical economics that was the common property of economists before Keynes's *General Theory*, holds that the economy has its own power of self-correction and that government efforts to influence the economy are generally ineffective. Monetarists think compensatory action by government is likely to do more harm than good. One contribution that Keynes made on the level of abstract theory is that he caused a basic reexamination of the underlying postulates of the classical theory. Those who thought his insights fundamentally flawed were forced to explain, in more precise terms, how the mechanisms of the free market give to capitalistic systems a self-correcting capability. A large part of the research effort of economists in the last two decades has been preoccupied with establishing what the professionals would call the *microeconomic foundations* of macroeconomics. Keynes stirred up debate, which is what all great thinkers do. In this sense, at least, his influence still lives four decades after his burial in Westminster Abbey. "Is Keynes dead?" Paul Samuelson was once asked. "Yes," he answered, "and so are Newton and Einstein."

In contrast to the New Classical economics and monetarism, the Keynesian view that government action to stimulate the economy can be appropriate remains a contender in the competition for public acceptance. Modern Keynesians have modified Keynes's basic model to conform to developments in economic theory. They also recognize that there is a large amount of recuperative power built into the capitalistic system, as the classical economists claimed. But they still feel that lags in response time and market frictions make the servo-mechanism of price and wage adjustment slow in its effect. Keynesians remain activist in sentiment on policy issues.

The implications of this professional debate for the role of government in modern industrialized societies are, of course, momentous. At the practical level of policy formation, leaders of the industrialized nations may disagree on the amount of intervention appropriate, but are clearly less inclined to leave it to the automatic forces of the market to correct an imbalance in the economy than they were before Keynes wrote. In the 1980s, U.S. leadership has not been reluctant for example, in an effort to increase the market for American exports, to urge the Japanese and West Germans to implement Keynesian types of expansionary fiscal action to accelerate their rates of economic expansion.

There was about Keynes's writing a depression mentality. The economy of the postwar period has not been—in sharp contrast with the economy of the 1930s—an economy of prolonged and widespread unemployment. No one thinks any more in terms of massive government intervention. There is also less confidence, particularly since the 1960s—even among those who lean toward a more activist role—in our ability to analyze problems and implement the proper cure. The idea of *fine tuning* the economy, which we associate with the days of Camelot, now strikes most economists as naive, if, indeed, the Keynesian economists of the Kennedy administration ever thought such a degree of control possible. Fiscal policy with a supply-side feature—tax benefits to business to stimulate investment—introduced by the Kennedy and Johnson administrations, is on the other hand espoused by a large percentage of economists, including some who would be reluctant to accept the label *Keynesian*.

At the practical level of economic forecasting, large-scale econometric models that were developed by Keynesian economists over the 1950s and 1960s, are widely used by most forecasters, although practitioners blend a good dose of intuition with the results derived from a large set of algebraic equations. There is a touch of irony here. It took economists a long time to convince practicing administrators that such models are useful. Just as they have become widely used by governments and businesses all over the world, a healthy dose of skepticism has developed among a large number of economists, even many Keynesians, about our ability to model the economy with this much detail and about the usefulness of such large-scale models for economic forecasting.

FISCAL AND MONETARY POLICY

Keynes fundamentally changed thinking about government deficits. It is now widely accepted, for example, that passive deficits are appropriate in times of recession. Even strongly-worded proposals for a balanced budget amendment have loopholes to allow for deficits during periods of business contraction. It is now commonplace that a recession is not the time to raise taxes in a futile attempt to balance the budget in the face of falling revenue. It is also widely recognized that the timing of changes in taxes and government outlays can affect the behavior of the economy and that when change seems desirable this impact should be taken into account in making budget decisions.

A more ambitious use of the fiscal tool for purposes of expanding economic activity is no longer widely supported. Even before the deficits of the 1980s, a large number of economists questioned the wisdom of a frequent use of fiscal policy to counter movements in the economy. We have spoken earlier of the time lag in completion of tax legislation that places a serious constraint on the effectiveness of decisions to adjust the budget to compensate for private spending. But in any event the huge deficits of the 1980s have neutralized the use of the budget as an important tool of government control. A deliberate decision to move the budget in the direction of a larger deficit for the purpose of stimulating the economy is now unthinkable. We have also learned that very large deficits can stimulate parts of the economy through their impact on domestic spending; they can also restrict other parts through the indirect effect they have on export industries. Our decisions will be constrained for most of the next decade by the twin deficits, the shortfall in the federal budget and the trade balance.

Quite clearly the view of Keynes and Keynesians up through the 1960s that monetary policy is of secondary importance in economic management is no longer accepted. In the last decade and a half, the monetary tool has come to be recognized by a broad spectrum of economists as the most important tool available to government for affecting the overall behavior of the economy. The monetarist school was primarily responsible for bringing about this change in thinking. But the victory has been bittersweet.

It will be remembered from the discussion in an earlier chapter that total spending depends not only on how much money is available but also on how fast it turns over. Total spending is the amount of money in circulation multiplied by the turnover rate, the velocity. Keynes thought monetary policy of limited effectiveness because changes in the velocity can offset variations in the money supply. If the Federal Reserve increases the money in circulation, but the turnover rate decreases, the two changes are offsetting. In the postwar period, up until the last decade or so, the velocity increased annually at a fairly constant rate, so that the effect of money changes could be predicted. In the last decade, the velocity has behaved less predictably and the Keynesian concerns have been revived. There is more reluctance to accept the monetarist policy prescriptions, particularly the prescription that the Federal Reserve be put on automatic pilot, expanding the money supply annually by a set rate. Variations in the velocity in the last decade have made an automatic expansion rule unworkable and have caused central banks in the United States and Europe to moderate the monetarist policies adopted in the late 1970s.

The Federal Reserve has been left in something of a quandary. If it is unwise to rely too heavily on changes in the money supply as the sole target of control, what target or targets should the Fed use in its day-to-day operations? The Federal Reserve is still searching for an effective target for its actions. It monitors the money supply, particularly money measures for which the turnover rate has been less erratic. It also monitors interest rate behavior and apparently some other indicators such as commodity prices. Monetarists are more unhappy with this situation than Keynesians. Keynesians have traditionally thought of interest rates as an appropriate target for the Federal Reserve and are not uncomfortable with multiple targets. Monetarists, on the other hand, deplore ambiguity on the part of the Federal Reserve in pursuit of its policies. They insist that the criteria used by the Fed for its actions should be well understood by the public so that there are few surprises. The problem of the moment is that it is not completely clear what the operating target for money management should be.

Despite the fact that monetarism has lost some of its influence on issues of central bank management, the central point that monetarists have succeeded in bringing to public attention will undoubtedly remain as one of the fundamentals of economic policy. A major cause of inflation, historically, has been too rapid an increase in the money supply. The Federal Reserve may have to depart from rigid adherence to a money target when the velocity becomes erratic, but it would be dangerous to stray too far from an emphasis on a disciplined expansion of the money supply as an important ingredient in a well-balanced policy regime.

THE QUALITY OF ECONOMIC LIFE

Keynes, becalmed in the eye of a major depression, lost his feel for the dynamic possibilities for economic expansion in modern industrial societies. His followers picked up the growth theme, but it has not been the main preoccupation of Keynesians just as it has not been a central concern of monetarists.

The practical importance of economic growth, in terms of its effect on the lives of human beings, is enormous. The difference between the masses of the Third World countries today and a century ago is that, while they are still poor, they now know, through the marvels of modern communication, that they are poor and that other people are not. A consciousness of poverty has developed and, along with it, what Adlai Stevenson once called "a revolution of rising expectations." The United States will be operating in the next decades in an international environment in which developing economies of the Third World will press their claim for their share of world markets and the less-developed nations will be struggling to join the growth process.

Here at home the political and economic climate for welfare legislation has been fundamentally changed. During the boom years of the postwar economy, up to the early 1970s, a rapidly expanding economic pie made it easier to get political acceptance for expansion of social programs and a widening of the safety net for the less fortunate in society. The slowdown in the growth of the economic pie since the early 1970s has weakened support for these initiatives.

New social programs in the 1950s and 1960s were financed by the fiscal dividend, the increase in federal revenues due to economic growth. The inflation of the 1960s and 1970s added to the increase in government income through *bracket creep*. Federal revenues benefited both from economic growth and from the inflation. Provisions of the tax code now allow for some indexing to compensate for inflation. In addition, the 1986 tax reform law reduced the number of income tax brackets so that bracket creep is at least partially eliminated as a source of federal revenues. With the slowdown in economic growth and the reduction in bracket creep, increasing revenues to finance an expansion in social programs are not as forthcoming. New programs will have to be financed by taking away from some other part of the budget.

The pressing need to move the federal budget in the direction of balance adds a further severe constraint on increase in aid to the needy. Despite the fact that the percentage of families in poverty has increased, and particularly the number of children, expensive proposals for expansion of the safety net are not likely to win political acceptance. The massive deficit has "taken away the allowance," although, perhaps, not in the way that President Reagan intended.

IS KEYNES DEAD?

We come back to our central question: Is Keynes dead? The answer is no. Many of his teachings have been modified and some rejected. But the controversy he provoked through his iconoclastic writings continues and his presence, to a degree that is surprising considering the time that has passed, is still felt within the inner circle of the debate.

An article in a recent issue of the *U.S. News and World Report* was headed: "Look Who's Making a Comeback." Standing there in a page length cartoon portrait was the hero of this tale, John Maynard Keynes. The rise and fall in the acceptance of economic theories partly depends, as we have said before, on the success of the competition. As monetarism has entered into a period of declining appeal, interest in Keynesian economics has revived.

It would be interesting to know what the master economist would make of all of this. Scholars who have delved carefully into the many volumes of Keynes's writings often point out that Keynes could be very flexible in the positions that he took on various issues, willing to change when convinced he was wrong or when he recognized that political constraints made a given course of action impossible. He would surely have modified many of his beliefs if he were living today and it is not at all certain what his opinion would be on a given problem. But with his unbounded curiosity and limitless energies, he would surely be in the thick of the controversies, winning over some with his charm, annoying others with the arrogance that was also part of his personality.

I also like to think of Keynes as still being capable of showing patience with a child who has thrown his hat from a cruise boat into the water.

NOTES

Chapter 1

Page   1   The source for Lucas's statement on the death of Keynesian economics is: "The Death of Keynes," in *Viewpoints on Supply-Side Economics* ed. Thomas J. Halistones (Richmond: Robert F. Dame, Inc., 1982), p. 3.

The Lucas "total chaos" statement is from Thomas J. Halistones, *Viewpoints on Supply-Side Economics*, p. 5.

Page   2   The Schumpeter quotation is from his *History of Economic Analysis* (New York: Oxford University Press, 1954), p. 41.

Klamer's *Conversations with Economists* is published by Rowman and Allanheld, Publishers, Totowa, New Jersey, 1983. The quotation is from page 238.

Page   2-3   The Keynes quotation is from: *The General Theory of Employment, Interest, and Money* (London: Macmillan Press, Ltd., 1973), p. 383.

Chapter 2

Page   5   For this chapter I have drawn on the large amount of biographical material on Keynes now available. Among the more important sources is a biography by Sir Roy Harrod, a student and colleague of Keynes: *The Life of John Maynard Keynes* (New York: Augustus Kelley, 1969). Keynes's nephew, Milo Keynes, edited a collection of papers on various aspects of Keynes's life: *Essays on John Maynard Keynes* (London: Cambridge University Press, 1975). Milo Keynes has also written a biography of Keynes's wife: *Lydia Lopokova* (New York: St. Martin's Press, 1983). The biography that will probably be the standard source for some time is: Robert Skidelsky, *John Maynard Keynes* (New York: Viking Penguin Inc., 1986). A second volume is in preparation.

Other biographical and historical material useful for those interested in Keynes's personal life include: Clive Bell, *Old Friends* (New York: Harcourt, Brace and Company, 1956); Quentin Bell, *Bloomsbury* (New York: Basic Books, Inc., 1968); Derek Crabtree and A. P. Thirlwall, eds., *Keynes and the Bloomsbury Group* (London: Macmillan and Company, 1980); Charles H. Hession, *John Maynard*

Keynes (New York: Macmillan and Company, 1984); Gertrude Himmelfarb, *Marriage and Morals Among the Victorians* (New York: Alfred Knopf, 1986); Michael Holroyd, *Lytton Strachey* (London: Heinmann, 1967, vol. 1, 1968, vol. 2); Elizabeth S. and Harry G. Johnson, *The Shadow of Keynes* (Chicago: University of Chicago Press, 1978); Francis King, *E. M. Forster and His World* (New York: Charles Scribner's Sons, 1978); Paul Levy, *G. E. Moore and the Cambridge Apostles* (London: Weidenfeld and Nicolson, 1979); Leonard Woolf, *Beginning Again* (New York: Harcourt Brace and World, Inc., 1963).

Schumpeter's memorial essay on Keynes appeared in the *American Economic Review*, September 1946. It is reprinted in *Ten Great Economists* (New York: Oxford University Press, 1951).

Page 7 The observation on the British educated class is from Robert Skidelsky, *John Maynard Keynes*, p. 120.

Page 8 The Keynes's quotation describing the impact of Moore's ethics on himself and his contemporaries is from: "My Early Beliefs," in *Essays in Biography* (London: Macmillan Press, Ltd., 1972), pp. 436–437.

Page 9 The quotation from the *New York Times* on the squares of Bloomsbury is from the February 23, 1983 issue, Sec. 10, p. 9.

Page 10 Quentin Bell's statement about the artists at Charleston is from *The Wall Street Journal*, August 19, 1986, p. 20.

The story on the Bloomsbury fund-raising expedition to Dallas is from: Jill Johnston, "Imagine a New Kind of T.V. Soap: Bloomsbury Comes to Dallas," *The New York Times Book Review*, Sec. 7, August 24, 1986, pp. 12–13.

Page 12 Keynes's statement on civilization as a "thin and precarious crust" is from "My Early Beliefs," pp. 447–448.

The quotation from the 1984 biography referred to is found in: Charles H. Hession, *John Maynard Keynes*, pp. X and XV.

Page 14 Keynes's comment on Wilson is from: "The Council of Four, Paris, 1919," *Essays in Biography*, p. 10.

Page 14-15 Keynes's comment on Russia is from: "A Short View of Russia," *Essays in Persuasion* (London: Macmillan Press Ltd., 1972), p. 258.

Page 18 Quentin Bell's remembrance of the hat incident is in: Crabtree and Thirlwall, eds., *Keynes and the Bloomsbury Group*, pp. 69–70.

Chapter 3

Page   21   The Charles Schultze quotation is from: Charles L. Schultze, *The Public Use of Private Interest* (Washington: The Brookings Institution, 1977), p. 18.

Page   24   Marshall Goldman's account of his conversation with the Russian economist is found in his book: *U.S.S.R. in Crisis* (New York: W. W. Norton and Company, 1983), p. 50.

Page   25-26   The Robertson story to illustrate the idea of the velocity of money is from: *Money* (Chicago: University of Chicago Press, 1959), p. 27.

Page   27   Keynes's comment on 19th-century orthodoxy appears in: "A Self-Adjusting Economic System," *The New Republic*, February 20, 1935, pp. 35–36.

Page   31   The observation about Socrates is from: David McCord Wright, "The Future of Keynesian Economics," *American Economic Review*, June, 1945, p. 285.

Chapter 4

Page   32   Samuelson's statement about the effect of *The General Theory* on young economists is from: "The General Theory," *The Collected Scientific Papers of Paul A. Samuelson*, vol. IV (Cambridge: The M.I.T. Press, 1966), p. 1517.

Page   33   Galbraith's account of how Keynes came to America is in: "Came the Revolution," *The New York Times Book Review*, Sec. 7, May 16, 1965, p. 1.

Page   34-35   Roosevelt's comment after his meeting with Keynes is reported by Arthur Schlesinger, Jr., *The Coming of the New Deal* (Boston: Houghton Mifflin Co., 1960) p. 406.

Page   35   Roosevelt's charge of fiscal irresponsibility on the part of the Hoover administration is discussed in *The Memoirs of Herbert Hoover, the Great Depression, 1929-1941* (New York: The Macmillan Company, 1952), p. 132.

Page   35-36   Senator Murray's original bill is: 79th Congress, S. 380. The Employment Act of 1946 is: 79th Congress, Public Law 304.

Page   39   James Tobin's comment on Kennedy is from his book *The New Economics One Decade Older* (Princeton: Princeton University Press, 1974), pp. 19 and 24.

Page 40 Walter Heller's conversation with President Kennedy is from "Walter Heller: Presidential Persuader," (interview by Kyle Crichton) of June 21, 1987. Copyright © 1987/88 by The New York Times Company. Reprinted by permission.

Page 42-
43 For a brief biographical sketch of Phillips see: C. A. Blyth, "Biographical Sketch, A. W. H. Phillips, M. B. E.; 1914–1975," in A. R. Bergstrom and others, *Stability and Inflation* (New York: John Wiley and Sons, 1978), pp. xiii–xvii.

Page 43 Phillips's famous article is: "The Relation Between Unemployment and the Rate of Change of Money Wage Rates in the United Kingdom, 1861–1957," *Economica*, November 1958, pp. 283–299.

Page 45 The Samuelson and Solow paper is: "Analytical Aspects of Anti-inflation Policy," *American Economic Review*, May 1960, pp. 177–194.

Page 48 The quotation from *Time* is from the December 31, 1965 issue, pp. 640–67B.

Chapter 5

Page 50 Keynes's statement on the damage of inflation is from: *The Economic Consequences of the Peace* (London: Macmillan and Company, 1971), p. 149.

Page 58 The Friedman-Schwartz statement is from their book: *A Monetary History of the United States, 1867–1960* (Princeton: Princeton University Press, 1963), p. 419.

Page 60 The Friedman/Meiselman statistical study of the relative effectiveness of monetary and fiscal policy is: "The Relative Stability of Monetary Velocity and the Investment Multiplier," in Commission on Money and Credit, *Stabilization Policies* (Englewood Cliffs: Prentice-Hall, 1963), pp. 165–268.

Page 61 Friedman's presidential address was published as: "The Role of Monetary Policy," *American Economic Review* March 1968, pp. 1–17. Phelps's research was first published in his paper, "Money Wage Dynamics and Labor Market Equilibrium," *Journal of Political Economy*, July/August 1967, pp. 687–711.

Page 64 John Muth's classic paper is: "Rational Expectations and the Theory of Price Movements," *Econometrica*, July 1960, pp. 315–335.

Chapter 6

Page 71 James Tobin's statement about Burns and Volcker is from *The New York Times*, Sec. 3, January 24, 1988, p. 25.

Page 80 The story of the combo known as the "Monetary Aggregates" is told in: Don Bedwell, "The Most Secure Job You'll Ever Have," *Georgia Trends*, October 1986, p. 43.

Chapter 7

Page 84 The phrase "the enormous anomaly . . ." is from: J. M. Keynes, "Economic Possibilities for Our Grandchildren," *Essays in Persuasion*, p. 322.

Page 87 There are a number of descriptions of the revolution in microelectronics available. See, for example, Ernest Braun and Stuart MacDonald, *Revolution in Miniature* (New York: Cambridge University Press, 1982); and Dirk Hanson, *The New Alchemists* (Boston: Little, Brown and Co., 1982).

Page 88 The *New York Times* announcement of the invention of the transistor is described in Dirk Hanson, *The New Alchemists*, p. 69

Page 90 For a short account of Schumpeter's life see: Arthur Smithies, "Memorial: Joseph Alois Schumpeter, 1883–1950," in *Schumpeter, Social Scientist* ed. Seymour E. Harris (Cambridge: Harvard University Press, 1951), pp. 11–23.

The Samuelson quotation is from his essay, "Schumpeter as a Teacher and Economic Theorist," in Seymour E. Harris, *Schumpeter, Social Scientist*, p. 48.

Page 91 The Schumpeter comment from the preface to the Japanese edition of *The Theory of Economic Development*. Authur Smithies, "Memorial: Joseph Aloris Schumpeter, 1983-1950, p. 18.

Page 92 The quotation on Schumpeter's visit to England is quoted in Arthur Smithies, "Memorial: Joseph Alois Schumpeter, 1883–1950," p. 18.

Page 96 The Keynes quotation from *The Economic Consequences of the Peace* is from the 1971 edition (London: Macmillan and Co., Ltd.), p. 12.

Page 97 The Schumpeter quotation on Keynes's "indictment of thrift" is from his essay, "John Maynard Keynes, 1883–1946," *The American Economic Review*, September 1946, p. 517.

Page 101- For a survey of world growth performance in the 19th and 20th
102 centuries, see: Lloyd G. Reynolds, "The Spread of Economic
Growth to the Third World: 1850–1980," *Journal of Economic
Literature*, September 1983, pp. 941–980.

Page 102 For a discussion of the convergence of growth rates, see William
J. Baumol, "Productivity Growth, Convergence, and Welfare:
What the Long-Run Data Show," *American Economic Review*,
December 1986, pp. 1072–1085.

Chapter 8

Page 104 For an account of the Washington Meeting of Laffer, Cheney,
and Wanniski, see: John Brooks, "The Supply Side," *The New
Yorker*, April 19, 1982.

Page 105- The references to *Time's* "Board of Economists" and the quoted
106 statement of the member of the Joint Economic Committee are
from the issue of February 22, 1971.

Page 111- Paul Craig Robert's inside account of the supply-side movement
112 is: *The Supply-Side Revolution* (Cambridge: Harvard University Press, 1984). George Gilder's book, *Wealth and Poverty*,
is published by Basic Books, 1981. Martin Anderson's book,
Revolution, is published by Harcourt, Brace, Jovanovich, 1988.

Page 112- The Schumpeter quotation is from: "John Maynard Keynes,"
113 *American Economic Review*, September 1946, p. 515.

Page 114 The Herbert Stein quotation is from *Washington Bedtime Stories*
(New York: The Free Press, 1986), p. 133.

Page 115 The Martin Anderson quotation is from his book, *Revolution*,
p. 162.

Page 118 For comments on the pattern of defense spending in the post-
Vietnam period, see Gregory B. Mills, "The Budget," in *The
Reagan Years*, eds. John L. Palmer and Isabel V. Sawhill
(Cambridge: Ballinger Publishing Co., 1984), pp. 111–112.

Page 121 For an account of the events surrounding the 1981 legislation,
see: Robert D. Reischauer, "The Congressional Budget Process," in *Federal Budget Policy in the 1980's*, eds. Gregory
B. Mills and John L. Palmer (Washington: The Urban Institute
Press, 1984), pp. 385–413. One should also read, for the insider's view, David Stockman, *The Triumph of Politics: Why the
Reagan Revolution Failed* (New York: Harper and Row, 1986).

The Moynihan quotation is cited in Thomas Edsall, *The New Politics of Inequality* (New York: W. W. Norton, 1984), p. 17.

Page 122 The article by William Greider is: "The Education of David Stockman," *Atlantic Monthly*, December 1981.

Stockman's description of the Rosy Scenario as a compromise to satisfy conflicting economic positions is cited in: William Greider, *Secrets of the Temple* (New York: Simon and Schuster, 1987), p. 367.

Page 127 Ricardo's statement on his speculative gain is from: John Maynard Keynes, "Malthus," in *Essays in Biography* (London: Macmillan Press, Ltd., 1972), p. 96.

Page 128 Robert Barro's equivalence theorem is in: "Are Government Bonds Net Worth?" *Journal of Political Economy*, November/December 1974, pp. 1095-1117.

Page 130 The 1986 act boasted federal revenues in fiscal year 1987 for several reasons, but this increase was not the original intent and was, for the most part, a one-time gain.

Chapter 9

Page 134-135 Wilson's book, *The Conquest of Copper Mountain*, is published by Atheneum, New York 1981.

Page 140 For a discussion of Keynes's role at the Bretton Woods conference, see: Richard N. Gardner, "Bretton Woods," in *Essays on John Maynard Keynes*, ed. Milo Keynes, pp. 202–215; and John Williamson, "Keynes and the International Order," in *Keynes and the Modern World*, eds. David Worswick and James Trevithick (London: Cambridge University Press, 1983), pp. 87–113. The quotation regarding U.S. dominance at the Bretton Woods conference is from Gardner's article, p. 203.

Page 145 Friedman's position on flexible exchange rates was presented in: "The Case for Flexible Exchange Rates," *Essays in Positive Economics* (Chicago: University of Chicago Press, 1953), pp. 157–203.

Page 158 The debate over the appropriate exchange rate level for the dollar has been a west coast-east coast affair with the west represented by Ronald McKinnon of Stanford who has argued that the dollar has fallen too much (see: "Fed Must Eye Money, Not Merchandise," *The Wall Street Journal*, August 24, 1988).

The east has been represented by Martin Feldstein of Harvard (see: "Unwanted Advice From Abroad," *The Wall Street Journal*, March 3, 1988; and "Redefining Dollar Stability," *The Wall Street Journal*, September 19, 1988) and Rudiger Dornbusch of MIT (see: "The Dollar: How Much Further Depreciation Do We Need?," *Economic Review*, Federal Reserve Bank of Atlanta, Sept./Oct. 1987) who have argued that the dollar needs to fall further.

Page 158-159   Rudiger Dornbusch has emphasized the changes in international trade relations that make it difficult for the United States to recover its trade surplus. See his article cited above.

Page 162   The statement about the number of forms signed by a European truck driver is from a report in *The Atlanta Constitution*, June 5, 1988.

Adam Smith's description of the assembly line in a pin factory appears in Book 1, Chapter 1, in *The Wealth of Nations*.

The discussion of modern pin manufacturers in the United Kingdom is found in Clifford F. Pratten, "The Manufacture of Pins," *Journal of Economic Literature*, March 1980, pp 93–96

Chapter 10

Page 165   Keynes's memoir on Marshall from which the account of the picture on Marshall's mantel is taken is: "Alfred Marshall," *Essays in Biography*, 1972, pp. 200–201.

Page 166   Keynes's statement on the faults of the economy in his day is found in *The General Theory*, 1972, p. 372.

Page 167   The book that started the debate over the current state of American industry is: Barry Bluestone and Bennett Harrison, *The Deindustrialization of America* (New York: Basic Books, Inc., 1982).

Robert Reich's book, *The Next American Frontier*, was published by Penguin Books, New York, 1983.

Page 167-168   The Boston Federal Reserve study summarizing research on the deindustrialization issue is: Gary W. Loveman and Chris Tilly, "Good Jobs or Bad Jobs? What Does the Evidence Say?" *New England Economic Review*, January/February 1988, pp. 46–65.

Page 168-169   For a useful summary of postwar changes in industry output and employment, see: Mack Ott, "The Growing Share of Services in the U.S. Economy—Degeneration or Evolution," *Review*, Federal Reserve Bank of St. Louis, June/July 1987, pp. 5–22.

Page 169-
170
For a summary of the behavior of income over time, see: *Trends in Family Income: 1970–1986*, Congressional Budget Office, February 1988.

Page 170
The phrase, "the quiet depression," is used by Frank Levy in *Dollars and Dreams* (New York: Russell Sage Foundation, 1987), p. 4.

Page 171
The numbers on monthly house payments are found in Frank Levy and Richard C. Michel, "An Economic Bust for the Baby Boom," *Challenge*, March/April 1987, Table 1, p. 37.

Page 173-
174
For a summary of the conflicting explanations of poor earnings performance, see Loveman and Tally, "Good Jobs or Bad Jobs? What Does the Evidence Say?", pp. 49–51. The view that wage deterioration is due to the shift of employment from manufacturing to services has been strongly argued by Bluestone and Harrison. The argument that the reason for low wages is found in changes in the age distribution of the population has been made by Robert Z. Lawrence. See: *Can America Compete?* (Washington: Brookings Institution, 1984). For a brief discussion of the research in the Labor Department, see: Robert Kuttner, "The Debate Over New Jobs Is Turning Into Mudslinging," *Business Week*, April 13, 1987, p. 22.

Page 173
For information on capital per worker in service industries and in manufacturing, see Mack Ott, "The Growing Share of Services in the U.S. Economy—Degeneration or Evolution," Tables 1 and 2, pp. 7 and 10, and the comments on p. 11.

Page 175-
176
The idea of the "product cycle" in which maturing industries migrate to low-wage production locations was developed in such classic treatments as Edgar M. Hoover, *The Location of Economic Activity* (New York: McGraw-Hill, 1948) and Raymond Vernon, "International Investment and International Trade in the Product Cycle," *Quarterly Journal of Economics*, May 1966, pp. 190–207.

Page 176
The *Business Week* article, "The Hollow Corporation," appeared in the issue of March 3, 1988, pp. 57–85. The statement that most of General Electric's consumer electronic goods are produced in Asia is on page 60 of this article. The statement about General Motors' purchase of services from Blue Cross/Blue Shield is on page 65.

For a short survey of what is known about the linkage between manufacturing and the rest of the economy, see: Randall W. Eberts and John R. Swinton, "Has Manufacturing's Presence in the Economy Diminished?" *Economic Commentary*, Federal Reserve Bank of Cleveland, January 1, 1988.

Page 178-179   For a critical view of the potential of industrial policy and a discussion of the Japanese experience, see: Charles L. Schultze, "Industrial Policy: A Dissent," *The Brookings Review*, Fall 1983, pp. 3–12.   The statment about Honda appears in Schultze's paper.

Page 179   "Murphy's Law of Economic Policy," is stated in: Alan S. Blinder, *Hard Heads, Soft Hearts* (Reading: Addison-Wesley Publishing Co., 1987), p. 1.

Page 180   Adam Smith's statement on the human propensity "to truck and barter" is found in *The Wealth of Nations*, Book I, Chapter II.

For a discussion of the effect of adjustment for taxes and other items on income distribution, see Levy, *Dollars and Dreams*, pp. 193–197.

Page 181-182   Information on the proportion of families below the poverty line can be found in: *Money, Income and Poverty Status in the United States: 1987*, Current Population Reports, Series P-60, no. 161, Bureau of the Census, 1988.

Page 182-183   For a survey of the Social Security program, see: Alicia H. Munnell, "The Current Status of Our Social Welfare System," *New England Economic Review*, July/August 1987, pp. 3–12.

Page 183   The gain in the per capita family income of elderly families is reported in the *Economic Report of the President*, 1985, p. 163.

For a positive evaluation of social security, see: Merton C. and Joan Brodshaug Bernstein, *Social Security: The System That Works* (New York: Basic Books, 1988). A useful review of this book by Gene Koretz appears in *Business Week*, April 18, 1988, pp. 12–18.

Page 183-184   For the change in the percent of the elderly and of women with a child under six years of age in poverty, see: Sheldon Danziger and Peter Gottschalk, "Work, Poverty, and the Working Poor: A Multifaceted Problem," *Monthly Labor Review*, September 1986, Table 1, p. 18.

Page 184-185   For a survey of the current welfare program, see Alicia H. Munnell, "The Current Status of Our Social Welfare System."

For a discussion of the income status of families headed by women, see: *Trends in Family Income: 1970-1986, Chapter III*, pp. 27–44.

Page 185-
186
For a survey of studies on welfare dependency and related issues, see: Greg J. Duncan, Martha S. Hill, and Saul D. Hoffman, "Welfare Dependence Within and Across Generations," *Science*, January 1988, pp. 467–471. The study of 700 welfare recipients is summarized in this article on pages 467–468. The study of the dependency rate of children from welfare families is also summarized in this article on page 469.

Page 186
The statement that some workers, even working year round, do not earn enough to remove a family of four from poverty is based on: Sheldon Denziger and Peter Gottschalk, "Work, Poverty, and the Working Poor: A Multifaceted Problem," p. 18.

Page 187
Keynes's statement on the efficiency of capitalism is from: "The End of Laissez-Faire," *Essays in Persuasion*, 1972, p. 294.

Chapter 11

Page 189
Samuelson's answer to the question, "Is Keynes dead?" is found in: "Liberalism at Bay," *The Collected Scientific Papers of Paul A. Samuelson*, Vol. IV, p. 874.

Page 190
For a review of the current state of economic forecasting, see: Stephen K. McNees, "How Accurate Are Macroeconomic Forecasts?" *New England Economic Review*, July/August 1988, pp. 15–36.

Page 194
"Look Who's Making a Comeback" appeared in the February 1, 1988 issue of *U.S. News and World Report*, pp. 43-45.

INDEX